THE STORY TELLERS

THE *STORY* TELLERS

STRAIGHT TALK FROM THE WORLD'S MOST ACCLAIMED SUSPENSE AND THRILLER AUTHORS

EDITED BY **MARK RUBINSTEIN**

BLACK STONE
PUBLISHING

Printed in the United States of America

First edition: 2021
ISBN 978-1-0941-3817-6
Literary Collections / Essays

1 3 5 7 9 10 8 6 4 2

CIP data for this book is available
from the Library of Congress

Blackstone Publishing
31 Mistletoe Rd.
Ashland, OR 97520

www.BlackstonePublishing.com

PETER JAMES

JOHN LAND

SARA PARETSKY

HEATHER GRAHAM

DAVID MAMET

CATHERINE COULTER

MARCUS SAKEY

JAMES ROLLINS

MARY KUBICA

JOSEPH FINDER

KARIN SLAUGHTER

LAURA LIPPMAN

SCOTT TUROW

STEVE HAMILTON

REED FARREL COLEMAN

DON WINSLOW

CANDACE BUSHNELL

C. J. BOX

DENNIS LEHANE

FREDERICK FORSYTH

JOHN SANDFORD

ROBERT CRAIS

GREG ILES

DAVID MORRELL

JAYNE ANN KRENTZ

ANDREW GROSS

LISA GARDNER

LEE CHILD

KEN FOLLETT

HARLAN COBEN

ACE ATKINS

WALTER MOSLEY

IAN RANKIN

STUART WOODS

PATRICIA CORNWELL

CLIVE CUSSLER

KATHY REICHS

SUE GRAFTON

SIMON TOYNE

MICHAEL CONNELLY

JONATHAN KELLERMAN

FAYE KELLERMAN

TESS GERRITSEN

J.A. JANCE

MEG GARDINER

DANIEL SILVA

CONTENTS

INTRODUCTION

Inspired by more than five years of author interviews for my Huffington Post blog, I wrote *The Storytellers* to share the personal stories of many of the world's most acclaimed authors, not only with their devoted readers, but with everyone who enjoys meeting creative people whose life experiences have deeply colored their art and outlooks on life itself. After completing the interviews published in the Huffington Post, I conceptualized this collection, then contacted many of the authors and interviewed them again. As a result, major parts of the conversations in this volume never appeared in the Huffington Post or elsewhere.

Here are brief excerpts from conversations with four of the forty-seven authors featured in this book:

> "Everything about the future frightens me . . . There's no end in sight for the creative things people can do to wreak havoc on civilization . . . I think being on this planet is a lonely experience, and without imagination, it's very isolating. For me, writing has been a gift."
>
> **—PATRICIA CORNWELL**

"I used to lay sod for a living, and I washed dishes. I didn't like it at all. So, when I found out I had a gift for writing, it saved me."

—DAVID MAMET

"I was an only child. My mother was an only child and my father was an orphan. There was a lack of interaction between and among us. I was alone a lot. That being the case, I had to fill up time, so I made up stories. And I think that has stayed with me all these years.

—WALTER MOSLEY

"The vast majority of what we call morality is simply fear of being caught."

—DENNIS LEHANE

Like the four authors quoted above, the writers interviewed for this book shared candid thoughts, opinions, inspirations, frustrations, backstories, and their sources of creativity.

Collectively, these writers' books have sold in the *billions*, and many of their characters are iconic. But this volume does far more than explore their writing: it lets you into these people's lives firsthand and in their own words. These internationally bestselling wordsmiths emerge as fully fleshed-out people whom you previously knew only through their fiction.

MARK RUBINSTEIN

LEE CHILD
REVENGE CAN BE SWEET

Lee Child has sold millions of books worldwide, and his Jack Reacher character has virtually become a household name. The series follows the adventures of former American military policeman Jack Reacher, a loner who wanders from place to place. Lee's first novel, *Killing Floor*, won both the Anthony Award and the Barry Award for Best First Novel.

In 1974, at age twenty, he studied law at the University of Sheffield though he had no intention of entering the legal profession. During his student days, he worked backstage in a theater. After graduating, he worked in commercial television and was involved in producing shows like *Brideshead Revisited* and *The Jewel in the Crown*.

But suddenly, at the age of forty, he was fired due to a corporate takeover and union-busting on the part of his new employer. That's when Lee's career as a novelist began. The rest is history.

Q. **Is it true that you created Jack Reacher from the smoldering embers of your own rage after you were let go by Granada Television?**

A. It's probably more accurate to say the adventures Reacher gets into are the product of that experience. I can't say that Reacher himself was specifically related to that. I'd been in the entertainment business for a very long time by the point I left Granada Television. I learned very quickly that you cannot be successful by compiling a laundry list of virtues. You can't say, "This is what the world is like; this is what I feel about it; therefore, I've got to have a protagonist with certain popular characteristics." If you start with a shopping list of traits, you end up with a wooden character with very little spark and with barely an identity of his own.

Clearly, what happened with Reacher is this: He's an archetypal character. He's a loner, a mysterious stranger with no history and no future, someone who just shows up on the day something has happened in a place. He solves the problem and then rides off into the sunset. That archetype is a perpetual character who's been around forever—in American Westerns, in the knightly sagas in Europe of the Middle Ages, in Scandinavian and Anglo-Saxon legends, even going back to religious myths where the Savior suddenly appears. This kind of character was in the back of my mind, but I paid no attention to any sort of preformed design. I literally refused to think about what the character needed to be because I wanted him to be authentic and organic.

One basic rule that applies is: it's not the writer who decides whether a character is cool; it's the *reader* who makes that decision. If a writer tries to force things—or lead the witness, as it were—the result is an embarrassing failure. So, really, I just metaphorically closed my eyes and wrote that first book, *Killing Floor*, and Jack Reacher emerged.

Q. **What has made you characterize the Jack Reacher books as "revenge novels"?**

A. Revenge is basically the common theme for most of the books. It's not necessarily Reacher taking revenge for himself. Often, it's on behalf of someone else or on behalf of a situation in which an arrogant and contemptuous person prevails in an evil way. Fundamentally, he takes revenge for the perpetrator's past felonies.

Q. **Do you personally share many of Reacher's qualities of silent masculinity, brute force, and the wish for good to triumph over evil?**

A. Well, I'm silent, certainly. I obviously wish for good to triumph over evil. Am I forceful and masculine? I'm an old guy now, but I do my best. [Laughter.]

Q. **You've talked about Reacher being the embodiment of a masculine fantasy, and a feminine one, too. Tell us more.**

A. When I wrote the first book and then looked at it afterward, I felt it would appeal to men. I didn't consciously plan it, but I'd created a situation of a man with no commitments, no responsibilities, and I felt that was a masculine fantasy. My thought was certainly borne out, since many men responded to that idea—no mortgage, no bills, no commitments. They could just walk away tomorrow. It appealed to a very powerful male fantasy.

But I also learned as the years went by that some women were not only attracted to that sort of man, but they actually wanted to *be* that guy. It was also a woman's fantasy—to be able to walk away and be somewhere else tomorrow. It's a universal fantasy.

Q. **Reacher has an active sex life. Tell us about that and about writing erotic scenes.**

A. Writing sex scenes is by far the hardest and most ridiculous thing a writer can ever do. It's virtually impossible to get it done with any plausibility. You know, Reacher loves women, like I do. One of the things I love about publishing is, generally speaking, almost everyone I deal with is a woman. I like them. Reacher likes them. And, of course, something about Reacher makes women respond.

I think part of Reacher's appeal for women is he's the ultimate safe affair. A woman can be guaranteed of a good time for twenty-four or forty-eight hours, and she can be guaranteed this guy will never call; he will never return. It's safe. In real life, many affairs are not safe: you get found out; you get a divorce; you lose your house and half your money. It's a nightmare.

In the fictional world, Reacher gets away with it. For everyone, for men and women, it's appealing for someone to have a nasty little secret—a two- or three-day fling, such as occurs in *The Bridges of Madison County*. I think many readers luxuriate in that same feeling. And Reacher, of course, will never get a woman in trouble by reappearing. It's a no-consequences affair.

Q. **I suspect it's no coincidence that Jack Reacher is exactly your height, six feet, five inches? How much of Lee Child is in Jack Reacher?**

A. Inevitably, we writers put a lot of ourselves in our protagonists. Anyone who writes will use a good deal of autobiography in a protagonist. It's part of the writing process and it's also fun to do. You can insert your own enthusiasm, jokes, and opinions.

But Reacher is not exactly my height. He's one inch taller than I am. And that is *very* typical: most male writers will make a hero an inch taller and considerably more muscular than they are. [Laughter.] Women writers usually give their heroines better hair and thinner thighs. [More laughter.] They're really idealized versions of ourselves. It gives us an alternative life where we can work things out a bit differently than they actually turned out.

Q. **I understand your knowledge of fighting isn't just from research. You got into quite a few brawls as a youngster in Birmingham, UK. Tell us about that.**

A. I always point out that my childhood was no different from anybody else's. I wasn't unique in having a bad situation as a kid; everybody's situation is bad. I grew up in a gray, industrial landscape where there was economic austerity and very little for a kid to do. In that city, violence was a response to virtually everything. In my case, it was a bit more complicated because my parents were very aspirational for us to get an education and do well. That put a target on my back in a neighborhood like mine.

If you're viewed as being above your station or too big for your boots, you become a target. So, I had a fight pretty much every day with some kid. I got a fellowship to a prestigious secondary school located on the better side of the city, so from the age of eleven onward, I had to fight my way out of the neighborhood in the morning and back in during the afternoon. [Laughter.] I was very good at it. It was a part of my day I quite looked forward to. Reacher's fighting ability really approximates mine at about age nine, when I was bigger than everybody else.

Q. **While your books depict well-choreographed fight scenes, I'm more impressed by Reacher's searing logic when thinking about criminals and their next moves. Will you talk about that?**

A. I love that aspect, too. I think that's a very strong strand in well-written crime or detective fiction: the sheer delight in watching a smart person figure something out. Of course, that dates back to Sherlock Holmes. Conan Doyle made many mistakes of detail in the books—errors in geography, or a mistake such as Watson's wound changing locations on his body, from his side to his leg, and elsewhere. But the most compelling aspects of the books are the *mental* machinations of Holmes. That phenomenon has dominated the genre ever since because people love it. Reacher is very much in that tradition. He must think ahead and figure things out.

Q. **You were born James Grant but changed your name to Lee Child. Do you use your pen name in everyday life?**

A. I've been in the entertainment business all my adult life and have used five or six different names over the years. You know, you may have a contract prohibiting you from doing something else, so you go ahead and do it under a different name. I was familiar with the idea of stage names, and it never occurred to me not to use one, to be honest.

It's now twenty-plus years of doing this as Lee Child, so almost everybody I'm in contact with apart from a very small handful of people knows me as Lee Child. So I just go with the flow. I think names are a weird thing anyway.

Q. How so?

A. The people who gave me my allegedly real name were people I didn't know at the time I was born. [Laughter.] And I didn't particularly like them later when I got to know them. [More laughter.] So why would I feel obliged to keep that name? I think when we turn eighteen, we should all rename ourselves.

Q. You've talked about your having smoked marijuana since 1969. Will you tell us more about that?

A. It was 1969. What can I tell you? [Laughter.] That's how it was. I liked it and found it to be an appealing sensation and quite liberating. It untangled the creativity a little bit. I have always enjoyed it and think it's absurd how we ban things so arbitrarily—you know, alcohol is legal, but marijuana is not. It works for me and hasn't done me any harm.

Q. Do you write while using cannabis?

A. I'll occasionally use it as an aide for concentrating, especially when I'm rereading something I've written.

Q. With your success, it's clearly no longer about the money. What keeps you writing the Jack Reacher books?

A. It used to be a financial need. I had a financial contract. Now it's an *emotional* contract. It's a contract with the reader. It's such a special relationship with the reader. The reader pays you the most important compliment—it's not the money spent for the book; it's the time the reader devotes to the book. If a reader doesn't like the book, it's not the wasted money I care about. It's the *time* the reader has wasted. These people have given me a day of their lives, or two or three days, and I've got to respect that. I feel I've got to give them the very best product I can. Right now millions of people are looking forward to a new Reacher book, and not to provide it would be insane. I think entertainment is fundamentally a two-way street. It's a transaction. The audience wants something, and the author supplies it. That's how it works. So yes, it's become an emotional contract. I used to be scared of going bankrupt. Now I'm scared of letting people down.

Q. **I understand that by the time you've finished the first draft of a novel, it's basically ready for publication. How do you do that?**

A. I start each day by reading through what I wrote the day before. I polish it and then move ahead. By the time I've reached the end of the book, it's been churned over many times. Every word has been examined several times and it's as good as I can get it. I never forget that I'm telling a *story*. When I've written a book, I firmly believe that what's written is exactly *what* happened. To change it retrospectively in a second draft or rewrite would seem to me dishonest. It would be like changing my own biography. My editor might say, "Wouldn't it be better if such and such happened instead of what you wrote?" I say, "Yes, probably, but it *didn't* happen." [Laughter.]

Q. **Speaking of editing and writing, what constitutes a good day of writing for you?**

A. A good day would be two thousand words in publishable condition. That would be an excellent day. I'm more comfortable doing twelve or fifteen hundred words. My sister-in-law is Tasha Alexander, the historical novelist. She can write five thousand words a day, but she must rewrite afterward. I don't. I go more slowly and it's more polished after the first draft. I fight for every single word.

Q. **Other than the obvious, how has Jack Reacher changed your life?**

A. He really hasn't changed my life. Some writers get too close to their heroes, or even fall in love with them. When that happens, the hero's appeal just falls off a cliff because the author is on the hero's side and is protective of him.

To avoid that, I aim to keep myself liking Reacher a little bit less than the reader will like him. That keeps him honest. And I refuse to think about him when I'm not writing. He's not a feature of my everyday life. He doesn't really have an impact on me. It's necessary for me to maintain some distance from him so I can get on with what I need to do on a daily basis.

Q. **Do you ever wonder to yourself in certain situations, "What would Reacher do?"**

A. [Laughter.] I don't need to wonder. I know exactly how he would react in any situation, since I'm the one who will make him respond. Occasionally, my wife and I will encounter some aggravating real-world situation and we'll look at each other and say, "What would Reacher do?" [More laughter.]

Q. **You're quite tall and recognizable. Are you accosted in public?**

A. More and more over the last five years. People recognize me now. Like most writers, though, it's a very low tempo compared to ballplayers or actors. Stephen King is probably the most physically recognizable author and he's identified frequently. For me, it's maybe once or twice a week. Someone will stop me on the street or at an airport.

Something else came along with that kind of recognition:

people relate to me as a person who's writing these books. But then something happens: a few unconsciously view me as a third-party independent phenomenon. For instance, a reader will say to me, "I loved your last book. It was really great. But the one before that was awful." It's said as though we're chatting about the weather. As though I'm some kind of impersonal force.

Q. **Well, your photo is on the cover flap of about half a *billion* books by now. So maybe some people relate to you as though you're the Eiffel Tower. [Laughter.]**

A. Yes, my photo is on all those books. However, I've occasionally sat between two people both reading my books and neither of them noticed me. [More laughter.]

Q. **If you could meet any three fictional characters in real life, who would they be?**

A. That's a tough one. There are three characters among my contemporaries whom I really like. Karin Slaughter writes about a guy named Will Trent. He's got quirks and handicaps that I don't have; I have some others. I like him a lot.

I'd like to meet Ellie Hatcher, who's been created by Alafair Burke; she would be a fun character to meet.

Then I'd like to meet Tess Monaghan from Laura Lippman's series.

Q. **You're invited to a dinner party and you can invite any five people, dead or alive, from any walk of life to join you. Who would they be?**

A. The thing is, when you achieve prominence as an author, you get invited to those dinners. I've met many famous people either at dinner or charity balls. I met Paul McCartney and

Barak Obama. They're very guarded and cautious in public. They can't really say what they're thinking. Honestly, if I were invited to such a dinner, I would politely decline and choose to stay home and watch television.

Congratulations on an enormously successful writing career, which has garnered you readers all over the globe.

LISA GARDNER
GOLDILOCKS AND WRITING TOWARD THE LIGHT

Lisa Gardner is a *New York Times* bestselling author of crime thrillers. She has more than twenty-two million books in print and is published in thirty countries. As Lisa Gardner, she writes the FBI Profiler series, as well as the Detective D. D. Warren series and several stand-alone novels. Under the pseudonym Alicia Scott, she's written romance novels.

A self-described research junkie, she worked as a research analyst for an international consulting firm and parlayed her interest in police procedure, cutting-edge forensics, and twisted plots into a streak of internationally bestselling suspense novels.

Her success crosses into television film with four of her novels becoming movies: *At the Midnight Hour, The Perfect Husband, The Survivors Club,* and *Hide.*

Our conversations took place between 2014 and 2016.

Q. How and when did you begin writing fiction?

A. I wrote my first book at seventeen. I was very lucky because it was published three years later. I started my career as Alicia Scott, writing romantic suspense novels. There was always a dead body and an investigation. I wrote seven or eight of those novels and got more and more interested in the suspense element of the books. I also grew more comfortable doing research and cold-calling detectives, prisons, and morgues. The more research I did, the bigger the crimes became.

I came up with the idea for a stand-alone thriller called *The Perfect Husband*. It featured a serial killer who broke out of a maximum-security prison. His revenge against everyone who put him there included pursuing his ex-wife. So even back then I was writing a kind of domestic thriller. That was my first Lisa Gardner book, and I've never looked back.

Q. What made you begin writing at the young age of seventeen?

A. I didn't know any better. [Laughter.] Seriously, I lived in Oregon. I'd never met an author, editor, or agent. In other words, I had no idea how hard it is to write a novel, let alone how impossible it is to get one published. On the other hand, I had an idea for a murder mystery. So I wrote it.

Q. How did you manage to get published by age twenty?

A. Once I started telling people I'd written a book, they asked when it was going to be published. This was a new thought for me. But a good friend helped me find a book on how to get published. This was back in the early nineties, when the paperback market was exploding, so demand for new voices was higher than it is now.

I followed the steps for submission spelled out in the guidebook. Several years and a number of rewrites later, my first book found a home. I'd told friends when my book sold, I was going to buy a Mercedes. [Laughter.] Big successful author, right?

My first lesson in publishing: my book did sell, and I earned just enough money to buy a computer, and even then, I had to wait for the computer to go on sale. But it was still absolutely amazing to hold the finished novel in my hands. It gave me goose bumps.

Q. **I understand that while writing your first crime/suspense novel, you were working in the food service industry. After your hair caught on fire a number of times, you decided to focus solely on writing. Tell us about that.**

A. Like many novelists at the beginning of a career, I was writing for love, not money. It took a good ten years for me to become an overnight success. [Laughter.] I had many jobs; one was as a waitress at a Greek restaurant. They had an appetizer called flaming saganaki, which is deep-fried cheese over which brandy is poured and then lit on fire. It was the nineties and a time when women wore really big hair. If you didn't pour the brandy properly, the fire could blow back and get onto your hair. It happened quite often. I got plenty of "pity tips" from patrons because of it. So, I'm really grateful every day that the writing thing worked out.

Q. **You once described your writing process as "out of the mist." Tell us what you mean by that.**

A. I'm not a plotter for my novels. I do lots of research. It's one of my favorite parts of writing because I was once a research analyst. I may know some key forensic points, but I don't like knowing what's going to happen next. If I already know who the good or bad guys are, then the reader will know, too.

For instance, with *Crash and Burn*, when I began the book,

I didn't know if Vero existed. I didn't know if Thomas or Nicky were good or bad. I prefer it when characters can go either way—good or bad. There's more complexity, and there are some secrets. One of the things that keeps me showing up each day and writing is that at some point I want to know the answer.

Q. You're known for doing a good deal of research. But you've also talked about the dangers of doing too much research. Will you comment on that?

A. I think doing research is the most fascinating part of my job. I get to speak with people who do really cool things for a living. I surf the internet and talk to experts, but at the end of the day, I must sit down and start writing. I have to produce a novel—I must tell a compelling story.

Q. Your website has some great information about the dos and don'ts of research. Will you share some of that with us?

A. When I was starting out as a novelist, I did an enormous amount of research for my first suspense book. I threw it all in the book. My editor at the time said it was too much. It wasn't entertainment. So, I heavily edited the manuscript. When I resubmitted it, she said, "There's nothing in there." It was too sparse.

Ever since then I've been a Goldilocks writer: the first draft has too much research material, the second has too little, but the third draft will be *just right*. I don't want to snow the reader with too much research detail. I love the Hemingway quote: "You must learn the glacier to write the tip.'"

Q. Your novels depict great villains, or as you've put it, "The Diabolical Prima Donna." Tell us about that.

A. I think people love a good villain. My point is that in so many books and movies, the villain is the one who sticks with you.

For me, a great suspense novel involves cat and mouse. If your detective is the cat, you've got to give him a worthy mouse. Otherwise, there's no tension and the novel lacks excitement. You want a villain just as clever as your detective. I also think the villain must be complicated and have some compelling attributes. For instance, Ted Bundy stands out as the ultimate, real-life bogeyman. He would slaughter poor young girls yet wouldn't drive an uninsured car. He was polite and adhered to nearly all of society's rules of etiquette and propriety. That kind of complexity made him interesting.

Q. **You're one of the most successful novelists working today. What has surprised you about the writing life?**

A. What's surprised me is that it doesn't get easier. With thirty books written, you would think I'd feel proficient, but each book is painful in its own way. To paraphrase Dorothy Parker's observation: I don't know that I like writing. I know I like having written.

I'm always just feeling my way to that other side—the completed novel. I feel I'm forever gnashing my teeth and banging my head against a blank computer screen. [More laughter.] I wish writing were easier. You would think that twenty-five years and seventeen books later, it would become easier, but it hasn't.

Each day, I start out writing with no idea what I'm going to say. Many other writers have a plan, an outline, a map, but I don't. And it isn't easy to write this way.

Q. **Does facing each day with no real outline or plan make you nervous?**

A. Absolutely. If there's one thing I've gotten used to in writing, it's this: I haven't gotten over the anxiety of writing. I've just become comfortable with it. The fear of the unknown is with me constantly.

Q. What do you love about the writing life?

A. I love that magical moment when it all comes together in a way I could never have imagined. I always think of writing as a giant leap of faith. There's that "Aha" moment when things just seem to fall into place. Those days are amazing and precious. The art takes over, it all comes together, and I've actually completed a novel despite myself.

Q. What would you be doing if you weren't a writer?

A. Probably some type of criminology. With all the research and consulting with experts, what's fascinated me most is the psychology of crime. What is the nature of evil? Is it inborn or acquired through the environment? Or is it a product of abnormal physiology, such as with the Texas bell tower sniper who had a brain tumor? I write fiction, but if I wasn't doing that, I think I'd be involved in criminology.

Q. Which authors do you enjoy reading today?

A. Stephen King, Karin Slaughter, Tess Gerritsen, Lee Child, Laura Hillenbrand, Kristin Hannah, and I read a lot of YA with my daughter.

Q. What, if anything, keeps you awake at night?

A. I'm a parent, so there are many fears that keep me awake. I think to a certain extent, *Find Her* involved my exploration of a parent's greatest fear. There are so many abductions in the news these days. Between the Jaycee Dugard case and the Elizabeth Smart case, and so many others, finding research material for *Find Her* was not a problem.

I think most of my books are about facing fear. The writing process, in some ways, lets me work out the kind of everyday anxieties that can keep a parent awake at night.

As parents, we have to have faith that our kids will find their ways through things.

Q. **Looking back on your career, is there anything you would have done differently?**

A. From a marketing point of view, it probably would have been better if I'd written my series books in consecutive order instead of alternating them with stand-alone books and other series.

It would have been more prudent if I'd written the books in a more cohesive way, instead of haphazardly, but it's interesting for me to see that readers have followed the characters.

Q. **As a bestselling author, do you worry about anything in your writing life?**

A. I'm lucky in that regard. I don't. As I said, time and experience have taught me to get comfortable with my own discomfort. If you're a professional, you learn your triggers. If I'm stuck, I go for a walk in the woods. Driving is also good for inspiration. Talking about the book with my agent or a friend can spur me on.

I don't wake up every morning thinking: it's 6:00 A.M. and I can't wait to get back to writing. [Laughter.] But I'm a professional writer and know the things that keep me focused and on track.

Q. **Do you ever feel guilty if a day goes by and you haven't written?**

A. I get more anxious if I feel I may not meet my deadline. I'm a very structured writer. I draft a novel in about six months.

Then I rewrite. I'm a big rewriter. If I get behind schedule, my husband and daughter will tell you I'm not fun to live with. [Laughter.]

Q. What question are you asked most frequently in interviews?

A. I'm most frequently asked from where do I get my ideas?

Q. Why do you think that's the most frequent question?

A. I think it's because when people look at me, they see someone who looks like an ordinary mom. They can't believe I come up with these horrifying scenarios. [Laughter.] My daughter is getting old enough to read my books, and so are her friends. I'm waiting for the day when the parents of my daughter's friends say, "I can't believe I left my child alone with this woman." [More laughter.]

Q. What, if anything, do you read while writing a novel?

A. I read all the time. I even read the Cheerios box. I have a thirteen-year-old daughter who's a huge reader and has introduced me to a number of amazing YA series. Many of them, like *The Hunger Games*, emphasize kick-ass heroines. I love reading suspense novels and especially enjoy reading books by Karin Slaughter, Tess Gerritsen, Joseph Finder, Lee Child, Harlan Coben, and my favorite new series right now is one by Gregg Hurwitz. It's sort of like Jason Bourne meets Jack Reacher.

I should say that while I'm writing a novel, I won't read anything similar in tone or subject to what I'm writing. I think I would worry about my work being influenced or even polluted by the other novel.

Q. **If you could have dinner with any five people, from any walk of life, living or dead, who would they be?**

A. One would have to be Stephen King. He's my favorite author and an inspirational voice in my career. I loved his book *On Writing*. I think he would be amazing and fun to talk to. I would like to invite Queen Elizabeth I, because she was a woman who ruled at that time in history and because of everything she accomplished. I'd love to have Grace O'Malley, the pirate queen, and Elizabeth's archrival at the dinner, too. Ben Franklin would have to be there. He was a great philosopher, thinker, writer, and an inventor, too. And then I'd love to have Sherlock Holmes to round out the dinner party.

Congratulations on writing gripping suspense novels. Harlan Coben described your books as involving "taut psychological suspense, intricate mysteries that are emotionally devastating and ultimately empowering." He was absolutely correct.

DENNIS LEHANE
MYSTIC RIVER, *CRIME, AND MORALITY*

Dennis Lehane is known to millions of readers. He was born and raised in the Dorchester neighborhood of Boston, the setting for many of his books.

His novels *Mystic River*; *Gone, Baby, Gone*; and *Shutter Island* became blockbuster movies. He wrote his first screenplay for *The Drop*, a film based on his short story, *Animal Rescue*. Between 2004 and 2008, he wrote teleplays for the TV series, *The Wire*.

A Drink Before the War won the Shamus Award. *Mystic River* won both the Anthony and the Barry Awards for Best Novel, and the Massachusetts Award in Fiction. *Live by Night* won the Edgar Award for Best Novel, and the Florida Book Award Gold Medal for Fiction.

Our conversation took place in 2015.

Q. You once said you knew you would be labeled a genre writer. You said, "And there's no way out of that, so let's just go all the way. It's been the greatest accident of my life." Will you talk about that?

A. I don't know if it's still true of me now, but it was certainly true when I came out of graduate school in 1993. The crime fiction genre was very much ghettoized. Sometimes it was for good reasons; in some cases, it was unfair. What I and others were rebelling against was the notion that literary fiction was the only kind of literature. Crime fiction was its own ghettoized genre, or it should have been, according to that kind of thinking.

I was growing very tired of what a writer once referred to as "stories about the vaguely dissatisfied in Connecticut." At the time, they were dominating literary fiction. I became enamored of writing about what Cormac McCarthy called "fiction of mortal events." That's why I drifted into crime fiction. I think crime fiction has social value, and I was very interested in writing about social issues such as race, class— you know, the haves and have-nots in American society. It seemed like a natural fit with the crime novel.

Now, twenty years later, while we may not have knocked the genre gate down, we've stormed it. Some lines of distinction between so-called literature and crime fiction have become a bit blurred. Now some crime fiction is allowed into the club. [Laughter.]

Q. In an interview some years ago, you said "my career track is really pathetic." What did you mean?

A. It's a case of falling butt-backward into luck. Okay, the Kenzie and Gennaro books sold, but *Mystic River* was a big surprise to me. It took two and a half years to write, and I didn't show the first draft to anyone. After seven or eight revisions, it was done. My publisher said the book was beautiful, but it would never sell. I really thought I'd never sell the film rights, but I couldn't resist the offer when Clint Eastwood called me after he'd borrowed the book from a friend. How's that for a lucky break?

Q. **Tell us about the Irish American storytelling culture in which you grew up.**

A. My parents came from Ireland and moved to a section of Boston where they were surrounded by their siblings and in-laws. We grew up with all our uncles and aunts nearby. They gathered every Friday and Saturday at one or another's house. They would sit around and just tell stories.

My brother and I began to notice that every six or seven weeks the same story would come back into the rotation. But it was *tweaked*. We began to understand—whether consciously or not—a good story wasn't necessarily concerned with facts. It was concerned with a *basic truth*. As an adult I realize what my parents, uncles, and aunts were doing by telling these stories again and again, all about the old country. They were trying to make sense of the Irish diaspora, to make sense of having left the place they loved.

Q. **Do you think they romanticized the old country?**

A. Oh, of course. When I went to Ireland, I expected to step back into the 1930s. You know, a lovely place where nobody got divorced, no one ever said a cussword, and everything was just perfect. That image was calcified in my home in Boston. But in Ireland, time had moved on. The people there were living their lives.

When I was in graduate school, my mentor would describe storytelling as "the lie that tells the truth."

Q. **Many of your novels are filled with moral ambiguity. Tell us about that.**

A. The vast majority of what we call morality is simply fear of being caught. Just look at any comment section in newspaper articles on the internet, where people remain anonymous and say whatever they think. Or watch people when they're driving their cars. Maybe a small percentage of us with moral fiber will categorically not do certain things, even if we're not being watched, but with the vast majority, all bets are off.

I don't know too many really bad people, and I don't know too many saints, either. I think most people fall somewhere in between. And that's what I write about. Bad people don't wake up each morning thinking "I'm a bad person." They think, "I'm a good person in my heart, even if I have to do some bad things." That's true of bankers, and it's true of stockbrokers who short stock. And that's true of gangsters, who short people. [Laughter.]

Q. **In 2001, *Mystic River* was your first novel outside the Kenzie-Gennaro series. It wasn't until 2010 that you brought the duo back in *Moonlight Mile*. Did you get pressure from fans to return to that series?**

A. I didn't really get pressure; I got wishes. Fans continue to show up at nearly every signing and want to know if Patrick and Angela will ever come back. My answer is, "I don't know." I haven't retired them. They've sort of taken these longer and longer vacations from me.

Q. **It seems to me you've taken a more expansive path in the last few years. Is that a fair statement?**

A. Yes. I would say that path began after *Mystic River*. For the first time in my life, I became aware of other people's expectations about what I would do next. I didn't respond well to that pressure. It wasn't why I got into writing in the first place.

So, I made a conscious choice to zig when everyone thought I would zag. After *Mystic River* I wrote *Shutter Island* just to change things up once again. Writing that book was really fun. I was able to do what I'd wanted to do for a very long time, which was to write about the Boston police strike. I've stayed on that independent path, despite knowing I've lost some fans along the way, but that's okay.

Q. **So, *Mystic River* changed your writing life?**

A. Yes. It changed the perception of me as a writer—almost overnight. Suddenly, I was viewed as a *literary* writer. Until that point people thought, "He produces really well-written genre novels." That was my label. After *Mystic River* I was suddenly writing *literature*. A lot of debates began after that. It was a strange and wonderful place to be. So you're right, it led me to decide to follow a more idiosyncratic path.

Q. **I saw the film *Mystic River* and then read the novel. As fine as the film was, the book was even more powerful. Did that film have an impact on your subsequent writing life?**

A. No. I don't ever, ever, ever think of films when I write. To me, writing a book is a very intimate conversation I'm having with an imagined reader. It's not a film script. A film script is just a blueprint—like an architectural diagram. And a film involves lots of input from so many different people with very different skill sets.

Q. **You once said, "Character is action. It's the oldest law of writing. It goes back to Aristotle. Plot is just a vehicle in which your characters act." Will you amplify that?**

A. I think a book is a journey by which a main character, or
    several characters, ultimately reach a reckoning with them-
    selves. The plot is just the car driving them down the road on
    that journey. I don't need a spectacular car. I just need one
    that's serviceable. I'm not a car guy.

    With the exception of *Shutter Island*, I never wrote an
    original plot. All I do is make the plot serviceable, like the
    car. I work really hard on a plot, because you need to work
    hardest at the things that don't come naturally. I don't work
    hard at dialogue. It just flows. It comes naturally to me. I
    barely rewrite it. Plot takes up the majority of my worry
    when I write a book because it's the last thing I consider. I
    think my talent is in dialogue, character development, and a
    sense of place.

Q. **What has surprised you about the writing life?**

A. What's surprised me most is that it's as cool as I hoped it
    would be. [Laughter.] You know, one of my favorite movies
    is *Broadcast News*. One scene describes my own life. There's
    an interchange where William Hurt says to Albert Brooks,
    "What do you do when your reality exceeds your dreams?"
    Albert Brooks says, "Keep it to yourself."

    That's where I find myself. I go on book tours; I'm inter-
    viewed by people, and it gets put in newspapers. Even twenty
    years down the line, it still seems surreal to me, surreal in a
    wonderful way.

    You know, last night at a book signing, someone asked
    me if I'd sign a paperback. I said, "Of course." And he said,
    "Some authors don't sign them." I said, "What the hell did
    they get into writing for?"

    I mean, there was a time when you were a complete nobody,
    and in your fantasy life you thought, "Wouldn't it be cool if

somebody actually wanted me to sign one of my books?" I still live in that place—where it all seems like a fantasy.

The thing is: I get paid to make shit up. I'd be doing it for free. I walk around thinking, "These lunatics actually pay me to do this." If a planeload of money was dumped on me, I'd continue doing what I do.

Q. **I was going to ask what you love about the writing life, but you've already answered that.**

A. They pay me to make shit up and I can keep my own hours. [Laughter.]

Q. **If you weren't writing, what would you be doing?**

A. Everybody has some fantasy about this kind of thing. I'm thinking I would be a carpenter. There's no reason for me to think that since I've never shown I can do anything with my hands. But I feel that's what I'd like to do if I wasn't writing.

Q. **You would certainly see the results of your labor.**

A. Yes. I need to see the results of anything I do, whether it's a book or a cabinet.

Q. **If you could have five people to a dinner party, from any walk of life, living or dead, who would they be?**

A. First, I'd have Gabriel García Márquez. I'd also invite FDR and Bill Murray. And then . . . Keith Richards. I would also like to have dinner with Joan of Arc.

Q. **What would you be talking about?**

A. With *that* group? What a party it would be. There would be no problem with conversation.

Congratulations on a stellar writing career and for following your own path. Many of your novels are multilayered and morally ambiguous explorations of family, blood, and betrayal. There are good reasons why you have such an enormous following.

MICHAEL CONNELLY
IS BOSCH AN ALTER EGO?

Michael Connelly's books have been translated into thirty-six languages and have sold more than sixty million copies worldwide. His novels have won many awards. His best-known crime fiction series features LAPD Detective Harry Bosch. His other hugely popular series features criminal defense attorney Mickey Haller, Harry's half brother.

Michael was once a crime reporter. In addition to the Harry Bosch and Mickey Haller series, he wrote the Jack McEvoy series, several stand-alone novels, many short stories, as well as some nonfiction books. He's also the executive producer of the television series *Bosch*, the most-watched Amazon Studios original drama series.

Our conversations took place between 2014 and 2017.

Q.   **I understand that at age sixteen your interest in crime was piqued. Tell us about that.**

A.   One night, I was driving my beat-up VW home from my job as a dishwasher and was stopped at a traffic signal. I saw a man running with something in his hand. As he passed a hedge, he shoved it into the hedge and kept going. When the light turned green, I made a U-turn, drove over to the hedge, and pulled out a shirt wrapped around a gun. I put it back in the hedge. This was before cell phones, of course, so I walked to a gas station and called my father.

Very soon, police cars with flashing lights descended on the area. I realized something had happened and flagged down a cop. I told him what I'd found and that I'd seen the guy run down the street and go into a bar. I became a partial witness to what had happened earlier, namely a man had attempted to hijack a car at gunpoint. His gun had gone off and the victim had been shot.

The guy I'd seen looked like a biker: he was big and had an unruly beard. There were a bunch of motorcycles parked in front of the bar. The police entered the place looking for a guy who fit the description I gave them. But all the guys in the place were big and had beards. The cops took them all to the police station. I spent most of the night looking at lineups, trying to identify the guy I'd glimpsed for only a few seconds. I was certain he'd gone into that bar and left through the back door. None of the men in the lineups were the one I saw.

The detective questioning me was a rough kind of guy. I could tell he didn't really believe me and thought I was a scared kid who was afraid of fingering somebody. It was frustrating—not being believed. The experience hooked me on the idea of learning more about detectives and their work. From that night on, I found myself reading crime stories in newspapers. I began reading true crime books looking for that rough kind of detective—like the guy who questioned me.

I had been reading some mysteries my mother read, but she preferred the soft-boiled, cozy ones. So, I began reading the hard-boiled stuff, which made me fall in love with the genre, and I'd fantasize that someday I'd write this kind of stuff. That's how it all began.

Q. **Tell us about the influence Raymond Chandler played in your writing life.**

A. At first my interest in crime fiction was reading contemporary stuff. I avoided old mysteries, and never read Raymond Chandler's novels. His most recent novel at that time was twenty years old, and there was stuff going back forty years. That just wasn't my cup of tea. So I never read anything by Chandler, even as I was immersing myself in crime fiction.

When I was in college, there were dollar movie nights. I went to see *The Long Goodbye*, which was based on one of Chandler's books, but was contemporary and set in Los Angeles in 1973. I loved the movie, which motivated me to read the book. As I read it, I realized it was set in the fifties, not the seventies. It was a great book. I then read every one of his novels in about two weeks. I got over this dumb idea of only reading contemporary crime fiction. I not only read Raymond Chandler, but I began reading all the crime fiction classics. I was hooked. A lightbulb went off in my head and I knew what I wanted to do.

Q. **You've said that you and Hieronymus (Harry) Bosch share some similarities. What are they?**

A. It depends on which Harry Bosch book you're reading. I've been so lucky to have written about him over a period of twenty years. When I first began with him, I didn't know if it would ever be published. So to make it interesting and fun, I wrote about a guy completely opposite of me. He's a smoker; I'm not. He's an orphan; I come from a big family. He's never been lucky in romance; I've been married for a long time.

I got lucky and the first book, *The Black Echo*, was published. I think I'm the luckiest writer on the planet: it's twenty years later and I'm still writing about this character. He's had to evolve, just like anybody would. In the process of his evolution, I started sharing more of myself with him, so it turned out he's not that different from me. It turns out he's left-handed, just like I am. He has a daughter who's the same age as mine. It's not only a sharing of these basic things, but Harry and I now share a world view.

Yet in some ways he's different from me. He's a reactive guy. He's undaunted and relentless. He's out there solving murders and carrying a gun. In those ways he's quite different from me. But if he stepped back and looked at the larger world picture, I think we would have a very similar take.

Q. **Harry Bosch is haunted by his Vietnam experience. What made you choose claustrophobia as a feature?**

A. My father was a builder. During my high school years, I worked for him. One summer, I was working with a guy who had just come back from Vietnam and had been a tunnel rat. He wouldn't talk about the experience, but it sounded really scary to me. There was no Internet back then, but there were some books about tunnel rats. It seemed to connect to my own life.

When I was a kid, I had some claustrophobia. I slept on the bottom bunk and felt like I was in a coffin. That always bothered me. Also, there was a rite of passage in my neighborhood where kids had to crawl through a storm drain. I had a fear about when my time would come to do it. So the idea of a tunnel rat played into my life long before I became a writer.

I moved to Los Angeles and worked at the *Los Angeles Times*. Just as I arrived, a big news story broke about a heist where the robbers used storm water tunnels beneath the city to get inside a bank. They then dug their own tunnel into the vault. As a police reporter, I was getting inside details from the detectives. It struck me that this could be the plotline of a novel. I could connect it to a detective whose past included tunnels. That became the framework for the plot of the first Harry Bosch novel. And it tapped into my own discomfort with enclosed spaces.

Q. **What made you name your most famous character Hieronymus?**

A. As a writer, you draw from stuff you know and from your own past. Realizing I wanted to be a writer, I took lots of English and art history classes in college. I had a humanities professor who was enamored of Hieronymus Bosch, the fifteenth-century painter. His work was very dark stuff and stuck with me.

So, fifteen years later, while putting together this book, *The Black Echo*, it seemed an appropriate name because this detective would be treading across terrain similar to those paintings. Bosch's paintings are about a world gone wrong and the wages of sin. You can ascribe these issues to a crime scene. And Harry Bosch would decipher crime scenes, the way fifteen years earlier in class we looked at paintings and tried to read them—understand what they meant. So his name, Hieronymus, came from that. I have some Hieronymus Bosch prints hanging in my house and office: *The Garden of Earthly Delights*, and the darkest one, called *Hell*.

Q. **You've said your "real" job is to write about Bosch. What did you mean by that?**

A. Bosch is my real focus. To keep writing about him, I need to move away from him at times. The Mickey Haller novels really derived from the need to keep Harry Bosch alive. The other books might have varying degrees of success, but my main focus is Harry Bosch. With the movie *The Lincoln Lawyer*, the Mickey Haller novels are now more successful than the Harry Bosch books, but Mickey was really born out of my need to take time off from Harry Bosch.

Q. **Mickey Haller is one of the most intriguing characters in contemporary fiction. Is he based on anyone you know?**

A. Writers take from everywhere. He really comes from three points. One is that years ago I met a guy—a lawyer—at a baseball game. During the game, we talked about our lives. And he's the one who told me he worked out of the back seat of his car. I thought that was an intriguing setup and someday I might write about that.

The other two sources for Mickey involved my doing research about a criminal defense lawyer. I went to a couple of lawyer friends. They allowed me to be a fly on the wall in their lives. So Mickey Haller came from these three lawyers.

Q. **Your fictional universe has Mickey Haller and Harry Bosch interacting. You've compared your work to a canvas with the characters floating across it as currents on a painting. Will you elaborate a bit?**

A. I compare these characters to the Hieronymus Bosch paintings. If you examine a Bosch canvas, you will see that it's busy with stuff happening in every quadrant of the painting. It's not all related, but yet somehow it is. In a Bosch painting, you can spend an entire day looking at one corner and look at another corner of the painting the next day. That infused my thinking about the series. Of course, the same character moves through the books, but I wanted a mosaic of interlocking characters, and if you look hard enough you find connections among them all.

Q. **Having read the Mickey Haller novels, it's difficult for me to believe you're not an attorney. What kind of research or collaboration do you do?**

A. I have more than just professional relationships with the lawyers I've consulted; they're friends. One was a college roommate. I run my ideas by them, write the book, and then they vet it for me. I have no legal experience, so I use this team of lawyers to make sure the writing is accurate.

Q. **Unlike many writers, you listen to music while writing.**

A. Music helps me get in tune with the character. Like Harry, I listen to instrumental jazz without lyrical intrusion because it's difficult for me to put words on a computer screen when there are vocals. There's something improvisational about jazz, and I'm improvising as I'm writing. It all works together for me in some way. It's a bit magical and hard to put my finger on it.

Q. **Harry Bosch is nearing the end of his career. What's going to happen to him?**

A. Harry's over sixty now, and he's going to retire soon. I think various developments in his story will give me some opportunities to take Harry in a new direction.

Q. **Let's talk about a relatively new aspect of your career. *Bosch* is now a police procedural television series produced by Amazon Studios. How did this project happen?**

A. Harry's had a checkered history when it comes to Hollywood. Early on there was interest in him. I sold the rights for a film in the 1990s. It was a long-term deal. Even though nothing came of it, I don't regret it because the Hollywood money permitted me to become a full-time writer. It allowed me to focus on Bosch's character in the books, which is a big part of why I'm still able to write about him. It was something of a deal with the devil, but I would do it again.

Years went by, and I finally got the rights back. By that time I'd written many books about Harry. It seemed clear that if I went back to Hollywood, the best way to tell the story would be in a television series. You know, in Hollywood word leaks out, and eventually Amazon came calling. A partnership was formed. From my standpoint, it was easy and painless. I wasn't drifting around Hollywood, trying to sell Harry Bosch. It all kind of fell in my lap.

Beyond the connection to bookselling, Amazon wanted me involved in the TV series. That's quite unusual in Hollywood. Normally, they take a book and say, "Be a good little fella and run along. We'll take care of this." But Amazon wanted my involvement to help nurture the visual re-creation of the character with whom I'd spent twenty years of my life. The prospect of participating in the television series was very attractive to me; it was basically a no-brainer.

I co-wrote the pilot with the showrunner. In television, the showrunner is the creative boss. I don't have experience with television, so we wanted to get someone who did and whose creative mindset was similar to mine. We went to Eric Overmyer who'd worked on *The Wire* and *Treme*, and who's worked on other shows I've loved. So, he's the boss—the show-runner. I'm his lieutenant. He runs stuff by me to get my take and to make sure we're on point with Harry Bosch's stories.

Q. **As a seasoned novelist, how does co-writing screenplays differ from writing novels?**

A. It's hugely different on at least two levels. The first is what you lose when you go from writing novels to writing for television. In the books, Harry's a very internal guy. One reason he's been around for twenty years is that people like the way he thinks.

In a television depiction, you can't go inside his head as you can with a novel. Everything on TV is about what he says and does, which is how a viewer determines whether or not he's likable. I think Harry has a kind of everyman's sensibility with which people connect. In the books, it comes out in his thinking process. But with television, it's really all about what he says and does. That's a big transition for me.

The other aspect is for twenty-five years, I've been in a room by myself, writing these books. Of course, I get edited when I turn a book in, but for the year during which I'm writing, it's me against the machine.

For the television series, I'm in a room with writers, and all four walls are covered with three-by-five cards showing every scene from each episode. It's very much committee work until everything's nailed down and plotted out. Then different scripts are assigned to various writers, who go off and work on those episodes. It's very different from the way I write. I don't even use an outline.

Now, I can go into a room and see every act and each beat of a scene, an episode, or the entire season right there on the wall. By the time I go off to write a script on my own, I pretty much know everything.

Q. How are you adapting to this sea change in circumstances?

A. They say you can't teach an old dog new tricks. But for me it's been a real breath of fresh air. I feel that after twenty-five years in a room by myself, I'm now writing differently. I'm having a great time with it. I think it's going to carry through in my writing future books.

Q. Since *Bosch* has been on Amazon TV, do fans tell you that when reading a Harry Bosch novel, they envision Titus Welliver as Harry?

A. It's interesting because Titus Welliver in real life and on the show is about twelve or fifteen years younger than the Harry Bosch about whom I'm currently writing. So, for me, there's still a distinct separation. As I'm writing, I don't see Titus. Then, when I watch the show, I *totally* see Titus as Harry.

When I write about Mickey Haller, I *see* Matthew McConaughey. It has nothing to do with the acting. It's a function of the fact that when McConaughey appeared in *The Lincoln Lawyer*, he was the same age as Mickey was in the book. So, perhaps by osmosis, the image filtered into my creative thinking. I assume it will happen with Titus, but it just hasn't happened yet. Also, I've been writing about Harry Bosh for more than twenty years before Titus was ever in the role, so *my* image of Bosch has been deeply cemented in my head. Titus has a hammer and chisel and is knocking down that image.

Q. Your Bosch novel *The Wrong Side of Goodbye* has an intriguing title. It reminds me of the noir novels of the 1940s. Tell us about the title.

A. You're right. I set out writing this book with a couple of goals in mind. The first was to open the story without there having been a murder committed for Harry to solve. And as for the title, I wanted to pay homage to my literary elders. I wrote the novel as a bit of a throwback to the private eye novels from the forties and fifties. These were the stories that made me want to become a writer when I read them years ago. The title could have just as easily been affixed to a Raymond Chandler novel.

Q. **What has been one of the most surprising things you've learned about writing in creating your novels?**

A. Basically, I write the story *I* would like to read. I write for an audience of one—myself. What's surprised me is how storytelling is so important around the world. So, a character trying to solve a murder and find his place in the world in LA can connect with someone in Dublin or Paris.

As I've had more success, I've had more opportunities to travel. It always surprises and fulfills me when someone stands up at a book signing in France and says they're very worried about Harry Bosch. It just connects to my heart that I've created this character with this almost universal appeal. It surprised me when it first happened, and it's remained a surprise to me.

Q. **If you were to have dinner with any five people, either in literature or history, living or dead, who would they be?**

A. An obvious one would be Raymond Chandler. The other one is easy: my father passed away before I was published and had any success, so I'd like to have a meal with him now. I was very close to a cousin who passed away when we were twelve. I'd like to catch up with her. And maybe I'd like to meet the real Hieronymus Bosch. But he might throw soup at me for taking his name.

Q. **What's in store for the future?**

A. When we've talked in the past, I always knew what I would do next. I usually start writing a new book on December first of each year, so I have nearly a month to decide what to do. I have an idea for a Bosch book and another for a Mickey Haller book, but I have this growing notion tugging at me and telling me to do something new. I don't want to keep writing only about Harry Bosch and Mickey Haller and would like to come up with something new before my storytelling days are over. So I might be putting a new character on the page.

Thank you for being such a prolific artist who has provided so much pleasure to millions of people for so many years. Both Bosch and Haller are enduringly fascinating characters.

DON WINSLOW
MASTER STYLIST FROM SHAKESPEARE TO CRIME FICTION

Don Winslow is known to thriller lovers everywhere, especially after his extraordinary novel *Savages*, which was made into a film directed by Oliver Stone. Don grew up in Rhode Island, and at age seventeen left to study journalism at the University of Nebraska, where he earned a degree in African studies. While in college, he traveled to southern Africa, sparking a lifelong involvement with that continent. Later, he obtained a master's degree in military history.

He spent time in California, Idaho, and Montana before moving to New York City to become a writer. He paid his bills working as a movie theater manager and as a private investigator. Later, Don joined a friend's safari firm in Kenya, where he led photographic expeditions. He also led hiking trips to the mountains of Southwest China. When not on safari, Don directed Shakespeare plays at Oxford during their summer program.

Don's first novel, *A Cool Breeze on the Underground*, was nominated for an Edgar Award.

Our conversations took place between 2015 and 2017.

Q. You have an extraordinary backstory. You've been a movie theater manager, a private investigator, led photographic safaris in Africa, hiking expeditions in China, and directed Shakespeare productions in Oxford, England. How have these experiences informed your writing?

A. I think—and you know this, too—everything we do informs our writing. That's what makes us writers. Everyday observations and experiences become grist for the mill. More specifically, I grew up on Shakespeare. I was reading and memorizing Shakespeare when I was eight years old. Having the chance to work with great people in England, working with language every day as a director, I had to make the language understandable and physical. I had to bring out the muscularity of the language. It definitely helped inform my writing. My involvement with the theater company was mostly before my first novel was published. I was still struggling to make a living. From seven in the morning until ten at night, I was either rehearsing Shakespeare, teaching it, or talking with other directors. I was constantly immersed in language—with its rhythm, sound, and with dialogue, all of which was a tremendous foundation for my writing.

The investigative work was not terribly different from what I do now, in the sense that I looked at lots of trial transcripts, read records, and interviewed people. I developed a capacity to search out certain details, looking for things that didn't quite match up. I looked for discrepancies between documents and people's testimony. That background informs my writing. For example, while writing *The Cartel* and *Power of the Dog*, I went through thousands of pages of records. Those were skills I learned as an investigator.

As a photographic safari guide in Kenya, my job was to

notice details. For instance, when trying to find a leopard for people to photograph, I had to keep in mind there would be a certain kind of tree at one time of day where a leopard could be found. And there was another place at a different hour to find the animal. In other words, I was always looking at details. I became a trained observer and would look at underlying reasons for things being the way they were.

In crime writing, there are the events, but then there are the underlying reasons for what has happened. And there are small details that are important, too. Providing that richness and those detailed elements are what I hope to give the reader.

Q. **Is there anything in your background that's made you so interested in crime stories?**

A. Sometimes I ask myself that question. I don't know that I can come up with the real answer. I guess the *hypotenuse* answer is that it's life in the *extreme*. I grew up during the New England crime wars, so as a kid, I knew about these kinds of guys in the neighborhood.

Q. **So, growing up in Rhode Island influenced you?**

A. Yes. When I was a kid, Rhode Island had a large Mafia presence, more so than it does now. It was always around, and I saw it. It was always written about in the *Providence Journal*, and Jimmy Breslin was a big influence on me. I recall being in high school and reading Breslin's columns and thinking *that's what I want to do.* In college, I was a journalism major. I wrote columns basically imitating Breslin's style. [Laughter.]

Q. **Your novels *The Cartel* and *The Power of the Dog* have astounding details about the Mexican drug trade and the so-called war on drugs. Will you talk a bit about your research for these books?**

A. Between *The Power of the Dog* and *The Cartel*, I spent ten years researching and writing about the topic. If you include *Savages* and its prequel, *The Kings of Cool*, it's more like fifteen years. Everyone had stereotypical images of the Mexican cartels, and like most stereotypes, some are true, but many aren't.

For me it was a matter of going after the details, trying to give these people real lives. My research technique partly involves my training as a historian. I try getting deep background, most of which won't show up in the book, but which informs how I write the novel. I didn't start with crime or cartel lore. I began with Aztec and Mayan history and the conquistador era. When I felt I had some understanding of the culture, I went to more recent history, extensively reading articles and books about the drug cartels.

I didn't want to approach DEA people, cops, former intelligence people or drug people out of ignorance. I wanted to master the background before talking to these people. You know, when you're writing, the research can be constant. As you write, you may be in the middle of a paragraph, when more questions arise. I even want to get physical details of what things look, sound, and smell like—everything.

The bizarre, surreal thing about researching the drug cartels was that most of it was already in the media and social media. By the time you get to the cartel era between 2004 and 2014, the drug lords were *advertising*. They were putting out demos on video clips. They were writing to newspaper editors and photographing banners over stacks of bodies, explaining what they did and why they did it. The drug wars became hyperviolent and widely known.

Q. **James Ellroy called *The Cartel* the *War and Peace* of dope-war books. You dedicated the book to more than one hundred named journalists who were murdered or who "disappeared" in Mexico during the period of the novel. Tell us about that.**

A. The cartels came to a point where they realized they not only had to fight the war with bullets, but they had to win the hearts and minds of people. They wanted to control the narrative, so they began killing journalists who told the truth. They began bribing journalists, army officers, and the police—it was a matter of "Take this money or we'll kill you." So, many journalists caved in and wouldn't cover the cartels' activities.

Q. ***The Winter of Frankie Machine* concerns a former Mafia hit man and is a smaller and very human story, in contrast to the epic proportions of *The Cartel*, *The Power of the Dog*, and *The Force*. Will you talk about that?**

A. It took me five years to do *Dog*. I came out of that experience mentally, physically, and emotionally exhausted. After that I wanted to do a smaller story—even though the story of Frankie Machine is about crime in Southern California. All the cases in the flashback scenes were real cases I fictionalized. It's a good changeup to play with scale. So, rather than telling the story of twenty-five people over fifty years, I decided to just get into the head of this individual and look at life through his experiences. If the reader gets some history, that's good, but I wanted the intimacy of one man's story. After the first twenty pages, you know Frankie and you *care* about him. I wondered if I could write about a guy whose job it was to kill people and make him human, and even likable.

Q. Shifting gears, you said when you wrote *Savages,* you wanted to write a book that "tore the cage a little, and maybe broke out." What did you mean?

A. [Laughter.] I'm a genre guy, and there's that slight stink on us. Literary fiction looks down on us. We're in something of a writers' ghetto. Over the last ten years, bloggers, critics, publishers, and editors have become very concerned with branding and defining what crime fiction should be. There are definitions and subdefinitions, and I felt all of these categories kept tightening the cage. You know, it's the notion that if you're a thriller writer, you *must* have your character in mortal jeopardy on page *one* or it's not a thriller. Or, by page 160, you *must* introduce a secondary character who has critical information regarding the case. [Laughter.]

I began wondering, *Who's setting these rules?* I felt we thriller writers were becoming cereal brands—like Frosted Flakes, Wheaties, or maybe Cheerios. People have had trouble categorizing me. Some stores have my books in the mystery section. Others have me in fiction. I wanted to break out of that box.

Q. Do you break any "rules" of writing with your novels?

A. I break the rules about point of view, switching them like a schizophrenic. Some writers try to figure out how to switch point of view inside a page. I'm trying to figure out how to do it inside a *word.* [Laughter.]

Q. You said about your most recent novel, *The Force,* "This is the book I've wanted to write my whole life." Tell us about that.

A. I was born on Staten Island, where Denny Malone lives. I was raised in Rhode Island, but as a kid I was always running down to New York. I lived and worked there in the late seventies and early eighties. New York has always been a home to me.

But it's more than that: the movie *The French Connection* is one of the reasons I'm a writer. I remember distinctly going into the theater on Broadway and seeing that film. I was just blown away by it, and by *Serpico*, followed by *Prince of the City*. Those were important and evocative works for me, both the books and the films. Having lived and worked in New York and having been so influenced by those movies, I always had an ambition to try writing this book.

Q. **In *The Force*, Denny Malone is a conflicted man: he uses drugs, is separated from his wife, feels guilty about his kids, and lives on the edge. Many of your protagonists can be described as "all messed up": Frankie "Machine," Ben and Chon from *Savages*, and Tim Kearney, a.k.a. Bobby Z. How do you manage to dig so deeply and depict such flawed and troubled people?**

A. [Laughter.] Yes, I guess they're pretty messed-up guys. Those kinds of people are more interesting than ordinary people. The edge is always more interesting than the center. I recall Michael Connelly and I were at some conference and he was talking about writing. He took a cup and put it on the center of the table. "It's not very interesting now," he said, and kept moving it toward the edge to the point where it was about to fall over and shatter. And then he said, "Well, *now* I have your attention. *Now* it's interesting."

He was dead right about that. He was talking more about *action* than about character, but I've always taken that concept and applied it to character. I think one of the great advantages we have in our genre of crime fiction is we write about people in extremis. We write about people in extraordinary situations. And they're often very flawed people. Before this, I wrote more about criminals than cops, but it's the same principle. The flaws in these people make them interesting and compelling. At the end of the day, the flaws make us love or hate them.

You and I have both been married to our wives a long time. You know that you get into a relationship because of someone's virtues, but after a while you begin to love their flaws. I often feel that way about my characters. I come to love them despite and *because* of their shortcomings. I often think our greatest strengths are also our greatest weaknesses.

That's true of Denny Malone: the same things that drive him to do great things also drive him to do bad things.

Q. **As do your other epics, *The Force* explores the drug trade, politics, police, and corruption. What has drawn you so intensely to these issues?**

A. I never started out to write about the drug world.

I live in California near the Mexican border, and back in the late nineties, a massacre occurred just across the border. I wanted to understand why it had happened. I found myself sitting at the keyboard and writing about it.

Living on the Mexican border, I eat more tortillas than bread. [Laughter.] The level of drug cartel crime is very real to me. In the course of researching and writing about it, I've met people who keep it vivid for me. It's one thing to talk about the heroin epidemic. It's another to go to the funerals.

As a writer, you want to write about the most interesting and important things happening today. I want to write about race relations, about police shootings, corruption, and drugs. In life, you can't separate things from each other; they're all interconnected parts of a larger piece.

Q. **Many of your novels are written in the present tense. What made you decide to use that approach?**

A. I remember the moment I first did it. It was in 1995. My career was flatlining. Working as an investigator, I was riding the train each day from San Juan Capistrano to downtown LA. I was writing on my laptop in the traditional third-person, past-tense, narrative style. But it seemed flat and dull. I was bored with *myself.* So I began writing the next page in the present tense. It opened up a whole new world for me. I began to have fun again. It turned into *The Death and Life of Bobby Z.*

The first few sentences of that book changed my writing life. Writing in the present tense is liberating. I love it. The next sentence is coming at you in the here and now. And it's cinematic. It immerses the reader in the immediacy of *now.* It's as though I'm saying to the reader, "Come with me on this cool trip. I want you with me. I'm not going to tell you, 'Here's what happened. It's too bad you weren't there when it occurred, so let me describe it to you.'" Instead, I say, "Let's travel this path together."

Q. **In one novel, you described an elevated structure as being "Carl Sagan high." In *The Cartel,* you describe an obese man as "one jelly doughnut away from a triple bypass." I'm blown away by your metaphors. They often reference popular culture and are absolutely arresting. Tell us about that.**

A. I think I use pop culture because I'm not that intellectual. I look for things people can relate to. We thriller writers write about a lot of really far-out things—stuff most readers never encounter in their lives. So I look for images and metaphors that *will* make it familiar. I also think they're fun. They just come to mind. And, of course, the rhythm of the writing is important—even a single syllable can make a huge difference.

Q. **Like "one jelly doughnut away from a triple bypass"?**

A. [Laughter.] Yes. It has a cadence, a rhythm of its own. At first I thought maybe it could be one jelly doughnut away from a heart attack. But then, I wanted to push it a little bit— maybe angle it off and take it one step further to make it more distinctive. The *triple bypass* reference is funnier.

Q. **Is it true you once said that for you, writing is an addiction?**

A. [More laughter.] I think it's true. Sometimes I think it's a good thing, sometimes, not.

Q. **How do you feel if a day goes by and you haven't written?**

A. Anxious. Very anxious. [Laughter.] I feel guilty. I think I should be home writing. I feel as though I'm shirking . . . It's a strange kind of dysphoria. I think this writing addiction is like a dope-driven rush. When it's going well, it's a real high. When it's going badly, it feels like it's just a job.

I try taking Sundays off. I *sort* of get away with that because I feel like I'm improving myself. [More laughter.] But I definitely feel as though something is wrong. Sometimes I just can't turn it off; I'm writing in my head. I'll be walking with my wife and she'll say, "What did you say?" I'll answer, "I didn't say anything." But it turns out I was speaking a char- acter's dialogue and wasn't even aware of it.

I walk nearly every day on this winding road with these wicked curves. One day I was so caught up in my thoughts, I literally walked off the edge of a little cliff. Luckily, it was a short drop. I was busily plotting something. [More laughter.]

Q. **Do you have a favorite among all your novels?**

A. That's a tough one. They're all my children. It's not a favorite, but I'm so attached to my first book, *A Cool Breeze on the Underground*. It was such a struggle and took so long to write. I have a fondness for *Dog* and *Cartel* because I spent so many years on them. And then there's *Savages*, which was such a dice toss. I just said "The hell with it. It'll probably end up badly." But it didn't. I really can't say I have a favorite. I love them all, but each in a different way. Picking a favorite is sort of like trying to pick your favorite child.

Q. **Or being asked which is your favorite dog?**

A. Yes. You know, it's been eight years since we lost our last dog. It was one of the worst days of my life. I haven't been able to get another one. I just can't go through that kind of loss again.

Q. **Is there anything about your writing process that might surprise our readers?**

A. I don't know if it's a surprise, but I treat writing like a job. I don't really believe in inspiration. Inspiration is for amateurs.

Q. **You know the old saying, don't you? "If you wait for inspiration, you're a waiter, not a writer." [Laughter.] "You can wait on tables at Le Cirque or at a diner, but you're still a waiter." [More laughter.]**

A. Let me tell you a cute story about Le Cirque.

Years ago, while working as an investigator, I stayed at the hotel where Le Cirque was located. But I wasn't going to eat at *that* restaurant, not at *those* prices. So I ordered in some Chinese food. When I got my hotel bill, there was a *forty-seven-dollar surcharge* for them having let the delivery guy come up to my room with the food.

So, the next time I stayed there, I ordered the food and asked the delivery guy to meet me in the hotel lobby. I ate my takeout in the lobby, right outside the entrance to Le Cirque. I stood there with a brown paper bag and ate the Chinese food. They told me it looked seedy and asked me not to do it. So I negotiated with them and they dropped the surcharge.

But getting back to the writing: to me, it's a deliberate process. It's not based on inspiration. The other thing that might surprise our readers is I don't start writing a book until I know the main characters well. I'll think about them— sometimes for years, like in the case of Denny Malone.

Q. *The Force* **and** *Savages* **are audacious pieces of contemporary fiction. Both are written in an edgy, lyrical, cinematic, even radical style. Will you talk a bit more about your writing style?**

A. As in architecture, form follows function. I think story dictates style. I try to write from inside the character's head. It's kind of sneaky: it's third person but it has a first-person point of view. Does that make any sense?

Q. **Yes, it does. And it's written in the present tense, which gives everything that sense of immediacy you mentioned earlier.**

A. Yes, when I began writing in the present tense, the story suddenly had a sense of immediacy it never before had. It was not like I was looking down at a table and describing what was there. So I've stayed with writing my novels in the present tense. That way of writing lets me *inhabit* a character. It dictates the style, the rhythm, and the choice of words. This may sound pretentious, but I try to pay attention to the musicality of the writing.

Q. **It doesn't sound pretentious at all. There *is* a kind of music to the words.**

A. Yes, there is. I go back to Shakespeare with that concept. You have to stage it. You have to put it on. You have to *hear* it. Sometimes when I was writing some of the chapters in *The Force*, I would listen to the hip-hop music referred to in the chapter and pump it up to the point where it was painful. I'd write while the energy and edge and anger of the music was pounding in my head. In other scenes, I'd listen to the jazz referred to in that chapter I was writing.

I think readers love *being* there in the midst of the action. That's particularly true in the crime genre. There's a powerful link between film and novels, especially in noir fiction.

Q. **I understand that *The Force* has been sold to Fox with James Mangold directing, and Ridley Scott is directing *The Cartel*, which is going to be a film. How have these events impacted your career?**

A. For me, it's been huge. To have directors of that stature is fantastic, and that sunlight reflects on me. The major effect is I now have the economic freedom to write all the time. That's been true since *The Death and Life of Bobby Z* was made into a film. I was six published books into my career before I could quit my day job. I always made a living. I wasn't going to penalize my family for my ambition, but as for how I approach my day? It's always been the same: *Get up and show up.*

Q. **What advice would you give to aspiring writers today?**

A. I'd simply say: *Write.* Like most things in life, it's a verb before it's a noun.

The second thing I'd urge is: *Don't write anything unless*

you have to. I would say you shouldn't write unless you feel an inner compulsion to do so. You must feel you *have* to do it. And then, don't listen to most people.

The third bit of advice is simple: Just read. Read good books. I just finished *War and Peace* for the fifth time in my life. I wanted to see how a great writer handles a multigenerational story. So, one has to read good things.

Another pointer: Don't pay attention to so-called peer reviews. It's too easy to get nibbled to death by ducks. [Laughter.]

Q. **Will you complete this sentence: "Writing novels has taught me_____?"**

A. Tenacity. It's taught me tenacity. [More laughter.] It's a marathon. It's like I'm at mile twenty-two and think, "I'll never make it." And you feel the same way the next time you're working on a book, but now you have the experience and can tell yourself you got through it last time and you'll get through it again. And it will come out pretty well.

Q. **You're having a dinner party and can invite any five people, living or dead, from any walk of life. Who would they be?**

A. Crazy Horse would by my first guest because I want to know what really happened at the Little Bighorn. Buddha would be next, because I feel I have to get noble here for just a second. Then I'd have Bruce Springsteen because I think he's *the* American poet. He's always, in a real sense, spoken to me. I'd have the late Art Pepper, a great saxophone jazz artist. Then I'd have Brendan Behan, the Irish poet, novelist, and short-story writer. He was so clever, he actually said, "I'm a drinker with a writing problem." [Laughter.]

Q. **What would you all be talking about?**

A. [Laughter.] Assuming we could talk…if I spoke Lakota, I'd be
probing Crazy Horse about what really happened at the Little
Bighorn. I wouldn't want Custer there because he was a liar.
I would love to hear Brendan Behan and Springsteen talk. I'd
be talking to Pepper about riffs in certain jazz songs. I don't
think I'd talk much. I'd just sit back and take it all in.

Q. **What's coming next from Don Winslow?**

A. I'll probably write another book. [Laughter.]

And I'll be the first to read it. It's been a pleasure talking with
an author whose novels are so original and resonate deeply with
realism, honesty, and sheer magnetism.

DAVID MORRELL
RAMBO AND THE DRAMATIZATION OF FEAR

David Morrell's debut novel, *First Blood*, written in 1972, became a bestseller and spawned the Rambo film franchise, starring Sylvester Stallone as the iconic figure. David has written thirty novels and his work has been translated into twenty-six languages.

He is acclaimed for his bestselling, action-packed novels, including *The Brotherhood of the Rose*, *Desperate Measures*, and *The Naked Edge*, to name a few.

David is rare among suspense/thriller writers, having received a BA in English from St. Jerome's University and an MA and PhD in American literature from Pennsylvania State University. In 1986, he gave up his tenure as an English professor teaching literature at the University of Iowa to begin writing fiction full-time. He also wrote the 2007–2008 Captain America comic book miniseries, *The Chosen*.

He was a finalist for the Edgar and Anthony Awards, received the Macavity and Nero Awards, and is a recipient of the International Thriller Writers Thriller Master Award.

Our conversations took place in 2015, 2016, and 2017.

Q. **Rambo is an iconic name in our culture. Amazingly,** *First Blood* **was your debut novel. How did your** *first novel* **become such a wild success?**

A. I have a graduate degree from Penn State. I studied at Penn State under a noted Hemingway scholar, Philip Young. I had an interest in thrillers, and it occurred to me that Hemingway wrote many action scenes: the war scenes in *A Farewell to Arms* and *For Whom the Bell Tolls* come to mind. But the scenes don't feel pulpy, as do so many in thriller novels. I wondered if it was possible to write an action book that wouldn't feel like a genre book if I used the kind of art Hemingway brought to his prose. He avoided clichés like "A shot rang out."

The tactic I used was to write action in a different way than had previously been done. I wanted to avoid all the vocabulary that had accumulated by that time.

With that intention, I wrote *First Blood*, allowing of course, that it was a very topical subject because there were so many returning Vietnam veterans in 1972. So, it was an attempt to reinvent the action book. The response was overwhelming. It was well reviewed in virtually every major newspaper and magazine.

Q. **And, of course, then came the movie.**

A. Initially, Stanley Kramer wanted to turn the novel into a film, but that didn't happen. A producer named Lawrence Turman, who had co-produced *The Graduate*, found the book in a bookstore and took it to Columbia Pictures, where Richard Brook began working on it.

After about a year, Columbia Pictures sold the movie rights to Warner Brothers. They brought in Sydney Pollack to direct Steve McQueen. That moved along for a time, but they suddenly realized Steve McQueen was forty-five years old and there were no forty-five-year-old Vietnam veterans. The men who fought there were eighteen and nineteen years old.

Finally, two producers, Mario Kassar and Andrew Vajna, had an agreement with Ted Kotcheff, a director of note. Ultimately, with Ted directing and Sylvester Stallone in the role, the film was released. And it did the same thing for action movies that the novel did ten years earlier for action books.

I should note that Sly himself didn't have confidence in the film and said it would probably be the most expensive home movie ever made. [Laughter.] But it was very well received when it was released in the fall of 1982. And the rest is history.

Q. **You once said, "My novels dramatize fear." Will you elaborate on that?**

A. One of the advantages of having gone to Penn State was having had a scholar for a mentor—Philip Young. Also, a professional writer named Philip Klass taught there. He was a science fiction writer whose pseudonym was William Tenn. As a professional writer, he brought wisdom to teaching because he'd done it for a living. He spent a great deal of time talking with me. One of the things he shared was, "The hardest thing for an author is to find a subject matter, a voice, and a distinct personality that will distinguish that author from everyone else."

Now when I teach writing I have a mantra: "Be a first-rate version of yourself and not a second-rate version of another author." This was what Philip Klass essentially said to me. He said one way to find that voice—that distinctive something— is to think that every person has a dominant emotion. For some it's pity. For others it's lust or anger. In his conversations with me, he determined my dominant emotion was fear.

And he was right. I had a terrible upbringing. My father

died in the Second World War, and my mother was forced, for a time, to put me in an orphanage. Then she remarried, but the marriage was horrible. There were terrible fights in the household. Many were the nights I slept under the bed, covering my ears so I couldn't hear them fighting. I told stories to myself in the dark. No wonder eventually—despite my academic background as a professor of American literature—I've become a thriller writer. I'm much happier doing that than writing academic literature. Basically, I have no choice because of how I was raised.

Philip Klass was right. My world view is that it can all go to hell in an instant and you have to be ready for it. That's pretty much the central theme running through my work. It's about people's awareness of how uncertain life can be and their trying to guard against that. So essentially, much of my work orbits around that theme as its core emotion.

Q. **So clearly, your personal life wends its way into the thematic infrastructure of your writing.**

A. Yes. The circumstances impinging upon each of us to make us who we are—I think about that concept a lot. I try to write novels that in some ways reflect my own life's events. The major event for me was the 1987 death of my son from Ewing's sarcoma, a rare bone cancer. Then, in 2009, my fourteen-year-old granddaughter died of the same disease. One could talk about unimaginable bad luck. It's generally not believed to be an inherited disease, so the fates really, really slammed my family. These terrible losses reinforced for me the fragility and unpredictability of life. So truly, it can all go to hell in an instant.

If you look at my work up until 1987, there was a theme of young people looking for fathers who usually disappointed them. After my son died, there were a couple of books where parents were looking for son figures. I know we're going to talk about this, but in my novel *Murder as a Fine Art*, we have a sixty-nine-year-old man, Thomas De Quincey, with a twenty-one-year-old daughter, Emily. Only *after* I finished the book did I realize Emily was actually a version of my *granddaughter*.

So, my books are very personal. What I try to do is use my writing as a way of discovering myself. Someone once said that if you read them in chronological order, you would have what amounts to an autobiography of my soul.

Q. **In psychiatry, we sometimes say, no matter how much he tries, the patient can never really change the subject.**

A. It's very true. Philip Klass said we all have a ferret darting around inside of us, not wanting to be discovered. But if we use our dominant emotion to try to identify that ferret, then we're on our way to finding our subject matter. So, Philip Klass's conversations with me were often self-psychoanalytic in nature.

Q. **This past summer we both attended a convention for suspense/thriller writers and devotees. You gave a talk called "Setting." I confess I first thought it would be a discussion about scenes and locales for a novel. But it was much, much more. Can you tell us what you meant by setting?**

A. If you think about the authors who have lasted, they have a world view and a kind of world within themselves—a setting, so to speak. We think of Hemingway in Michigan or Key West, or Paris, Fitzgerald in New York, or Faulkner in Mississippi.

Philip Klass encouraged me to think of setting as having a finality—that a novel could stand alone, simply on how its setting was handled in terms of the research that went into it. For instance, in *Murder as a Fine Art*, it was fascinating to discover how different London was in 1854 from what it is today. The setting helped establish the character for everything else in the novel.

When talking about ideas for a story, I put a lot of stock in daydreams because they're examples of our subconscious burbling up to the surface. I've noticed that in my daydreams the settings are as important as the situations. So, I ask myself why a certain setting comes to me. On a simple level, imagine lying on a beach with a pleasant breeze and listening to seagulls … Clearly there's a subconscious text having to do with feeling tired and the need to rest. But I began looking deeper in the novel to detect psychological issues by its setting. It's complicated, but it can make all the difference between a superficial book and one that goes more deeply into the subject.

One other thing I said was that in addition to place—or physical setting—one must consider how to describe things in a novel. If you use the sense of sight exclusively to describe things—which is what many authors do—you will have a one-dimensional, flat atmosphere. But if you put three or four senses into a setting by taking the sense of sight for granted and using others, such as smell and touch, you will, by adding those elements, have a multidimensional setting. It sounds so obvious, but I see it all the time in published books—authors using only the sense of sight in their settings.

Q. **You departed from the thriller genre when you wrote *Murder as a Fine Art*, the first novel of your Victorian trilogy. I was struck by the change in venue, by the time frame of the novel, and by how you described people's clothing and other things in 1854 London. Will you talk a bit about your excursion into Victorian England?**

A. Some years ago, *Creation*, a film about Darwin, referred to Thomas De Quincey. Charles Darwin had a nervous breakdown when he was writing *On the Origin of Species*. It had to do with the death of his favorite daughter. His wife suggested that maybe God was trying to tell Darwin not to write the book. He had fevers, he couldn't eat, and his ills didn't match any disease known at the time.

We know about it now: it was his subconscious in relation to his daughter's death. In the film, there's a line that said, "You know, Charles, there are people like De Quincey who know we can be controlled by thought and emotions beyond our awareness." I thought, this sounded very much like Freud, but the movie was set in the 1850s, long before Freud. So, I thought I'd like to learn more about Thomas De Quincey.

I fell in love with the guy. He preceded Freud by more than seventy years and invented the word *subconscious*. We know that Freud read De Quincy. I mention this because the issue of the subconscious is so vital and there's a suspicion that some of what developed in psychoanalysis was inspired by De Quincy.

Not only did he create the word *subconscious*, but he was the first person to write about drug addiction; the first who used a psychological approach to understanding *Macbeth*; he was obsessed by the first publicized mass killings in England—the Ratcliff Highway murders in 1811, way before Jack the Ripper; and he wrote about these killings in a fifty-page, blood-soaked essay.

In essence, he invented the true crime genre. In addition, he inspired Edgar Allan Poe, who in turn inspired Sir Arthur Conan Doyle to create Sherlock Holmes. De Quincy has never been given his due because of his drug addiction. I decided to write a novel about the Ratcliff Highway murders. The basic concept of the novel was that someone had read De Quincey's 1854 essay about the original murders, which occurred in

1811, and replicated the murders using De Quincey's essay as a blueprint. The question was, why was the killer doing it? De Quincey would have to use his psychological innovation to identify why this person was committing the crimes.

I wanted to write a novel about a real person and wanted to set it in 1854 when that essay was published. I realized to do this, I needed to study the period as if I were working toward a PhD, because people would jump on me if I got it wrong. I spent two years doing sort of a PhD thesis research about 1854 London. I had an 1851 map of London, and believe it or not, now I can get around 1851 London the way some Londoners can get around their city today.

It was just a joy to do the research. For me, form and content must go together. The only thing that wasn't typical of the time was De Quincey's daughter, Emily, who didn't conform to the male-dominated Victorian dictates of the era. It was great fun having her make some of the men look very foolish.

Q. **You're known as a writer of thriller fiction. The De Quincey trilogy was a significant departure for you. What was your goal in writing these novels?**

A. I wanted to escape the modern world. I started the research on *Murder as a Fine Art* in 2009, shortly after my granddaughter Natalie died at the age of fourteen from Ewing's sarcoma. As I said, many years earlier, that same disease had killed my son at age fifteen. Unstrung by this double grief, I was seized by the notion to escape into 1850s London and try to hypnotize and protect myself from the reality of what had occurred.

I think it was my attempt to escape from grief by disappearing into that Victorian world. A friend of mine said to me, "It struck me that Emily, De Quincey's daughter, is a version of Natalie. Whether you knew it or not, you were reincarnating your granddaughter in these novels."

Q. **After having immersed yourself in Victorian England and the De Quincey saga, what feelings do you have about now moving on to something else?**

A. It's been difficult. For the last few years, I've been immersed in Victorian London. I feel as though I've come out of the depths of the ocean back into the modern world. Looking around at the vitriol of our current political situation, it reinforced for me how much more pleasant it was to be in 1850s London. I must admit, I feel somewhat adrift right now.

Q. **David, you've been such a successful novelist. What has surprised you about the writing life?**

A. What comes to mind is how much things have changed in the writing world. This is my forty-third year as a published novelist. When I started in 1972, there were no book signings. Novelists didn't go on tour or do publicity. There were hardly any bookstores—certainly none of the chain bookstores existed. There was a time when ten or fifteen book warehouses existed in each state; they serviced mom-and-pop grocery stores and stationery stores. Those warehouses disappeared. The chain bookstores appeared. And, of course, we now have the e-book revolution. That allows many more writers to get out and self-publish. I've seen a great deal that's changed in the writing world. That's what has surprised me most of all.

One of the things these changes have taught me is to take the long view of the writing life. There are peaks and valleys. As I said before, I've always felt you must be a first-rate version of yourself, not a second-rate version of another author. I also believe it's foolish to chase the market, because if you do, you'll always be looking at its backside.

I've always written what I love to write. Some authors told me not to write historical novels such as *Murder as a Fine Art*, *Inspector of the Dead*, and *Ruler of the Night*. These books would be a departure from my contemporary American subjects. They felt readers wouldn't go with me. They wanted more Rambo or more of *The Brotherhood of the Rose*.

But I didn't want to keep writing the same kind of novels.

This is my forty-first year as a published novelist. That's an eternity in the publishing world. The usual publishing life of many authors is fifteen or twenty years. They fall out of favor because they keep writing the same novel over and over again.

Q. **What's the most exciting thing about being a successful novelist? Is it recognition? Fame? Satisfaction? Are there any specific instances you can talk about?**

A. There are a couple of ways to look at this. If we want to look at the false value of fame, which always changes, I guess I have to smile. There were five thriller characters from novels and films in the twentieth century who became worldwide icons. They were Sherlock Holmes, Tarzan, James Bond, Rambo, and Harry Potter.

I grin a little at the idea that I created a character in that pantheon. In a slightly different way, my *Brotherhood of the Rose* was the first novel of a trilogy to be filmed as a miniseries. It's the only miniseries to this day that was broadcast after the Super Bowl. Soon after its publication, *Murder as a Fine Art* rose in ranking until it was the number one book in the entire Kindle universe on Amazon. These things were exciting.

But this really points to the false value of fame. It can all change. The universe is filled with people who were popular at one time and not at another. You must have a steady sense of yourself and a core of validity, so that as the world changes, you can remain unfazed.

The most exciting thing for me, and the one with the most lasting value, is to have a chance to research subjects in which I'm deeply interested. These subjects make me a fuller person because they require me to explore topics for my fiction, which allows me to understand myself and the world more fully. It helps me move forward as a human being. Writing fiction—researching and then exploring the story, its emotions, and ideas—is the payoff. Hopefully, I become a fuller, better person through these projects. It all keeps me fully grounded.

Q. **What do you love about the writing life?**

A. It's an opportunity for me to exercise my imagination. As I said, as a child I spent a lot of time at night beneath my bed, afraid of hearing my mother and stepfather fighting. Covering my ears, I told myself stories in which I was the hero.

When I grew up, I discovered I still had this need to tell stories. I got to do it, and even earn a living doing it. It's a wonderful opportunity to benefit from my daydreams in a culture that doesn't value daydreaming. I think our best ideas come to us when we give ourselves permission to go into that kind of trance. I love the opportunity to let messages rise up from my psyche.

Q. **If you weren't a writer, what would you be doing?**

A. When I was young, I wanted to be like Nelson Riddle, the famous orchestrator. As a teenager, I had music lessons and absorbed a great deal about harmony, musical theory, counterpoint, and orchestration. But something happened at age seventeen: I lost interest in music and realized my passion was in telling stories. I sometimes think the musical training in structure was helpful in terms of writing novels.

Q. **If you could have dinner with any five people from history—either writers or others, living or dead—who would they be?**

A. That's a loaded question because I'd love to have dinner with my son and granddaughter more than anyone else. But if we step aside from that, Thomas De Quincey would be high on my list, as would Benjamin Franklin. My mentors, Philip Young and the screenwriter Stirling Silliphant, who wrote *Route 66* would be there, too. If we're talking about the great minds, I think Saint Thomas Aquinas would be at the table. I'll leave it at that.

Q. **What's coming next from David Morrell?**

A. I don't really know. I'm suffering from Victorian withdrawal. I'm catching up on my contemporary reading, and we'll see where that leads me.

Congratulations on having written the Victorian trilogy in addition to the stunning contemporary thrillers in your oeuvre. The De Quincey books were exquisitely rendered and atmospheric, and were reminiscent of Poe.

PATRICIA CORNWELL
KAY SCARPETTA AND THE COURAGE TO FAIL

Patricia Cornwell is the internationally bestselling and award-winning author of more than thirty-three books, the most famous and widely read being the novels of the Kay Scarpetta series.

She has won nearly every literary award for popular fiction and has authored twenty-nine *New York Times* bestsellers. Her novels center primarily on medical examiner Kay Scarpetta, along with her tech-savvy niece Lucy and investigator Pete Marino. Patricia researches cutting-edge forensic technologies that inform her Kay Scarpetta novels.

Our conversations took place between 2015 and 2017.

Q. **Your Kay Scarpetta novels are so richly detailed in medical forensics, it's hard to believe you're not a physician. How did you learn so much forensic pathology?**

A. People sometimes mistakenly call me "Dr. Cornwell." I was an English major in college. For thirty years, I've been a self-educated student of medical forensics, ballistics, and all things related. It's my avocation. I constantly cruise the internet looking for new information. I have consultants on whom I rely for the latest technologic advances. I also do field research. For one novel, I went to Texas firing ranges to test high-tech assault rifles and ammunition, the things readers will find in the book. That's how I continue to learn. While I wouldn't qualify as an expert witness in court—I don't have the pedigree—there's nothing to stop me from educating myself.

Q. **What do you think so fascinates readers about forensic work?**

A. I think it's the same thing that's so fascinating about archae-ological excavation. Or, your own discoveries when you find an object like an old arrowhead buried in your backyard. You start wondering about and re-creating the scenario of how it got there. Why is it here? What happened? Did someone live or die on this very spot? Our human nature demands that we be intensely curious about these mysteries and we try to piece together our surroundings so we're better informed. That's what forensics is all about.

To me, this goes back to our tribal survival instincts. If you can re-create a situation in your mind about what happened to someone, how that person died, there's a better chance it won't happen to you. I think it's part of the life force compel-ling us to look death in the face. We're the only animal with an understanding that someday we'll die. I think we all want to make our temporary stay on this planet less mysterious, more knowable. We want to learn what happened here, so we'll feel less vulnerable about the same thing happening to us. It's the kind of curiosity that propels us to study monsters. And I think that kind of curiosity is what makes people so interested in forensic matters.

Q. **Your first book, *Postmortem*, is considered the first forensic thriller. I understand you had an interesting experience at your first book signing. Will you tell us about that?**

A. It was so bad, it was really about not being invited to the dance. [Laughter.]

Postmortem was accepted very tentatively by the publisher. It had been rejected by almost every other major house, which by the way, isn't uncommon for unknown writers. When it was finally published, there was no marketing budget or publicity plan. I went to a local bookstore and got to know the owner. He agreed to have me appear at the store for a book signing. By the way, it was a religious bookstore, so it was the completely wrong venue for a forensic thriller. [More laughter.]

Well, on the day of the signing, I got there on my lunch hour at the appointed time, and not a single person showed up. One lady came by and held out a tissue. I asked if I could help her and she said, "Yes. Please put this in the trash for me."

I said to myself, "My future is not looking very bright."

Q. **Your Kay Scarpetta novels have influenced TV programs such as *CSI: Crime Scene Investigation* and *Cold Case Files*. Do the television writers ever ask for your advice?**

A. I don't really want to be a consultant on other people's shows. However, I'm writing a pilot for a CBS show called *Angie*

Steele. It's about a woman investigator who went to MIT but decided to become a cop. So, I'll be a consultant for that show, but I don't have an interest in consulting for other shows.

Q. **Your writing style has varied in the Scarpetta series—from past to present tense, from first person to omniscient narrator, and you've gone back and forth. What brought about those stylistic changes?**

A. I think a writer looks for different ways to explore abilities and skill sets. I always want to evolve, and my goal has always been to get better at writing. I'm constantly exploring different ways to do it.

In writing a series, there's a lot of latitude for experimentation, opportunities to stretch your wings. In 2003, with *Blow Fly*, I switched to a third-person point of view. The fans didn't like that. They wanted to be inside Scarpetta's head. I write these books for my readers. So I switched back to the first-person point of view. I'm quite sure I'll continue writing in the present tense. I've always thought of writing as a glass windowpane through which the reader enters a new world. I try honing my writing style to be as immediate, physical, and tactile as possible, almost like the reader is watching television.

For me, the present tense lends immediacy to the work, makes it almost cinematic. The great challenge for writers is to draw the reader into the novel as though it's a movie. When you're reading, the brain must translate printed words into sights, sounds, smells, and taste; whereas you don't have to do that as much in movies. A movie gives you an immediate emotional response. The limbic system is on fire when you're watching a movie or when you're at a rock concert.

When reading a book, the brain has to do the work of getting the reader to that place. So, I do whatever I think is necessary to help the reader make the transition to those emotional responses. In a sense, you can call me an emotional facilitator. [Laughter.]

Q. **You're very prolific. Do you ever struggle with procrastination or writer's block?**

A. I most certainly do. I like to remind people not to judge me based on what they see on the outside. Prolific and successful people have the same problems others do. I absolutely have days where I'll find every excuse under the sun not to sit at that desk and write.

Q. **Why is that?**

A. Because writing scares me. It's hard. And if the characters are being uncooperative, I just move words around uselessly. At times like that, I wonder who stole my characters. Or I think they've gone on vacation.

I don't feel I control that world. I don't think you can be creative if you try to control what you're doing. You have to allow psychological spaces in your mind—ones you don't even know exist—to let things surface on their own. It's far easier to do almost anything else than to write.

Sometimes I have writer's block where I'm stuck in a scene. When that happens, I need to go back to where the script *was* working. I've probably taken a wrong turn, and some part of my brain is saying "You don't want to go any farther. You're on the wrong track." When I'm at that kind of dead end, I go back and fix it.

But writer's block is a terrible thing—whether you're a journalist or writing fiction. It's debilitating and depressing. I always say the genius within us all is the *child*. That's where all the good stuff comes from. So, writer's block may very well be a matter of your little child not being happy. And if the child isn't happy, he's not pulling out his crayons. [Laughter.]

Q. **Yet you're producing a Kay Scarpetta novel each year. How do you remain so prolific?**

A. It's not easy. The actual sitting down and writing a novel requires intricate work and can be painstakingly exhausting. I can do it when I have the time, but occasionally, something else comes up, like book promotion, and finding time to research and write becomes more difficult.

Q. **Your recent novels have a good deal of technology in them. Will you talk about that?**

A. When you think of things we're afraid of in today's world, they're quite different from what they were twenty years ago. Much of it has to do with technology and terrorism. Years ago, it was more the fear the Ted Bundys of the world might crawl through your window.

The things we fear today have changed. With technology, the Internet and social media—with identity theft wiping out people's bank accounts and events like that—we don't necessarily know what's *real* or *true* anymore. Everything's electronic: these aren't things you can hold in your hand. We're not dealing with tangible items. How do we know what's true? If someone wants to manipulate us, how preventable is it? I coined the term *data fiction* to describe this phenomenon.

The changes in technology in our world have caused me to dramatically alter what I do in my books. Kay Scarpetta is our contemporary, so she has to worry about cybercrime— not only personally, but its impact on her cases. And look at what's going on right now with ransomware.

Q. **Your recent novel *Chaos* depicts some frightening possibilities about technology and the use of weapons. Tell us about that.**

A. In the first decade of my career, the main character in the novel was the *forensics*. In my writing, I spent a great deal of time showing readers things with which they were totally unfamiliar. For example, in the midnineties, no one gave a thought to the possibility of biological terrorism and weaponizing a plague like smallpox. Now we worry all the time about this kind of scenario.

When I started writing, I seized upon the idea of having some malevolent person or organization exploit the wonders of technology by perverting them to achieve catastrophic ends. That kind of situation puts the characters through unimaginable stress to try to figure out how to prevent a cataclysmic event from happening.

This formula has served me well, and I'm even more inspired now than ever before because technology is proliferating at lightning speed. I can barely keep up with all the developments and advances. There's a technology war going on, and that's what I use in my stories.

Q. **Speaking of technology, especially concerning weapons, does anything about the future frighten you?**

A. Everything about the future frightens me. The possibility of creating weapons for which we have no defense is immense. There's no end in sight for the creative things people can do to wreak havoc on civilization. Whether it's cyberattacks on an election or on the power grids, these are vulnerabilities that if creatively exploited would be devastating to our society. I sincerely believe that if you allow yourself to think about it, someone will *try*.

Q. **What scientific resources do you use to stay so current about forensics and technology?**

A. I have a whole team of consultants available to me. Over the years I've amassed a network of the best and the brightest people out there—whether it's expertise on DNA, medical examiner's techniques, microscopic or trace evidence experts, I've had the privilege of being in the company of some of the best and most skilled professionals in the world.

Q. **You have so many interests. What's a typical day like for you?**

A. I love scuba diving and flying helicopters, but if I did these things every day, I wouldn't be able to write books. I've been dabbling with television and Hollywood, which is fun and takes up some time, and I make sure I exercise every day.

If we're in the same place, my partner, Staci, and I almost always have dinner together, and we enjoy watching television.

My favorite kind of day is a quiet one. I get up, go to my desk, and write. If it's a lovely day, I'll take a break and go for a walk. I don't listen to anything while walking—I don't want to get hit by a car—and I use the silence of the walk to let my mind roam free. In our busy, need-to-be-connected world, you miss out on the pleasure of solitude if you're constantly looking at your cell phone while walking.

I give myself an hour to think and just be still. Then I'll go back and write some more. That's the essence of a good day for me.

Q. **What, if anything, keeps you awake at night?**

A. What keeps me awake or restless while I'm working on a book is, I can never get away from it. I'm lying there and have this anxiety: "Oh, I've got so much left to do," or "I'm only on page ten," or, "Will I ever finish this thing?" When

I'm writing a book, it feels like I'm always living with it. And when I'm finally finished with a novel, I'm instantly starting another one.

Q. **More than one hundred million copies of your books have been sold; they've been translated into thirty-six languages and are available in one hundred twenty countries. After all this success, what has been most striking to you about writing?**

A. What's struck me most is the process of creativity. I've been fascinated by where ideas come from. I feel when we really open ourselves up to our urges and get our conscious brains out of the way, we're almost channeling things from areas we don't begin to understand. It's both a scary and amazing experience.

I've been repeatedly surprised how secret parts of my mind are creating something without my conscious knowledge. Hemingway was very aware of this phenomenon. He had an ironclad habit: when he had written a very good sentence and knew where he was going next, he would quit writing and not think about it until he went back to it the next day. He wanted to give his subconscious mind enough time to work on the story.

That continues to amaze me: this ability the human mind seems to have. It even goes to the issue of genetic memory. We channel things creatively that really come from someplace that's part of our genome, our primal heritage.

Q. **What does writing novels do for you emotionally?**

A. I love the way it keeps me company. I find no matter what's going on in my life, I don't have to wait on somebody else to fill my time or give me satisfaction. If I have an hour or two,

I can sit at my desk, open something I'm working on, and be transported to the same world I want to take the readers. I probably developed that ability for a very good reason. As a child, writing was my best friend. If I wrote a poem or an illustrated short story or described the scenery while I looked out over a valley in North Carolina, where I was brought up, it made me feel less by myself.

I think being on this planet is a lonely experience, and without imagination, it's very isolating. For me, writing has been a gift. Creative expression is a great coping mechanism if you're sad, scared, or lonely, much as I was as a child. Writing was my retreat. I played sports and all that, but the thing that healed my soul and touched those parts of me nothing else could had to come from within myself. If you can reach inside yourself and create something—a painting, a drawing, a book—it can be healing and very life affirming.

Q. **What's the most important lesson you feel you've learned about writing?**

A. I think the most important lesson I've learned is the power in letting go. You have to learn not to try to control the process of writing. You've got to free-fall, and adults don't like to do that. But if you think about how you started writing as a child, you'd get a piece of paper, a pencil or a crayon, and you would just start with whatever came into your head. You didn't plan an outline or do storyboards.

Then, when we become adults, we feel we must control the process. The more you try to control creativity, the less successful you're going to be. It doesn't mean you can't have structure or logic, but if you overthink things, you won't be creative. Thinking can be dangerous. The worst stuff I write is something I thought out instead of writing what just comes out of me. It's really more intuitive than anything else.

Q. Who are the authors you read these days?

A. I'm an eclectic reader. I read a lot of biographies. I love nonfiction, especially history. In fiction, I enjoy reading Lee Child, Dan Brown, Michael Connelly, and Harlan Coben. It has to be something very engaging; otherwise my attention will wander.

Q. What advice would you give to writers starting out?

A. My advice would be this: You'll never be good at anything if at first you're not bad. That pertains to writing or anything else in life. You must have the courage to fail. Be willing to be really bad. [Laughter.]

I would also say, "Rejection is not a measure of your worth." If it were, I'd be worth nothing because I've been rejected so many times. I wrote four novels before one was finally published.

Q. If you could have dinner with any five people, living or dead, from history, politics, or literature, who would they be?

A. I'd love to have dinner with Dickens. I'd love to have dinner with Agatha Christie. I'd love to have met Lincoln. I'm so sorry I never got to meet Truman Capote. I think *In Cold Blood* is one of the greatest true crime books ever written. I think dead people might be my specialty. [Laughter.] And then there's Harriet Beecher Stowe. She's supposedly a relative—allegedly, an ultra-removed aunt of mine. It may be part of my genetic heritage, because she and I write basically about the same thing: abuse of power, whether it's slavery or anything else. I visited her home in Connecticut and can honestly say I felt a kinship, something almost like channeling something from her.

Q. **What would you all be talking about at dinner?**

A. I'd be fascinated about their writing processes. I'd love hearing how they started their days and the things that compelled them to write what they did. I know Dickens was influenced greatly by his childhood—working in a bootblack factory by the age of twelve. It would be fascinating to talk with Agatha Christie. I understand she was incredibly shy and introverted. Becoming a celebrity was difficult for her because she was happiest staying at home and writing. Also, both Dickens and Agatha Christie were heavy into research, so we'd have a great deal in common. If she were writing today, who knows? Miss Marple might have been a medical examiner.

Congratulations on a writing career that's gained worldwide attention and has mesmerized millions of readers with the wonders of forensic science and the character of Kay Scarpetta.

HARLAN COBEN
THE MASTER OF MISSING PERSONS

Harlan Coben is known to readers everywhere. His first novel was published when he was twenty-six years old. After two stand-alone thrillers, *Play Dead* in 1990 and *Miracle Cure* in 1991, he began writing the popular Myron Bolitar series.

His 2001 stand-alone novel, *Tell No One*, was hugely popular. In 2006, film director Guillaume Canet made the book into the French thriller, *Ne le Dis à Personne*. The movie was the top box office foreign-language film of the year in the United States, won the Lumière [French Golden Globe] for best picture, and was nominated for nine Césars [French Oscar], winning four awards.

Harlan Coben has gone on to write many more stand-alone novels. His books regularly appear on the *New York Times* bestseller list, and more than sixty million have been sold internationally. He was the first writer to receive the Edgar, Shamus, and Anthony Awards.

Our conversations took place between 2015 and 2017.

Q. The plots of your novels are quite intricate and replete with twists. How do you structure them?

A. When I start to write, I know the beginning and the end, but I don't know much in between. I've often compared it to traveling from my home state of New Jersey to California. I could take Route 80—the most direct route—but chances are I could go via the Suez Canal and stop at Tokyo. But I always end up in California.

E. L. Doctorow once said, "Writing is like driving at night. You can see no farther than your headlights, but you make the journey." That sums up my writing process when it comes to structure.

Sometimes I'll outline one or two chapters ahead as I go along, but generally I don't outline.

Q. Many of your novels involve someone who's gone missing. Actually, Harlan, I view you as the "Master of the Missing Person." What draws you to this scenario?

A. I think it's an intriguing scenario. Just think about it: a missing person could be alive or dead. You don't know. There's always hope. I love writing about hope. Hope can make your heart soar or can crush your heart like an eggshell.

For me, missing people ratchet up the emotion. Unlike in a murder mystery, there's *more* than justice being served in solving the crime; you can have full redemption when the person is found. I love the possibilities disappearances present.

Q. Any idea about what makes thrillers so appealing to so many readers?

A. I think good thrillers have gripping stories and compelling characters. I think the real key is the emotional layer in the story, beyond simply stirring the reader's pulse; a good thriller stirs the heart and makes the reader really care about what happens to the people in the book.

Q. **Your thrillers don't involve the usual protagonists— soldiers, detectives, lawyers, CIA agents, or spies. They're about ordinary people whose lives change in a few dramatic moments. Will you talk about that?**

A. I enjoy writing about that sort of Hitchcockian ordinary man who finds himself in extraordinary circumstances. That situation is more compelling, and the reader can relate more readily than if the character is some kind of superhero.

I want the reader to be immersed in the protagonist's world and not be able to leave it. I want the reader to be in the protagonist's shoes, to feel what he or she is feeling and thinking. It helps if the protagonist is the kind of person who lives down the street and is less classically heroic. I try to keep the reader up all night, wanting to know what's going to happen next.

Q. **Do you feel the most frightening things are those that could actually happen to anyone?**

A. Yes, I do. Almost all my ideas come from something that happens in my regular life. I then think, "What would happen if . . . ?"

For instance, in my book *The Stranger*, I didn't make up the Fake-A-Pregnancy website. There are sites that actually sell "bellies" and fake sonogram readings, along with bogus pregnancy tests. That being the case, my mind says, "What would happen if someone found out his wife was never pregnant and just faked it?" It's basically the real-life "what-ifs" that can be so intriguing. That's how all my books start.

Q. The first sentence of *Fool Me Once* is, "They buried Joe three days after his murder." And the first sentence of *The Stranger* is, "The stranger didn't shatter Adam's world all at once." Tell us your thoughts about the importance of a novel's first sentence.

A. The opening sentences of a thriller are crucial. I want to hook the reader as fast as possible. If I can accomplish that with the first sentence, that's what I want to do, but it's a heck of a challenge. I think the first sentence sets the tone for the rest of the novel. It's like I'm saying to the reader, "Strap yourself in; we're going on a very fast roller-coaster ride." I love the way the opening line and various twists in a novel can mess with the reader's mind.

Q. Speaking of "messing with the reader's mind," your novels have mind-boggling twists. What makes twists so important in thrillers?

A. I think we all love the "gasp" moment in a book—that instant when we literally see everything from an entirely different perspective. If done correctly, we enjoy being fooled. But there's more to it than simply being misdirected; it must work on an *emotional* level. A sleight of hand is fine—it's like watching a card trick—but I hope the book emotionally blindsides you as well, so you *feel* something. I'm not satisfied with simply writing a fast-moving plot if the book lacks real emotional impact.

Q. As for emotional impact, you once said reading William Goldman's novel *Marathon Man* was a life-changing event for you. Tell us about that.

A. I was fifteen or sixteen. I hadn't read many adult novels; mostly, I read the classics and read books for school. My father gave me a copy of *Marathon Man*. I found myself racing through it. You could have put a gun to my head and I wouldn't have been able to put that book down.

While I didn't try to become a novelist until years later, I think subconsciously there was something inside me that said, "What a cool job it would be to be able to make people feel the way I'm feeling right now, reading *Marathon Man*."

Q. **Any thoughts about your successful career as an author?**

A. It's been a very interesting climb for me. I didn't hit it right away. I took all the steps along the way—being published by a small house, then by a slightly larger one; then came a bit of recognition; then a little bit more sales, and then more, until the last seven novels have debuted as number one on the *New York Times* list.

I have a true appreciation of how lucky I am. I think one of the surprises is that as a bestselling author, I can still have a normal life with my wife and four kids, living in the suburbs.

Q. **You mentioned living a normal life. You're a huge guy with a very distinctive look. Are you ever accosted in public?**

A. No, not really. Like most writers, I enjoy living my life in anonymity.

Q. **Is writing fiction as much fun now as it was when you were starting out?**

A. Yes, but it's a different kind of fun. Up until a few years ago I was still playing basketball, but it was a different type of fun than when I was a college player. But it's still something that I'm compelled to do, that I'm inspired to do, and that I love doing.

The thing I love the most about writing is when the book is done and readers get to read it. There's an old saying, "I don't like writing. I like having written." I think that very much applies to me. It's not a book until you read it. When a book comes out and people read it, the characters come alive in people's heads—and for each reader, it's a different experience. That part of the writing life still jazzes me—when I get that one-on-one connection with the reader.

Q. **What do you love about the writing life?**

A. I think the short answer would be "What don't I love about it?" There's no downside for me. I guess I'd rather not have to do so much traveling, and writing never gets any easier. It always torments you. There's that insecurity, the feeling I'll never be able to do it again. Unlike some other jobs, you can never, for a second, just show up. You really have to work at it, and you find yourself feeling some doubt with the beginning of each new novel. But really, for me, there's very little downside, and I love what I do. It's been a dream come true.

Q. **What would you be doing if you weren't writing?**

A. I have no other marketable skills. I'm disorganized, forgetful, and easily distracted. I don't know what I would be doing. Frankly, that's part of what makes me a writer. Writing is a form of desperation. Most writers aren't capable of handling a real job in society. This is all we have. So, this is what I do.

Q. **What's the most important lesson you've learned about writing?**

A. It may sound like a cliché, but you have to write. You have to turn off that voice in your head telling you it's not working, or you need more time to get this novel right. You have to put words down on paper and remember that you can always change them. You can always fix bad pages; you can't fix no pages.

Q.   **Is there anything about your writing process that might surprise our readers?**

A.   I don't know if it's a surprise, but I write much faster toward the end of a novel than at the beginning of the book. The last forty pages of my most recent novel, *Don't Let Go*, were written in one sitting and were barely rewritten. It's because I knew how the book was going to end from the first day I began writing it. I get so excited toward the end, I write in something of a frenzy.

Q.   **What, if anything, keeps you awake at night?**

A.   I sleep pretty well. I have four kids, and like any parent, I worry about them all the time. But I've learned to not take it to bed. I worry about things I can control and have stopped worrying about those I cannot.

Q.   **If you could have any five people from any walk of life, living or dead, join you at a dinner party, who would they be?**

A.   Well, I'd love to have my parents with me. If I chose writers, I'd invite those I've known personally, who have passed away: David Foster Wallace, Elmore Leonard, Donald Westlake, and Ed McBain. They were writers whose work I admired greatly and whom I personally admired enormously.

Congratulations on having written pulse-pounding bestsellers that have mesmerized readers for years. It's been a pleasure talking with you.

SUE GRAFTON
WRITING FROM SHADOW

Sue Grafton is best known for her alphabet mystery series (*"A" is for Alibi*, etc.) with her feisty nature-hating, fast-food-loving protagonist Kinsey Millhone. NPR's Maureen Corrigan said the forthcoming conclusion of the alphabet series "makes me wish there were more than twenty-six letters at her disposal."

Sue's books have been published in twenty-eight countries and in twenty-six languages—including Estonian, Bulgarian, and Indonesian. Books in her alphabet series, beginning with *"A" is for Alibi* in 1982 and most recently, *X*, are international bestsellers with readership in the millions.

Named a Grand Master by the Mystery Writers of America, she has also received many other honors and awards, including the Lifetime Achievement Award from the Private Eye Writers of America, the Ross Macdonald Literary Award, the Cartier Diamond Dagger from Britain's Crime Writers' Association, the Lifetime Achievement Award from Malice Domestic, the Anthony Award given by Bouchercon, and three Shamus Awards.

Our conversation took place in 2015. Sue died in 2017 and never got to write a "Z" novel.

Q. What inspired the Kinsey Millhone books and, in particular, what made you think of writing an alphabet series?

A. Growing up, I read the Nancy Drew books and all of the Agatha Christie novels. But the book that really made an impact on me was *I, the Jury* by Mickey Spillane. Reading that book was something of a revelation for me, and I think it was when the idea of Kinsey Millhone came alive in my mind.

As for the idea of an alphabet series, I must give credit to *The Gashlycrumb Tinies* by Edward Gorey. It was a rhyming book where twenty-six Victorian children were killed in very bizarre ways. "A is for Amy who fell down the stairs; B is for Basil assaulted by bears; C is for Clara who wasted away; D is for Desmond thrown out of a sleigh." It gave me the idea of each book and its theme involving the succession of letters in the alphabet.

Q. Here's an obvious question: *X* is the twenty-fourth Kinsey Millhone novel and the first one that doesn't have a defining alphabetical word in the title. How come?

A. Originally, I thought *X* would be for *xenophobe*, but as I wrote the book I realized there wasn't a foreigner to be seen anywhere in the novel. Wherever possible, I used X words; but at the end of the book I couldn't see any of these X words encompassing the entire story. I think it's best if *X* represents the *unknown*.

Q. In *X*, the serial killer is identified early on. Will you discuss that device in contrast to the reader *not* knowing the killer's identity, which seems to occur far more frequently in mysteries?

A. Technically, there are two kinds of mysteries: one is called *open* and the other is called *closed*. In a *closed* mystery, the reader is in the same position as the detective, sorting through clues and interviews, trying to arrive at the identity of the culprit.

In an *open* mystery, the identity is a given. The reader knows early on who the culprit is, and the question becomes, how is the sleuth going to nail him? A good example of an *open* mystery is the old *Columbo* TV series, where the viewer knew the villain's identity right at the beginning.

Q.   You once stated the last novel in the series will be *Z is for Zero*. What does that mean?

A.   I used to say, "*Z* is for Zero, and then I'll use numbers." But Janet Evanovich started using numbers, which she'll greatly regret because you can never get to the end of numbers. I'm limiting my run to twenty-six novels. I'm now trying to catch my breath so I can gear up and write the last two. It takes me two years per book. So we've got four years to go before I sign off.

Q.   When you say, "sign off," do you mean you will no longer be writing mysteries?

A.   I'll no longer be writing them with alphabet titles. Miss Millhone dominates my life. It's both a curse and a blessing. [Laughter.] We'll see what she comes up with. I know I'm not going to be allowed to write about anybody else. She's a very jealous mistress. If I continue with the series, I think I'll do stand-alones. I may at some point get bored or burned out, and then I'll stop writing.

Q.   I'm sure you know that Arthur Conan Doyle was sick of Sherlock Holmes and wanted to kill him off.

A.   I'll never get sick of Miss Millhone. She's largely based on me. Who can get sick of oneself?

Q. Much like Kinsey Millhone, you're known for having paved your own independent career path: writing screenplays, TV movies, and, of course, novels. Will you talk about that?

A. I got to Hollywood because of two novels I had published early on in my career. One was sold to Hollywood. I worked there for fifteen years. Toward the end I became very unhappy. I realized that I cannot write by committee, which is what's involved in writing movies in Hollywood. I felt it was undermining my autonomy and authority as a writer. I knew I'd better get back to solo writing before I was ruined. To get back to writing alone, I decided to do a mystery because my father had published mysteries back in the forties.

It just turned out to be what I was born to do. "A" is for Alibi was the first mystery I ever wrote. Reaching publication was a miracle in itself. At the time I had no notion there would be other novels thereafter. I was very fortunate to have been picked up by a great editor, Marian Wood, at Henry Holt and Company. She had never before edited a mystery novel, so it was a fresh turn for both of us.

Q. Speaking of Hollywood, have you ever wanted to see Kinsey Millhone on the big screen?

A. No, not at all. I know how things are done there. I'd never let those people get their hands on my work. They'd go ahead and ruin it for everyone, me more than most.

Q. What, if anything, has been difficult for you in your writing life?

A. I'm an introvert. I love that about my life, but it's part of my job to get out in the marketplace and promote my books. I had to go to book signings and talks. It surprised me to learn it was expected of me, and though it didn't come naturally to me, it surprised me even more that I've become quite good at it.

Q. **What's the most important thing you've learned about yourself because of your writing?**

A. The most important thing is I've learned to operate out of *shadow*. I've learned to understand and accept that about myself. The term is part of Jungian psychology involving the juxtaposition of *shadow* and *ego*.

Shadow is the unconscious—our wants, our needs, our intuition. It's the melting pot of all our venom and it's the dark part of our natures. In that stew of petty jealousies and homicidal urges lie all the creative energies a person can possibly summon.

I reached a point in writing *"J" is for Judgment*, where I drifted into *ego*. I got too worried about whether the critics or my editor would approve of what I wrote. And, frankly, it shut me down for a while.

So, I spent some time learning to get out of my own way. The problem is I lose sight of that lesson whenever I start a new book. I have to go back with each new novel to relearn the technique of writing from the soul—from *shadow*. It's also the equivalent of learning to write from the right side of the brain as opposed to the left; the right is the creative part, while the left is the bean counter.

I learned that I can write really bad sentences. [Laughter.] When I first write them, I think they're wonderful. But when I go back the next day, I'm appalled. Writing is really all about buffing and polishing what you've written. Actually, writing is rewriting. That's been an important lesson for me.

I also learned to have patience and to make my own way with my books. I wrote seven novels before I began writing the alphabet series. Of those seven books, only the fourth and fifth were actually published. The others are in the trash. As I said before, *"A" Is for Alibi*, the first in the alphabet series, was my eighth book and, fortunately, it was my ticket out of Hollywood.

Q. **What, if anything, keeps you awake at night?**

A. Coffee. [Laughter.] But seriously, there is something that can keep me awake at night. Toward the end of a book, when I am totally engaged, I will wake in the night. It's like I'm having a visit from *shadow*. I can hear lines of dialogue. I get up and go to the bathroom with a flashlight and write the words down. I'll get back in bed, and the next thing I know, *shadow* says, "Wait. I have another really good suggestion."

There's something exhilarating about that process—about operating from that mysterious place—from shadow. That voice in the night gives me cogent bits of information, like bread crumbs in a forest. It keeps me on track.

Q. **Has that experience ever changed the trajectory of a story?**

A. [Laughter.] It's caused me to *dump* stories. There were a couple of books where I had a few hundred pages written, or maybe fifteen thousand words done, and *shadow* would say, "I don't like this." I always argue with *shadow*, but she always wins. The hardest thing to do is dump a book, but if it's not working, there's no point in wasting time on it.

Q. **Have you ever suffered from writer's block?**

A. I suffer from writer's block every single day.

I used to fear it and fight it. Now I consider it *shadow*

giving me the message that I'm off track. So, instead of complaining, I listen very carefully and start backtracking in the manuscript's narrative to figure out where I went astray.

I think writer's block is actually a gift. It's dreadful when you're in the midst of it. You just think you're going to die. But, as a rule, you don't. The answer is always there—somewhere within the manuscript—and you must have the patience to pursue it.

Q. **As an eminently successful writer, what advice would you give to writers starting out?**

A. I would say learning to write well takes years. In this day and age, where there is so much instant gratification, people sit down to write thinking it will be smooth, easy, and effective.

Generally, we all speak fairly well and there's a tendency to think writing isn't that hard. People surmise, "I'll just write what I would say." But the truth is what happens on the page is very different from what happens in the brain. The translation process is very tricky, and it doesn't come easily.

I don't believe in shortcuts. Novice writers must accept it will be a struggle. They need patience and must be willing to persevere.

Q. **You're hosting a dinner party and can invite any five people from any walk of life, living or dead. Who would they be?**

A. I'd invite Mark Twain. Then Nora Ephron, a heroine of mine. I adore Anthony Trollope and would want him, too. I'd be very tempted to put H. L. Mencken on the list. And I'd love to invite Raymond Chandler.

Q. **All are writers. What would you be talking about?**

A. I hope we would be talking about our suffering as writers, sharing our misery, and giving each other a little comfort. [Laughter.]

Sue Grafton did not complete her "alphabet series" of novels featuring private investigator Kinsey Millhone. She died in December 2017, after a two-year battle with cancer.

DAVID MAMET
PLAYS, MOVIES, NOVELS, AND CON MEN

David Mamet is one of the most acclaimed and eclectic writers of our time. As a playwright, he has won a Pulitzer Prize and received Tony nominations for *Glengarry Glen Ross* and *Speed-the-Plow*. Other plays have included *The Duck Variations, Sexual Perversity in Chicago,* and *American Buffalo.*

Feature films he's written and directed include *House of Games, Things Change, Homicide, Oleanna, The Spanish Prisoner, The Winslow Boy, State and Main, Spartan, Redbelt,* and the HBO film *Phil Spector.*

His screenplays include *The Postman Always Rings Twice, The Untouchables, Hoffa, The Verdict, Wag the Dog, The Edge, Ronin,* and *Hannibal.*

He's written poetry, essays, and novels. He's written for television and radio and is the creator, producer, and a frequent writer for the television series *The Unit.*

Our conversation took place in 2015.

Q. **Your dialogue has been called street-smart and edgy. It's even called Mamet-speak. How does it come to you?**

A. There's an old joke about a guy who comes home and finds his business partner in bed with his wife. And he says, "Sam, I *have* to . . . but *you* . . . . ?" [Laughter.] That's not about my marriage . . I'm married to a goddess, and I thank the Lord every day for the last twenty-five years.

But the idea is simply . . . I *have to*. I just don't know any better. That's the dialogue that comes out of me. That's how I write. I'm a bit of a freak. There are times I recraft it, but sometimes it just comes out the way it does. I just do it until it's done.

Q. **Language seems so important in understanding and appreciating David Mamet.**

A. Well, you know, a play is basically a long, formalistic polemic. You can write it without the poetry, and if you do, you may have a pretty good play. We know this because we see plays in translation. Not many people speak Norwegian or Danish— or whatever guys like Ibsen spoke, or Russian—yet we understand Chekhov and the others. We don't get the poetry of it because it's been translated. So we follow the plot and get the idea.

On the other hand, you can also write it in what's essentially poetry that's going to stick in your mind. The test of that is whether or not people remember what's been said in the play. People remember Shakespeare's words all their lives. We remember the rhythm of it. You're a psychiatrist, right?

Q. **Yes.**

A. So you know this: Freud said it's polymorphous perversity. It's a priori . . . We can't get beyond the fact that there's something in music that gets to us. And for me, poetry is the music of speech.

Q. **Your dialogue has been considered a form of street poetry.**

A. Maybe so. I wrote an essay about rap music, which is the operative poetry of our time. Speaking of street poetry, it has many precursors. I've been reading this great book by George MacDonald Fraser, a Victorian writer. He quotes many of the old Scottish border ballads that were simply folk music of the times. It's clear he was influenced by and immersed in Sir Walter Scott. He was regurgitating the Scottish border ballads. By the way, if you read those ballads, you realize you're partly reading Kipling, and that's where Kipling got many of his ideas. It's the music of the people. And I guess that's the way I write.

Q. **Is some of your music the music of your own people— the primary culture of David Mamet—meaning your own family as a kid? You once said you developed your penchant for dialogue from early family discussions.**

A. Well, my family is Jewish. We're newcomers—we've been Jews for only about seven thousand years. But the Jewish family, like the larger Jewish community, operates through disputation, because that's our great talent. Argument! That's what the Talmud is, and that's what the Jewish legal system is. You take two completely opposing views and try to find some middle ground.

Q. **Was there a great deal of disputation in your family— plenty of shouting at the top of people's lungs?**

A. No. I think that's the Italians. We just bear grudges until the end of time. [Laughter.] My father was very fond of the phrase "Shut up and sit down." So there you have it. But I did go into poetry because that's where the money is. [More laughter.]

Q. **Can you compare writing a stage play with a screenplay as opposed to a novel?**

A. Writing a stage play and a screenplay have very little to do with each other. A stage play is just dialogue. One has to be able to communicate the play through disputation. A stage play is basically a form of überschizophrenia. You split yourself into two minds—one being the protagonist and the other being the antagonist. The playwright also splits himself into two other minds: the mind of the writer and the mind of the audience. The question is, how do you lure the audience in so that they use their reasoning power to jump to their own conclusion, so that at the end of the play—as Aristotle said—they're surprised. It might even involve leading the audience to its own destruction. So, writing a play might be compared to the workings of psychopaths, who can be the most charming people in the world and who move you step-by-step to your own destruction.

Q. **And writing a novel differs in what way?**

A. Writing a novel is an incredibly free experience. One puts one's self in a narrative mode. You can go off in any direction—the past, the future, or go laterally, or include one's own beliefs. It's total freedom.

Q. **So then, disputation, or conflict is at the heart of it all?**

A. Yes, of course. That's what a play is about. That's why it has the capacity to cleanse. Here's what happens in a play. You get involved in a situation where something is unbalanced. If nothing's unbalanced, there's no reason to have a play.

Let's look at it this way: if Hamlet comes home from school and his dad's not dead, and his father asks him if he's had a good time, it's boring. But if something's unbalanced—like his father's dead and may have been killed by his uncle and his uncle is sleeping with Hamlet's mother—then you have an unbalanced situation that must be returned to order. The task of a play is to return to order that which has come unbalanced. In *Hamlet*, Shakespeare not only has conflict between people, but he brilliantly conveys conflict inside Hamlet's head. But yes, conflict is the essence of it.

Q. Which is easier for you: writing a play or directing?

A. There are certain things I can do naturally. Writing dialogue comes easy to me, and like most people, I enjoy doing what comes easily. But there's also great enjoyment in doing the thing that comes with difficulty.

Q. So, directing is more difficult for you?

A. Not necessarily. When it comes to writing, plot can be a pain in the ass. I work very, very hard on that, but I enjoy working on it because it has great rewards. But there's no doubt that I love directing.

Q. Your plays and films often deal with duplicity, theft, manipulation, and con games, like *House of Games* and *Heist* or in a play like *Glengarry Glen Ross*. Is this your view about our times?

A. Well, it's a view of *every* time. Some of my plays deal with conflicts in the business world; some deal with marital conflicts or conflicts in growing up. Perhaps you're talking about the better-known plays. There always has to be *some* conflict. If you keep writing the same play, why not just go home.

Q. But there's something about the con, the con game that seems to attract you.

A. Yes. That does attract me. You see, the con game, like the play, lures the mind on to its own destruction. Step A is correct; step B seems correct; step C makes sense, and then I wake up and realize I just gave all my money to a total stranger. How does that happen?

In a movie—which is a different kind of play—you lead the audience on. Or, as my friend Ricky Jay, the great magician says, "At some point, you just gotta ask for the money." You've got to lure them on to the point where they—unconsciously—make a leap of faith, and then there's the reveal, which is completely absurd.

Q. So to some extent, is all art manipulation?

A. Maybe so. You know, magic is manipulation for which one signs on. A healthy person doesn't go to a magic show and think, "I'm gonna find out where that dove actually came from." Right? They go in order to be fooled. They suspend disbelief. Basically, they trade their power to disbelieve for their power to be amused.

Q. You were once asked what you would have done if you hadn't become a writer; you said you'd have probably become a criminal. Can you tell us more about that?

A. It was a dramatic thing to say. I didn't really mean it. My mother used to say—and my wife says it now—"Why must you dramatize everything?" And I say, "Well, that's my nature." My good friend Patti LuPone performed at a concert, and this guy came in—morbidly obese, obviously unhappy, badly dressed—and there was something pathetic about him. But he must have chosen to be the way he was. He could have made different choices. And I thought, that's like me . . . I had choices, and I made them.

Q. Your choice was to become a writer, a poet, a filmmaker, a director—not a criminal, although you've written extensively about criminals.

A. So did Brandeis, but he didn't become a criminal. [More laughter.]

Q. You once said, "There's no such thing as talent; you just have to work hard enough." What did you mean?

A. It's not true. You know, you can practice forever, but you're not going to throw a fastball like Sandy Koufax did. He spent time explaining the ergonomics of the fastball, and it made perfect sense to him, because he could throw that fastball.

I was doing a movie with Helen Mirren and we were on the set. She said, "Oh, David, when you direct, you kind of act." Which is what a director does; he kind of acts out the piece for his actors. She said, "You must have been an actor." I said, "Yeah, I was a kid actor."

She asked how I was, and I told her I was *terrible*. She said, "But it's so easy." And I said, "Yes, Helen, for *you* it's easy."

So, if you've got talent, some things are easier. I think Eric Hoffer is the one who said, "The talentless think everything happens without effort."

Q. Clearly, you make an effort at what you do, but you do have that inborn talent.

A. Yeah, I do. I thank God every day for that. I used to lay sod for a living, and I washed dishes. I didn't like it at all. So, when I found out I had a gift for writing, it saved me. If I didn't have writing, I'd have become a much more compromised individual than I am. I took this obvious gift and worked very hard. I didn't want to end up like that guy at the concert.

Q. **Speaking of working hard, David, some people say writing is really rewriting. Does that characterize your writing, or does your writing just flow from you and require relatively minor revision?**

A. There are some things I work on forever. They can literally take years and years and years. Others may require relatively little effort.

Q. **Looking back on your body of work, would you say there's any overriding theme?**

A. I hope not. One of the reasons I go to work is to amuse myself. If I can't amuse myself, it's very hard to work. Someone once said, "Steal from anybody but yourself." I don't want to take away the pleasure of writing by trying to pound home some theme. That's a reason I've written nonfiction and a few novels . . . I just go and knock myself out.

Q. **What effects have Hollywood and mass media had on the theater today?**

A. In my lifetime television has been at war with the movies and seems to have wiped the movies out. They're dying in the face of the internet and other media. And theater is pressed to the wall now and again.

When I was a kid there were the little theaters, and there was amateur theater. Then there were regional theaters—such as Bob Bruestein at Yale—which spawned a resurgence of the American theater ... Joe Papp and people like that. But now maybe theater's back is to the wall a bit.

But despite the internet and electronics, stage plays will

always be relevant, just as rap music has reinvented the idea of poetry. If someone had something important to say, it was said within his or her cultural milieu. Similarly, stand-up comedy born in the Borscht Belt in the forties and fifties spawned improvisational theater. It's become a staple of world entertainment. So I don't think stage theater will ever die.

Q.   **Do you feel a novel or play should be accessible to a wide audience?**

A.   I've been making a living writing for close to fifty years, and I never met a stupid audience. I never read a good book that's inaccessible. I think it's a status notion if we writers posit that people are dumber than ourselves. I read children's literature because my last teenager is still at home . . . and the literature makes me want to throw up. The idea that kids are stupid and we must write down to them is ridiculous. But it's a great receptacle for second-rate writers.

Q.   **Which writers do you enjoy reading most?**

A.   I feel almost anyone can write a book, but not everyone can write a good sentence. My collection of novellas, *Three War Stories*, is an homage to Patrick O'Brian, who wrote some of the greatest adventure stories in the English language. If one goes back to the history of literature, there's a whole bunch of them. I adore Hemingway, Kipling, Patrick O'Brian, the Trollope books, George Eliot, Jane Austen, Tolstoy … all the great nineteenth-century novelists.

Q.   **Let's talk about your latest work, *Three War Stories*, in which the novellas deal with three wars spanning centuries and continents. Why write about war?**

A.   [Laughter.] Well, I'm going to have to revert to being in kindergarten. I wrote one novella and thought "That's kind of cute."

Then I wrote another and thought that if I write a third, I might have a book. So I wrote three. It just happened like that.

Q. **So there was no statement you were making by writing about war?**

A. It's not my job to make a statement. I know there are writers who do that, but as someone once said, "If you want to send a message, send a telegram."

Q. **If you could have dinner with any five people or writers from history—dead or alive—who would they be?**

A. I would choose my family. Writers don't like to talk with each other. We don't like talking with anybody; that's why we write, for God's sake. [Laughter.]

Q. **Will you indulge me . . . ? Family aside, who would you like to have dinner with?**

A. You know, when I give a talk or lecture, people want to speak with me afterward. But there's nothing I really have to say to the audience. For them it's the longing to get close to someone provocative or mysterious. For me, to talk to the audience is like the audience wanting to know how a magician does the trick. The magician can't tell them, because if he does, it ruins the trick. He has to resist the urge to confess, which is what I'm not doing very well with you today.

Q. **But you do talk to audiences and impart knowledge of your craft.**

A. Actually, not. What I'm really doing is just showing off. Because the things I can't tell them are like the things one doesn't tell one's children. They can't understand. They may understand as a memory—like later, when you say to yourself,

"God, now I see what my dad meant." But at the moment, there's an unbridgeable gap.

Q. **Some writers say, "The art speaks for itself. I have nothing more to say. It's far more interesting to read my book or look at my work than to speak with me." Does that pertain to David Mamet?**

A. Of course. I'm not Beau Brummell—a society wit. You know, someone sitting morosely in a corner at a raucous dinner party is probably a writer.

Q. **As an artist living in an absurd world, how do you respond to it?**

A. Existence *is* absurd. So I try to find some meaning in it by doing my job. Christians say, "In my father's house are many mansions." You're never going to get to the middle of the artichoke.

Q. **So you find meaning in your work, and I assume, in your family?**

A. Yes. I'm also a big fan of the Bible. It seems to address most of our ineffable questions.

Q. **And, of course, it's poetry.**

A. Yes, but there aren't enough pages.

Q. **Let me ask you about actors. Are there any you've found most interesting to work with?**

A. I find all actors interesting. The job of a director is to work with actors. It's about how one speaks to them in a way to help them play the part and motivate them to go down the road you've conceived

Q. **Have you dealt with actors who don't really get what you meant to convey?**

A. One hires them not because they can get it right, but because they can act. The subsequent question is, can they act *this part*? The actor wants to know what's going to help him understand and be good in the part. It's the director's job to communicate it. But you know, an actor may keep blowing a line because the line is no good.

Q. **Has an actor ever convinced you a line is "no good" and you've changed it?**

A. Sure. The better an actor is, the more he or she understands—intellectually or not—the text. It's happened many times, and actors are right more often than they're wrong.

Q. **What's next for David Mamet?**

A. I'm going to shoot this thriller I wrote, and will direct, with Cate Blanchett, and I hope to do a new, original play next fall in New York with Al Pacino.

It's been a pleasure talking with you, and I appreciate your telling me a little about how you do your magic tricks.

JOHN SANDFORD
ARCHAEOLOGY, ART, LUCAS DAVENPORT, AND VIRGIL FLOWERS

We know him as John Sandford, but that's his nom de plume. As journalist John Camp, he won the 1986 Pulitzer Prize for his five-part series about an American farm family faced with an agricultural crisis. After turning to fiction, he's written many *New York Times* bestselling books, including twenty-five Prey novels featuring Lucas Davenport. He's also penned four Kidd novels, nine in the Virgil Flowers series, three stand-alone books, and three YA novels co-authored with his wife, Michele Cook.

Our conversations took place between 2015 and 2017.

Q. You grew up, were educated, became a journalist, and won a Pulitzer Prize as John Camp. Because another writer's name was the same as yours, you became John Sandford and are now famous. Does John Camp ever feel cheated?

A. No, he really doesn't. I was a newspaper columnist for a while and I didn't much care for it. I'm a reporter type, not a celebrity type. I don't like people looking at me; I'd rather be watching people.

As a columnist, my picture was at the top of the column, so when I was in the downtown area of Saint Paul, people recognized me and would talk to me. A woman once said she saw me with some friends at a restaurant—and how "literary" we looked. It was supposed to be flattering, but the thing is, it disturbed me that people were watching me while I was eating. I don't know how celebrities deal with that sort of thing. So I'm perfectly content to be John Camp 99 percent of the time and John Sandford when I write.

Q. So, you still remain John Camp in everyday life?

A. Absolutely. I'm John Camp in terms of everything except the books.

Q. A while back, you left the Prey novels and began writing others. Then you returned to Prey. Tell us why you did that and if it might happen again.

A. I think it will happen again. That is, if I keep writing. My health is good, but I'm getting older. My first wife died a few years ago and I've remarried. Michele and I have—basically because of an interest she has—been involved in writing a young adult book. It's called *Uncaged*. I'll be doing a twenty-fifth Prey novel, but I'd like to do other things at this time.

Q. Have you found any problems in writing the Prey novels, a twenty-five-book series with a recurring character?

A. There are problems. It just seems like I've done so many Prey books. You begin wondering what the tolerance of the readers may be for yet another story about Lucas Davenport. I know my audience. Many of my readers are women; they tend to be affluent and educated. One of the things both men and women seem to be interested in is some kind of *romantic* aspect to the novels. And Lucas is getting older. We both started out at age forty-five. He's now fifty and I'm seventy. [Laughter.] I've kept his aging process slow, but I don't know if I can keep doing it. He's getting out of that romantic target age. So, I don't really know what's going to happen with Lucas. I want to keep my readers,who I really value. And you know, twenty-five novels in a series is quite a big, round number.

Q. Any special time of day for writing?

A. Usually late at night. I fool around all day. I play golf and hang out. I go around and look at stuff.

Q. Your recent Lucas Davenport novels feature a great deal about technology in tracing and tracking criminals. How have you kept up with these modern techniques?

A. One thing I realized when I began the book is that it's impossible to write an old-fashioned crime story like those featured in the sixties and seventies. It doesn't work well anymore. Those people left clues that can no longer be contested in court. Take DNA for example. It's impossible to refute if it's found.

   If you write contemporary police procedural novels, it's tough for anyone to get away with anything.

Consider the iPhone: it tracks every place you've been. That means the cops can accurately place you at the crime scene, and it's the same thing with the GPS navigation system in your car.

For me, technology is almost a character in the book, albeit a very complicated and omnipresent one. Yes, I do research, but I'm also struck by how people are so consumed by it and connected to it. You can't walk down the street without encountering people on their cell phones texting or talking.

Q. **In addition to Lucas Davenport, you write books about Virgil Flowers. He's a fascinating character. Will you give us a brief description?**

A. He's a smart man who's not all that comfortable with his role in law enforcement. He's a tall guy with long blond hair. He was a baseball player in college and graduated with a degree in ecological science. He also writes occasional magazine articles on outdoor topics.

Q. **How has he evolved over the years?**

A. He used to chase a lot of women, but for the last couple of books, he has had a permanent girlfriend . . . which may be a mistake. [Laughter.] He hasn't been terribly successful with women. He's been married and divorced three times, and none of those marriages lasted more than a year or so. He still maintains good relationships with his ex-wives, but he's had chronic problems with women. I don't know what's going to happen with this relationship with his current girlfriend.

Q. **Why did you say his having a permanent girlfriend may be a mistake?**

A. Because I have a lot of female readers and many of them have come up to me at readings and have expressed their dissatisfaction with that fact. [Laughter.] The problem with Virgil is *he likes women*—not in a predatory way—he enjoys their company, but he's also sexually attracted to them, and then . . . Virgil falls in love. I think women readers like that he doesn't take women for granted. It all seems kind of odd, even to me. [More laughter.]

Q. **I couldn't help but notice that your *Virgil Flowers* books have significant elements of humor. Tell us about that.**

A. When I was a newspaper reporter, I heard the funniest stories from cops. Many cops have good senses of humor. You almost have to have that to do the job. Some very weird and funny things happen on the street. Virgil has a sense of humor, and I try working that into the books.

Many of the things that happen in the books are more stupid than just plain funny. If you work with cops for a long time, you realize that a lot of the people they come in contact with are really dumb. And they do really dumb stuff, repeatedly. Many times, it leads to tragedy, but some of these stories are really a complex mixture of comedy and tragedy.

Q. **Who do you find more compelling to write about: Virgil Flowers or Lucas Davenport?**

A. I don't find either one more compelling than the other because they're totally different from each other. Virgil is a guy who is sort of left in the past. The killings he gets involved with are more mundane than those in which Lucas is involved. The perpetrators are usually the losers in society. They're not clever criminals. Virgil allows me to use my sense of humor much more than Lucas does.

Lucas Davenport is much more intense and far darker than Virgil Flowers. I like writing both of them. Virgil is very much of a release for me after writing about Davenport because I can have fun with him as opposed to the intensity of Davenport.

Q. **Your villains are quite unique. How do you construct and develop them?**

A. My villains are more of an engineering construct than anything coming from inspiration. When I'm setting up a book and thinking about what I want the villain to be, I'll survey a range of possibilities. Will these be impulse murders? Is it going to be someone who's had a psychotic break? Are the murders done for money, love, power, or sexual gratification? I pick the gender of the person—it can be either a man or woman. The killer was a woman in my novel, *Silken Prey*. Then I assign the villain certain characteristics, which are mostly taken from people I didn't like in the past.

Many things can make a villain interesting. You know, a typical killer so often described in thrillers is despicable from start to finish: his nose drips; he's pure evil. I tend to construct villains who were shaped to some extent by forces they couldn't control—many of them have had deprived pasts. I think the most appealing villains are those who act badly but aren't totally bad human beings. Interesting villains have more than one dimension and have different facets to their personalities.

Q. **Do you plot the elements of a story in advance or let the plot evolve as you write?**

A. The plot pretty much evolves on its own. When I've tried to outline ahead of time, it hasn't worked for me. It makes the pace of the book way too fast. I prefer a kind of cinema verité quality to the novel, which comes from struggling with its direction—you know, hitting a bunch of dead ends because detectives are trying to figure out a complicated situation.

When I outline a plot, things get solved really quickly. The books are around a hundred thousand words long, and at around the seventy-five-thousand-word point, I tend to outline so I can rush up to the climax.

Q. **After all these years, are you still learning things about writing?**

A. I'm learning about writing all the time. Every time I write a book it feels like I'm doing it for the first time. I think the most important lesson for first-time writers is the value of persistence. I have little tricks to keep me going—I write down how many words I write every day. I do that because it tells me I'm making progress and I'll get to the end of this project if I just persist. I can get lost in the middle of a long book, but if I know it's progressing, it makes the writing a little bit easier. I think some novice writers sit and stare at a screen. What I find helpful is to lie down on a couch, eat an ice-cream cone, and just think about what I'm trying to do. [Laughter.]

Q. **From what you've said, it sounds like you feel each book is its own arduous journey.**

A. It is. Each book is a struggle. There have been times when I've been writing and I'm halfway through a book and I stop short because I say to myself, "This just doesn't feel right." And I think a lot of other authors have had the same experience. Writing a novel isn't something that happens on a straight line. You go back and look at what you did, and then you change things. Then you go forward a bit more, then back, then forward again.

Q. **Have you seen changes in the thriller genre over the years?**

A. The novels have become more sophisticated and far more violent. The writers I read as a kid, like John D. MacDonald, didn't create villains like the ones being created now. The villains really set the tenor of a thriller or crime novel. I don't like certain kinds of villains—the remorseless killers who are so smart they evade every effort made to capture them. They're almost supernatural. I think we see more of that today than ever before.

I also don't like some of the heroes we encounter today: American military guys who are superheroes—the ones who go in against tremendous odds and manage to survive with nothing but a torn shirt. I just don't like that kind of stuff. That's why I liked the movie *Zero Dark Thirty* so much and *Black Hawk Down*. They seemed so real to me.

I like thrillers to be fairly real. Every one of my main characters has been shot. Their wives freak out and worry about them. They have marital problems because of their jobs. In other words, they're human. I'm a commercial writer, but I do like to keep at least one hand on reality.

Q. **What's in the future for John Sandford?**

A. I'm seventy-two now. I'm thinking ahead about three years. I'm working on a new Lucas Davenport book. The thing is, for the last three years, I've written three books a year, which has been really intense. Now that I'm back to the two-books-a-year schedule, things have kind of loosened up a bit. I've gotten back into the habit where for a few hours a day, I'm able to read for enjoyment.

Q. **You mentioned your age. Are you thinking about retiring?**

A. I don't know if I'll ever retire. They'll probably carry me off the job. But I've got some other interests I'd like to indulge. I'd like to drop back to a book a year, so I could have time to do other things.

Q. **But you're still writing at a torrid pace.**

A. I'm going to have to cut back sooner or later because the pace really does hurt, and it keeps me from doing other things. I sit at the computer for hours every day, and even when I'm not actually writing, I'm thinking and talking about it. Let me give you an example: last night, my wife and I sat down and had a protracted conversation about the possibility of writing two other novels. We discussed all the complications of establishing the plots. When I'm doing two books a year, even when I'm away from the computer, I can't get away from the writing.

For instance, when I walk around on the street, I look at signs, trucks, and bumper stickers, all of which contribute ideas for the books. Even when I'm in the car just out for a cruise, I'll see something interesting and make a mental note of it. And it all comes down to the fact that I can't get away from the writing and find it very hard to relax.

I'd like to be able to pursue other interests, like play a round of golf, which I used to enjoy. Writing demands a great deal of my time and soaks up my physical and mental energy.

Q. **Speaking of other interests, tell us about your involvement in an archaeological dig.**

A. In the early nineties, I was reading a great deal of history, which has always been a passion of mine. I studied American history in college. I then studied European history and eventually got to the history of the Bible.

The question with those stories has always been what part is history, what's myth, and what's actually tendentious religious politicking? I thought there might be enough actual history there to be very interesting. So I went to the Holy Land to look this over.

While I was in Israel, I ran into a man who was the head of the Department of Archaeology at the Hebrew University in Jerusalem. We look quite a bit alike—enough so that people would mistake us for each other. It turned out his grandparents came from the same town in Lithuania where mine came from. I'm a Roman Catholic and he's a Jew, but there had to be some crossover someplace along the line. We really hit it off, and he convinced me to join the dig at a site called Tel Rehov. We were investigating the era of Solomon and David, trying to determine if the stories about them were credible.

The dig went on for fifteen years and I would go there for a period of time each year. It was grueling and fascinating work. I loved it. We now have three or four large volumes about what we unearthed, and we'll have an exhibition of our findings from Tel Rehov at the Israel Museum next winter. That archaeological dig was one of the great times of my life. And I also have other hobbies.

Q. **Besides history and archaeology? What are they?**

A. I'm a painter; that's the main thing. I was painting with oils but grew allergic to the volatile spirits, so I changed to acrylics. I recently decided I need to write some music. But I don't know anything about music, so I started studying music theory and bought a guitar. I've been told since I was a child that I can't sing, so now I'm going to see if I can learn to sing.

Q. **Is there anything about your writing process that might surprise our readers?**

A. I don't think there's anything about the process itself that might surprise readers; however, perhaps they don't realize it's very hard work. I'm sitting at a computer many hours every day. Because the work is so consuming, I have to make an effort to get away from the novels. I have to force myself to take a break to exercise. I didn't exercise yesterday; I sat at the computer for most of the day, and as a result, today I have a sore back. Writing is actually very hard work. I don't just type a few words and then go out for a latte. [Laughter.] I know people appreciate when the book is good, but I think they don't understand how hard it is physically and mentally to write.

Q. **Tell us something about your *life* that might surprise our readers.**

A. I read about a lot of writers who've struggled and fought to succeed—people who have had rough times in their lives. Of all the people I know, I probably had the happiest childhood. I had parents and grandparents who loved me. I loved them. My parents were good people. I loved my brothers and sisters. We had interesting lives. I'm very grateful for the life I've had.

When I think about trauma in my life, it's only been there because I've *looked* for it. As a reporter I covered traumatic stories that have become part of my writing DNA and have served me very well. But those were traumatic events I sought out—crimes, murders, and disasters like plane crashes.

I'm certain I speak for millions of readers when I say I'm very glad you work as hard as you do and have provided us with so many suspenseful novels.

SARA PARETSKY
V. I. WARSHAWSKI AND DOUBT

Sara Paretsky is the award-winning author of the V. I. Warshawski detective novels. In 1982, when Sara wrote *Indemnity Only*, she revolutionized the mystery novel by creating a hard-boiled woman investigator.

Growing up in rural Kansas, Sara came to Chicago in 1966 to do community service work in the neighborhood where Martin Luther King Jr. was organizing. Sara felt that summer changed her life, and after finishing her undergraduate degree at the University of Kansas, she returned to make Chicago her home.

She received an MBA and a PhD in American history from the University of Chicago.

Sara shares her heroine's passion for social justice. In 1986, she founded Sisters in Crime to support women mystery writers. She established a foundation to support women in the arts, letters, and sciences and has endowed scholarships at the University of Kansas, as well as mentored students in Chicago's inner-city schools.

She has received many literary awards, and her novels have been translated into nearly thirty languages.

Our conversations took place between 2015 and 2017.

Q. In reading your novels, I'm struck by your vivid descriptions of Chicago. Your integration of character with environment has been compared to that of Hammett and Chandler. Will you talk about setting in your novels?

A. Chicago is the city where I came of age. The summer of 1966 was probably the most intense experience of my life. I got very involved in the neighborhood where I was living in the city itself. Even though it was a violent summer, I always think of it as the summer of hope and passion and the summer when I grew up. I think that's why Chicago plays such a big role in my books. For me, it's an emotionally important place.

Chicago is like a set of small towns and neighborhoods. When I worked with kids who had never been downtown, they weren't terribly impressed by the big buildings or Christmas lights when we took them there. The details they saw through children's eyes were drunks passed out on rooftops or wildlife running along the elevated train tracks. I learned from them that what makes a scene come alive is close-up detail, and that's found its way into my books.

Q. How has V.I. evolved as compared to *Indemnity Only*, the first novel in the series?

A. When I wrote *Indemnity Only*, there weren't women, either in real life or in fiction, doing what V.I. was doing. The year it was published, 1982, was the first year women could serve in Chicago's regular police force instead of merely being matrons at detention centers. So V.I. had a chip on her shoulder and was much more in-your-face than she is now. V.I. had to prove her worth, but now she's dealing with other problems.

She and I are both older, more mature, and I guess, more worried about things. I'm a self-taught writer and don't think out what a protagonist should or shouldn't be doing. V.I. tends to reflect more of my own emotional life at the specific time I'm writing.

Q. **Your latest novel, *Fallout*, has V.I. leaving her comfort zone, Chicago, and going to Kansas. You mention in a note that this is part of your own "origin story." Tell us more.**

A. I set the story in Kansas because much of the story had to do with research on biological weapons, which is a field of study in which my father had been involved as a cell biologist. I could only imagine placing the story at the University of Kansas, where he did his research and also taught. So I devised a way to get V.I. out of Chicago and have her travel down the Mississippi and over to Kansas. I grew up in eastern Kansas and am very familiar with the area.

Q. **The issue of race appears in *Fallout*. You mentioned you relied partly on your own memories with regard to this history. Will you tell us more about that?**

A. My father was one of the first Jews hired at the University of Kansas. When my parents had enough money to buy a house, the realtors told them there was one section of town where the Jews and African-Americans lived. Because my parents didn't sound Jewish, they were shown homes in other areas. They opted out of the area and bought a house in the country. But that was my first exposure to issues of race in the city. We didn't have a large African-American population, but they were barred from college-bound classes at the high school and couldn't live in certain college housing. My father was intent on bringing students of all races and nationalities into his lab at college. Things began coming to a head in the late 1960s and early '70s, so awareness of racial issues was part of my early life.

Q. As *Fallout* progresses, medicine and bacteriology come into play. How did this idea come to you?

A. My dad worked on an organism that causes Rocky Mountain spotted fever. It's closely allied with typhus, which is one of the diseases the Soviets were interested in developing as a bioweapon. Two labs doing work similar to what my father was doing were located behind the Iron Curtain. He never got permission to visit those labs.

In the midsixties, there was a conference about this organism held in Czechoslovakia. He attended and persuaded a technician to inject him with their strain of this organism so he could bring it home in his bloodstream in order to study it. I wanted to write that story and did so in a short story in a collection called *Ice Cold*, edited by Jeffery Deaver. My father got off the plane from this conference with a fever of *one hundred and five*. He didn't start antibiotic treatment until his lab technician could take a blood sample from him. He didn't endanger the other passengers on the plane because the disease can be transmitted only by a tick bite.

I don't know if he was a hero, an idiot, insane, or a combination of the three. So, this found its way into *Fallout*.

Q. As you pen more novels about her, how do you find different issues to challenge V.I.?

A. I know my books are described as issue-driven, but they don't come to me that way. They unfold for me as stories. For instance, in the novel *Brush Back*, the idea came to me when I met someone in charge of arranging tours of Wrigley Field for Chicago Cubs fans. He told me about the underbelly of the stadium. That sparked the idea for the book. I had to build a story, and it evolved out of V.I.'s old neighborhood. Even though I'm not a native of Chicago, stories from the old neighborhoods grip me. I get letters from people from these neighborhoods, and they often *drive my thinking about the stories.*

Q. V.I. isn't getting any younger. Will she retire? And if she does, will there then be a new character?

A. Right now I'm taking the coward's way out on V.I.'s age. She's going to hover around fifty for a while. If she retires, she'll probably end up blowing up the nursing home that she's incarcerated in. I can imagine creating a new character, but I just can't imagine leaving V.I. behind.

Q. So, she's part of your life?

A. Of course she is.

Q. You've been noted for writing crime novels with a feminist perspective. Will you tell us about that?

A. I grew up in Kansas, a very conservative state. My parents were old-fashioned in their views about what girls should aspire to. I have four brothers, and it was a struggle for me to have the same opportunities life provided them by birth. These issues mattered very much to me personally.

When I began writing crime fiction for publication, I was part of the first generation of women to do so and had to deal with a certain amount of resentment. Sue Grafton and I were writing hard-boiled books in what had been a masculine genre. That personal history has always shaped how I see the world, and it goaded me into starting Sisters in Crime.

Q. Which, if any, aspects of Sara Paretsky are embodied by V.I. Warshawski?

A. Oh, I would say that V.I. is the tough, tenacious person I would be if I weren't something like Hamlet, "sicklied over with a pale cast of doubt." V.I. says the kinds of things I sometimes blurt out, but more often I only imagine saying them.

Q. **With nineteen V.I. Warshawski books, do you have a favorite?**

A. *Hardball* is right up there. It deals with torture done by the Chicago police, which went on in real life for about twenty years. I think in some ways it's my strongest novel because it drew on my personal history.

My very favorite is *Critical Mass*. Everything about it was so very personal for me. It's about a scientist whose life was derailed by the Nazis in a way similar to how my family's world was upended. Actually, they were all murdered. The only people in my family to survive were my grandparents, who came to America before the war broke out.

Q. **As president of the Mystery Writers of America, what, if any trends do you see now in mystery fiction?**

A. Publishing is in free-fall. Nobody knows where anything is going. Will e-books transform everything? Will self-publishing be the fate of all writers except for James Patterson and a few others? The big casualty in this brave new world has been the loss of opportunity for African-American, gay and lesbian writers, and to a lesser extent, women writers. Back in 2000, there were probably twenty-five black writers published by the big houses. Today there are three or four. We're trying to develop ways to bring all writers to the attention of readers.

Q. **What, if anything, keeps you awake at night?**

A. Way too many things do that. [Laughter.] I worry my career's disintegrating. I worry whether people will buy my books, or if I still know how to write a book. I have to start a new book, since I'm under contract. It just never gets easier. In fact, it gets harder as you go along.

Ruby Rich, who used to review for the *Village Voice*, said, "Writing is a form of auto-sadomasochism—first you tie yourself to the bed, and then you beat yourself up."

When I begin each new book, I think, "Oh no. I can't do it again. They'll hate the new one."

Q. **What has surprised you about the writing life?**

A. That there's such goodwill among crime writers. There's really a great deal of mutual support. In the world of the important literary writers, there are always feuds and endless quarrels, such as the classic one between Norman Mailer and Gore Vidal. Crime writers fly below the radar. We're not viewed as being as important as so-called literary writers; that creates a different and more collegial atmosphere. It's been a surprise to me, and I feel very happy to be where I am.

Q. **Is there anything about your writing process that would surprise our readers?**

A. I wish my process weren't so tormented. I always feel you can smell burning rubber when I'm writing. [Laughter.] I spend an inordinate amount of time trying to work out story lines. For example, right now I'm working on a book, and when I got to page ninety, I realized it isn't working. So I must burn more rubber before I can go any further.

Q. **So, the excruciating aspects of your writing process might surprise our readers?**

A. Exactly. By the end of a novel, I send it off with a certain amount of dread because there's chewing gum and Scotch tape holding the manuscript together. [Laughter.]

Q. **If you could read any one novel over again as if it were for the first time, which would it be?**

A. Of the books I've read within the last decade, certain ones stand out: *Gilead* by Marilynne Robinson and *Wolf Hall* by Hilary Mantel.

Q. **Which of the books you read as a youngster has stayed with you?**

A. *Little Women* was the iconic book of my childhood. I first read it when I was seven or eight. It was a bit above my reading level. Later, I read it many, many times. It was a magical book for me.

Q. **In your memoir and in an earlier interview, you said you want to do more than just write, and suggested that writing alone is insufficient. What did you mean, and do you still feel that way?**

A. I can't believe that just my words on the page are enough to change the way things are. I ought to be out physically keeping abortion safe and legal, restoring the Fourth Amendment, and getting clean water back into Flint, Michigan, and Kentucky. The list goes on and on. I think writing about crime and social issues may not be enough to bring about real change.

Q. **You're hosting a dinner party and can invite any five people, living or dead, from any walk of life. Who would they be?**

A. I'd invite P. D. James. I didn't know her well, but she was one of the wittiest, liveliest people I've ever encountered. Politics notwithstanding, our core values were very much alike. She once took me to the Athenaeum Club in London. She was the first woman to be admitted as a member. We had such a great time making all the old stodgy members go "tut-tut."

Another person I'd invite would be the historian Daniel Boorstin, who was appointed Librarian of Congress. To please my husband, who's a physicist, I'd include Galileo, his favorite scientist. I'd invite another beloved crime writer who died last year, Dorothy Salisbury Davis. I was with her when she was dying. She was born Catholic and said, "I know which saint I want to greet me when I cross the river—Saint Teresa of Ávila. I want her because if God could put up with her rebellious spirit, he could put up with me." And I'd include Teresa of Ávila along with Dorothy. And I'd include Martina Navratilova, one of the greatest tennis competitors of all time.

It's been a pleasure talking with the author of so many intellectually lively mysteries about a gutsy protagonist whose stories are driven by political causes and social issues.

ACE ATKINS
FOOTBALL AND FICTION SOUTHERN STYLE

Ace Atkins has written fifteen books over the past fifteen years. A former football star at Auburn University, he became a crime reporter for the *Tampa Tribune*, earning a Pulitzer Prize nomination for covering a cold case from the 1950s. He published his first novel, *Crossroad Blues*, at age twenty-seven, becoming a full-time novelist at age thirty.

He has written stand-alone novels and is known for his Nick Travers series and his Quinn Colson series. Two of his books have been nominated for Edgar Awards.

In 2011, Ace was chosen by the estate of Robert B. Parker to continue writing the Spenser series of novels.

Our conversations took place between 2015 and 2017.

Q. **Before we talk about books and other things, let me ask how you got the name** *Ace.*

A. It was my dad's name. He was a professional football player in the old AFL and the NFL. A sportswriter dubbed him Ace, and it became his name. So, when I was born, that nickname was given to me. In a sense, it's a family name. The only time I'm called by my given name, William, is if I'm pulled over by a cop for speeding. [Laughter.]

Q. **Did you always want to be a writer?**

A. I became passionate about books when I was in high school. I discovered Ian Fleming. For a fifteen-year-old boy to discover the world of Ian Fleming was astounding. Not only were they great travelogues and adventure stories, but there were pages of descriptions of naked women. [Laughter.] I also read books by authors like Fitzgerald and Hemingway.

Then I got into Chandler and Hammett, but Ian Fleming was my gateway drug into the larger world of loving books, which made me want to become a writer. I read about Fleming's life and thought it would be exciting to research things, travel to places, and write about new locations.

Another writer I thought was fantastic was Gregory Mcdonald, a former journalist, who shaped the idea of my wanting to become a journalist. Fleming and Hemingway had, of course, been journalists, too. I loved the idea of the journey of the hero.

Q. **You were a high-profile varsity football player at Auburn—a defensive end—and when you graduated, you said you wanted nothing more to do with football. Your father had been a football coach. Were you rebelling?**

A. I think I was. My father was not only into football, but he worked for the NFL for thirty years, so football was a huge part of our family. Football was pressed onto me. So, what do you do? You rebel against your dad and become a journalist and then a writer. [Laughter.]

Q. **How did journalism come about?**

A. It wasn't easy. [Laughter.] My biggest motivator was I didn't want to become a football coach. I majored in mass communications, studying screen writing, and also took English and Southern literature courses.

I had a friend who said, "If you want to become a writer, the best place to do it is to go into the newsroom." I thought about people like Hemingway and Graham Greene and other writers I respected who honed their craft as journalists. I was living in Florida, and I took a job with the *St. Petersburg Times*. I was scraping by earning pennies writing stories. I'm not kidding. I was paid thirty bucks per story. If I got fifty bucks, it was a windfall. Eventually, I became a full-time reporter.

It took a few years before I got my sea legs because I didn't have a journalism background. It was also a bad time with the recession. Reporters were being laid off, but eventually I became a staff writer at the *Tampa Tribune*. That experience was valuable because the editors helped me hone what I was doing and I became a much better writer.

Q. **How did your career as a journalist prepare you for writing fiction?**

A. One of the things I see with amateur writers, or those who haven't been in the news business as print journalists, is a failure to *get to the point* of a story. As a journalist, you learn that words are cheap, and everything you put on the page is *not* magic. Having worked with some very tough news editors, I learned how to get to the point of a story. For instance, in a news story,

I might end up getting a hundred quotes, but I had to decide which were the *best* quotes to use in a story. I learned the meaning of dialogue and which words had the most impact. I learned how to write good sentences and to write with clarity and color.

Those were the lessons that prepared me to become a fiction writer, drawing on my training and experiences writing news feature stories.

Q. It's been said your novels contain parts of yourself—friends, colleagues, family members, and personal heroes. Tell us a little more about this.

A. That's more related to four books written before the Quinn Colson series: *White Shadow, Wicked City, Devil's Garden,* and *Infamous.* They're all based on true stories. The first was about a killing that occurred in Tampa in the 1950s. I'd been a newspaper reporter and was hanging out with retired cops and journalists who told amazing stories. So I wrote a book about it. The cops and journalists in the book were based on real people and experiences. In fact, when I was writing those novels, I got a really nasty letter from the son of a Mafia hit man. He not so subtly suggested I write about thugs and rednecks from Alabama, my home state. I thought that was a great idea. So the next book I wrote was based on members of my family who had a rather unsavory history. Those are the personal connections found in those four novels.

Q. One of the striking things about the books in the Quinn Colson series is how the small town of Jericho almost becomes a character. Will you talk about setting?

A. I'm always struck by how many novels today focus on international intrigue and involve superheroes. While I enjoy reading them, I try to write a different kind of novel. I write about ordinary people living in a small town such as Jericho, Mississippi. I love capturing the atmosphere of Southern life with its unique ambience and everything that goes on—the good, the bad, and the unexpected.

With each successive book, I can expand and dig deeper, so six books into the series, Jericho's corrupt underbelly has been more vividly exposed. I believe Jericho is emblematic of small-town life in America. I think it's a very Southern novel. There are many issues specific to the American South, but I could adapt the story and change it to another region, like Iowa or Kansas. There are certain archetypal characters and power brokers existing in small-town America everywhere.

Q. **You anticipated my next question. In the Quinn Colson novels, is Jericho a microcosm of the larger world?**

A. Yes, absolutely it is. You don't have to be in Paris, London, or New York, and you don't have to write international thrillers to experience corruption, intrigue, brutality, and criminality. It's as much a part of life in a small town as anywhere else. So, as you said, the fictional town of Jericho is a microcosm of the larger world. And a protagonist like Quinn Colson has all the flaws and warts you would expect to find in people anywhere: he's had a problematic off-again-on-again relationship with a married woman, has issues with work, and must sort out complicated relationships with his father and sister.

Q. **Your writing is quite lyrical and has been compared to James Lee Burke's and Pat Conroy's. It's also been described as an accurate rendering of the Deep South in Faulkner country. What do you think of these statements?**

A. James Lee Burke was an early influence on me. He taught me there are no limits to writing crime novels. You can be a crime writer and have as much depth and literary license as you want in telling these stories. He was one of my early heroes. I think it will take another fifty years before I can get into the realm of the skill set of James Lee Burke and Pat Conroy.

Living in Oxford, Mississippi—the world of Faulkner—has been helpful. I really learned from him to pay attention to the world around me. The people I write about are essentially the descendants of Faulkner's characters. Instead of their being at the general store or town square, I may overhear them in Walmart. I try to write about a modern South, not an embellished one. I learned from Faulkner and Flannery O'Connor that you find a lot of humor and characters simply by observing people.

Q. **So there really *is* "Southern writing"?**

A. Absolutely. I think there's certainly a set of themes and points of style emblematic of the Southern novel. I'm drawn more to the rough-hewn South, not mint juleps and the genteel South. The books that appeal to me are those by Faulkner, such as *Intruder in the Dust*.

Another favorite writer was Larry Brown, now deceased, who wrote about the real, gritty, modern South. I think there's a certain comedic edge to Southern writing, including the works of Flannery O'Connor and Barry Hannah, a master of the Southern short story. The Southern landscape offers a tremendous amount of organic soil, rich with history. You don't have to go very far to find ugly, sordid events. As a writer, that's what you really want to dig into.

Q. **The dialogue in your novels is strikingly authentic. How do you approach writing dialogue?**

A. I think it goes back to observation. It derives from what I've learned as a journalist. The writers I've admired so much,

McDonald and Hemingway, were awesome dialogue writers. They had been journalists.

So my ear is always attuned to eavesdropping. I listen to people all the time. I've gotten so good at it, people don't realize I'm listening to them. I may be in the grocery store and find myself in aisle five, overhearing someone explaining a relationship issue. That can become part of a novel. It's a matter of listening to people *really* talk, not learning dialogue so much from reading other books or watching movies. I listen to people every day, and can't turn it off.

I think dialogue is the engine driving a novel. It propels the story and bespeaks character. A novel's characters are made *real* by their dialogue more than by anything else. I've always felt dialogue is not just what people *say* to each other; it's what they *do* to each other with words. I love walking around and jotting down little bits of dialogue I overhear, whether it's at the general store, standing in a supermarket line, or sitting in a restaurant.

Without trying to eavesdrop, I hear the most amazing bits and pieces of conversation, some of which I can fit in a novel. A short while ago, while walking around, I heard a man and woman talking. From their conversation and the tones of their voices, it was clear they knew each other very well. She gave him a gentle punch on the shoulder and said, "How dare you sleep with another woman." He laughed and said, "What can you expect? I was in jail for a month." [Laughter.]

By listening to conversations taking place anywhere, a writer can find a treasure trove of dialogue that might wind up in a novel.

Q. **What's been the biggest surprise to you about writing?**

A. The biggest surprise for me is that each novel presents its own challenge. I'd have thought that working on the seventeenth or eighteenth novel would be easier. But every book is still tough. I'd like to say years of experience have made the process easier, but it's just not true. I think if you're going to challenge yourself as a writer, you try to make each project better. You find new and interesting obstacles with each book. When beginning a new novel, there's always a great deal of uncertainty—even some anxiety—but wanting to get paid trumps any anxiety I may feel.

Q. **Your writing style in the Quinn Colson series is literary. In the Spenser novels, it's hard-boiled, Boston noir. Tell us about that.**

A. Detective and crime fiction were my entry point into loving books. I'm from the South and went to Auburn University. Coming from that region, I was surrounded by notions of Faulkner, Flannery O'Connor, Robert Penn Warren, and other Southern writers. Those two worlds kind of melded into the type of books I write.

For the Spenser books, I'm following a Hammett/Chandler path. All those novels influenced me, but Hammett, Chandler, and to some extent, Hemingway inspired me in writing the Spenser books.

Q. **You write a Quinn Colson novel and a Spenser book each year. Last October, you told me about different ways you approach writing each one, even including the beverages you drink. Will you share that with us?**

A. To be frank with you, I'll drink anything put in front of me. [Laughter.] When I'm working on Spenser, I do drink more beer. It's a bit of a mental trick, but having a Sam Adams makes me feel like I'm in Boston.

Q. Spenser and Quinn are such totally different characters. Are there other mental tricks you use to get into one mode or the other?

A. You're right. It's a totally different thought process going from one to the other. It's like speaking two different languages. One little trick I use is music. When I'm writing a Robert B. Parker book, I listen to the music he really loved. That's classic jazz—Ella Fitzgerald, Mel Tormé, Louis Armstrong, or John Coltrane. When I hear that music, it sounds like Spenser to me.

When I write about Quinn Colson and the American South, I listen to country music—Johnny Cash, Charley Pride, and Loretta Lynn. The music helps me refocus and think in a different way.

Q. If I didn't know better, the Spenser novels would make me believe you've lived in Boston for years.

A. My parents are Southern, and I've spent most of my life in the South. But when my dad became a football coach, depending on the team, we lived in different regions—San Francisco when he worked for the 49ers, Detroit when he was with the Lions, and Buffalo when he coached for the Bills. I had to adapt to a new culture with each move.

Going to Boston and really soaking it up is not only extremely important, but I'm very familiar with doing that kind of thing. When I was a newspaper reporter covering central Florida, learning about a city was simply part of what I did.

Boston's a very different city from when Bob Parker was alive. For the Spenser books, it's part of my job to get it right and capture the city's ambience. So I spend a lot of time there. I want to make sure the novel has authentic descriptions. If I haven't been to a specific place, I would never put it in a Spenser book.

Q. **So you wouldn't just use Google Earth for describing streets and locales?**

A. [Laughter.] No. If I write about a place, I've *been* there. Fortunately, it's not tough for me to do because most of the Spenser stuff takes place in good restaurants and bars. [More laughter.] That's been one of the great perks of this job because Boston is such a terrific city. I love going there every few months. Two things have been great about writing the Spenser series: one was getting to know Boston, and the other was getting to know Bob's widow, Joan Parker.

Q. **What challenges did you face continuing a series with a preformed character, style, and setting?**

A. As a fan of the Spenser books for many years, I found the biggest challenge to be, most of all, *continuity*. I wanted to create an authentic Spenser novel where the feel of Bob's books was replicated. I wanted the reader who'd finished Bob's last book to pick up a Spenser book I wrote and feel it was written by him. The important thing was for Spenser to live on.

Q. **More generally, do you break any writing "rules" when crafting your novels?**

A. When I was a young writer, I used to read lots of stuff about what to do and *not* do when writing. I try to conform to the rules I like. [Laughter.] I think the best rules I ever read for a writer came from Elmore Leonard. He was a stylistic genius. His most famous rule, and the one I try to live by, is "If it looks or reads like writing, take it out and rewrite it."

As a young man, I tried to be fancy with my prose, but two of my favorite stylists were Parker and Leonard. They wrote spare, compact prose, and their word choices were economical and just perfect. The corollary to that first Elmore

Leonard rule is "I cut out the parts most people skip over." It's sometimes tough to do, but I try to follow those two rules.

Q. **Do you have a favorite among all your novels?**

A. I do. It's a novel called *Infamous*. It's the story of George "Machine Gun" Kelly. I did enough research for that one to write a nonfiction book, so the novel is based on truth but has a natural story arc. Parts of the book are almost verbatim renderings of actual events. It's like a Coen brothers screwball comedy.

Let me tell you about an interview I had with a 102-year-old man who, as a bank teller in 1932, was held up by Machine Gun Kelly. Kelly held a .38 behind the teller's ear as he emptied the cash drawer. I commented, "You must've been scared to death." The old gent said, "No, not at all. Kelly was polite and kept apologizing." Actually, Kelly's wife was really the mastermind, a Lady Macbeth type, and she was almost like a press agent. In fact, she's the one who came up with the moniker *Machine Gun*.

At some point I hope to return to writing creative fiction based on fact.

Q. **You mean *faction*?**

A. Yes. I really love it. I love doing the research and writing about historical periods and people. *Infamous* was the fourth faction book I'd done, and I hope to get back to that kind of writing.

Q. **If you weren't a writer, what would you be doing?**

A. I'd be unemployed. [Laughter.] I was a journalist. When I left the newspaper business, little did I know it was the final phase of that long and proud tradition. If I didn't have my writing, I'd probably be working for a magazine. I'd be a reporter in some capacity. I've got no other talents. Or, I'd be a gumshoe.

Q. **As a successful novelist, what's the most important lesson you would want to convey to young writers?**

A. The most important thing is to *work, work, work*. I work on my books every day except when I'm on vacation. To be a professional novelist means you want to improve with each project, and there's no substitute for always working and trying to write better prose. I've been doing this for almost twenty years, and it's a constant struggle to keep at it and grow as a writer.

Q. **Do you have mixed feelings about the life of an author?**

A. Sometimes I love it and sometimes I hate it. [Laughter.] I do love the freedom the writing life allows, but as a professional writer, I've got to make deadlines. I have to deliver a manuscript on time and it has to be good, sharp, and right. My editors expect a solid book, not a rough draft. So, while I love being my own boss and having independence, the writing life also confers responsibilities.

Q. **Can you complete the following sentence? Writing novels has taught me_____.**

A. I think it's taught me to understand people more than I did before. I would like to say that it's given me empathy. It's helped me understand the motivations of people—even the bad guys. It's allowed me to explore human nature. So, sort of like Quinn Colson, I'm evolving, too.

Q. **If you could have dinner with any five people, writers or figures from history—living or dead—who would they be?**

A. Definitely, one would be Hemingway. Billy Wilder would be another. Burt Reynolds has had a fascinating life, is a very funny guy, and made some great action pictures. He used to hang around with guys like Orson Welles. I'll bet he has some great stories to tell. I'd also like to sit down with Dashiell Hammett. My last choice is an easy one: Raquel Welch.

Q.   **What would you be talking about?**

A.   We'd be talking about Raquel Welch, of course. [Laughter.]

Congratulations on writing the suspenseful and compelling Quinn Colson suspense thrillers and for keeping Robert B. Parker's Spenser series alive and well.

ROBERT CRAIS
WRITING FOR AN AUDIENCE OF ONE

Robert Crais is the award-winning author of twenty-one novels, seventeen of them featuring Elvis Cole and Joe Pike. Before turning to writing novels, he wrote scripts for various television series, including *Hill Street Blues*, *Cagney & Lacey*, *Miami Vice*, *Quincy*, *Baretta*, and *L.A. Law*. His novels have been translated into more than forty languages and are global bestsellers.

He credits Raymond Chandler, Dashiell Hammett, Ernest Hemingway, Robert B. Parker, and John Steinbeck for influencing his writing style.

Our conversations took place in 2016 and 2017.

Q. **I get the feeling from reading your last few books that Elvis Cole is still evolving. Will you talk about that?**

A. He's evolving because *I* am. My first published novel, *The Monkey's Raincoat*, came out in 1987. I'm not the same person now as I was then. One of the reasons I've stayed interested in Elvis and Joe—maybe the primary reason—is I expect them to evolve over time, as people do. That's why, to me, they've remained fresh. There's always something new and interesting impacting their characters—helping to define who they are as people.

Q. **You've created two iconic characters in Elvis Cole and Joe Pike. Will you describe their relationship over the course of the series?**

A. It's dependable. At its core, the series is about friendship and loyalty. It's about having someone you can trust regardless of the situation. Elvis and Joe grew out of my love for the Hollywood notion of the buddy picture or the *bromance*. It goes back forever—with Pancho and the Cisco Kid, and much earlier.

There's a reason people respond to this situation: in the darkness, we want a person we can trust at our side. At our core, we're pack animals, like gorillas or wild dogs. We want to gather, have a family. Elvis and Joe are representations of *family*. They're partners; they're each that friend we all wish we had. I think that unfaltering friendship is worth writing about. I like to see it grow and evolve over time. I like to explore how they came to be as people and as friends. I think that's what I've done over the course of the series.

Q. **It seems the driving force in your novels is Elvis's character.**

A. Yes. I think of myself as mainly a character writer. While reviewers have always spoken highly of my plots—which I want to roll along—all the stories derive from the protagonist's character. Above and beyond the excitement and energy of the plot, the moments that bring a tear to the eye are the primary motivating factors for me.

Q. **The Elvis Cole and Joe Pike novels have fascinating villains. What can make villains interesting?**

A. To be interesting, they need to be complex and not cardboard cutouts. They must also be accessible. While my villains are actually horrible people, initially the reader doesn't know how horrible they truly are. They're presented as people you might bump into on the street. But little by little, I draw the reader in until there's the revelation of just how hideous they are. It should be unsettling for the reader as the hooks gradually sink in and the reader is compelled to read on and see what the villain will do next.

All writers, including me, are readers first. I was a voracious reader before I became a writer. I'm still a reader and I love to be entertained. Hence, I'm my own audience. So, when I write villainous scenes, I try to make them entertaining and then eventually transform the character into someone who's horrifying to *me*. If *I'm* entertained, hopefully the reader is entertained.

I recall an old saying that goes something like this: "No tears in the writer, no tears in the reader."

Q. **The dialogue in your novels is crisp and realistic. Talk to us about a novel's dialogue.**

A. I wrote a lot for television. It was my good fortune to have worked with and for some of the most talented people on television at that time—actors like Jack Klugman, Tyne Daly, and Sharon Gless, and producers and writers like Steven Bochco. Working with them on such character-rich shows taught me how drama should unfold, and actors like Tyne Daly and Jack Klugman gave me an appreciation of how dark dialogue should sound. Those lessons became ingrained in me and have infiltrated the books.

I usually don't think about dialogue. It just happens in my head. It unfolds. Of course, I revise it many times and always speak it aloud to myself. I constantly read my work aloud, which sometimes draws odd looks when I'm writing in a Starbucks. [Laughter.] I find that hearing it helps me make it more precise and more real.

Q. **In some of your novels about Elvis and Joe, you've augmented the private detective first-person POV with a combination of first- and third-person narratives, along with multiple points of view. Will you talk about that?**

A. I think it makes for a richer reading experience. To me, employing those writing techniques is the same as a painter using different colors. The backdrop of the novel is my canvas. I want the fullest possible experience for the reader and a full writing experience for myself. I'm the artist who writes the stuff, but I'm also my own first reader.

I work my way through the characters and their evolution over the course of the year it takes to complete the novel. I want to be entertained and need to stay interested in what I'm doing. The more "colors" I use, the richer the canvas becomes. If I've done the dance correctly, by the time a reader finishes the book, the experience will have been deeper and fuller.

Q. **You once said, "I gave up this artsy thing when writing novels and went back to what I knew." You described your first two novels as being on the "worst ever" list and decided to change your storytelling technique. Will you tell us about that?**

A. You mentioned my TV work. At a fairly young age, I got involved with television. I loved it and plunged headlong into writing for mainstream television, and did it for ten years. Over that period of time, the stresses of TV production began to tell on me.

I'd always had the desire to write books—things that would be mine as opposed to collaborative pieces, as they are in Hollywood.

I adopted this "literary" point of view in contrast to the way television writers approach a story. They plan things out, make a pitch to others on the project, then wait until people sign off before they can write it. That's how the business works.

I had this notion that a novelist—an *artist*—just sits down, goes into a trance, has no idea what's going to come out, and starts to type on the keyboard. And a few days later, there it is: he's created *art*. When I attempted to write my first novel, that's how I approached it. After being a TV "hack" for so long, I was going to be an *artist*. I started typing, just creating stuff out of whole cloth. I ended up with a five-hundred-fifty-page manuscript. It was a disaster. A couple of years later, I tried again, and the same thing happened. It was a big mistake.

After those two strikeouts, I thought maybe art is for *other* people. The TV thing had turned out okay, so maybe that would be how I'd write the third book. I wrote *The Monkey's Raincoat*, which really worked out.

Q. **So, it's safe to conclude you outline your novels?**

A. Yes, I do that. What I've learned over the years, after talking with so many writers in all genres, is this: we are all different. There's no one correct way to write. Some people can sit down without a thought in their head and begin to write and it comes out as a beautiful story. That's how it works for them. But it doesn't work for me. I have to know where I'm going. Looking back at twenty novels, I can't complain.

Q. **You also once said, "The beginning of a novel is the most difficult part for me." What did you mean by that?**

A. The beginning of the novel is when I'm figuring out what the book will be about. The shorthand way of saying it would be to use the word *outline*. To this day, that's the hard part for me. I've learned people have different definitions for the word *outline*. People who like to make it up as they go are terrified by that word.

Often, the implication is that it's some sort of linear act, where each chapter is successively outlined. That's not true for me. I take an organic approach, thinking about the characters and the story, and slowly develop different thoughts, scenes, and chapters, the majority of which wind up in the trash. It's a way of growing the story over time. It can take many months. Once I have that story line—that collection of themes and characters that gets me from the beginning of the piece to the end—I'm off and running. Typically, the actual writing is far less stressful.

Q. **You wrote for various television shows. Is there one you enjoyed writing the most?**

A. That's easy: *Cagney & Lacey*. That's because of the people who were involved and because, as a group, our talents melded so well. I was involved in the first full season [1982–83] as part of the writing staff, and I really think we were doing some of the best writing on television at that time. They're great people and are still my close friends.

Q. **What would you be doing if you weren't a writer?**

A. Oh, we're going to play that game. [Laughter.] Let's see, if I weren't a writer I'd probably be a cargo pilot in the South Seas, or an architect. Yeah, an architect. They create and construct.

Q. **What's surprised you about the writing life?**

A. If I pretend I don't know what happened, what surprised me is that I would be as disciplined as I am. Writing really takes an enormous amount of self-control and discipline. There are plenty of more fun things to do than to sit at your desk every day and write.

Q. **I assume you successfully deal with the near-universal temptation to procrastinate?**

A. Absolutely. The reality is—especially on a bad day, but really, on *all* days—it's a job like any other. Only, you're your own boss, and the boss, meaning you, is the person who must keep the writing-you in the chair, focused and committed to getting the task accomplished. You have to consistently force yourself to keep writing.

Q. **What do you love about the writing life?**

A. What I love about the writing life—despite the bad days when I have to force my way through—is when I'm *there* "in the moment," when what's happening on the page is *real* and *true* and *good*, and I'm *there* with Elvis Cole or with Joe Pike or with Maggie and Scott and I'm in complete touch with my emotions. That's when things come together and may burst into something I hadn't necessarily planned. There's no better feeling. That's what it's all about.

After twenty books, I think I've learned who I am as a writer and how I have to go about writing my books. I don't measure myself against other writers. If I have anything to offer as a writer, it's my world, my point of view, and my sensibility.

Q. **Is there anything about your writing process that might surprise our readers?**

A. While the books are fast-paced and things seem to happen quickly, it might surprise readers to know the end result comes only after months and months of writing, rewriting, and revising the original script. I can spend twelve to fourteen hours a day for months on end writing and revising.

If a book is three hundred pages long, I've probably written fourteen to sixteen hundred pages. I once actually kept the printouts from all the chapters in a novel. I kept them in a stack on the floor. When the book was finished, I took a side-by-side photo of the finished manuscript: it was four inches thick, with a *three-foot tower* of the drafts standing beside it.

Q. **If you could meet any fictional character in real life, who would it be?**

A. Elvis Cole. [Laughter.]

Q. **Absent Elvis, anyone else?**

A. Joe Pike. [More laughter.] You have to understand, these guys have been in my life since 1987. Elvis Cole and Joe Pike are in my head every *day*. I spend so much time with them because I find them fascinating. I wish these guys were my friends. I'd love to drive over to Elvis's A-frame, sit out on the deck and have a beer with him and Joe. Maybe Elvis would grill some steaks. Believe me, these guys live a far more interesting life than I do. [Laughter.]

Q. **Will you complete this sentence: Writing novels has taught me_____?**

A. Patience. I'm an impatient person. I'm always in a hurry and on edge. Novel writing is a slow-motion endeavor. It takes about ten months for me to write a novel. And I haven't found a trick that allows me to speed up that process. For me to stay focused on a project for that long is enormously frustrating and challenges my temperament. I'm just not cut out for it. [More laughter.] I've learned to corral my impatience so the book can unfold.

Congratulations on your enormously successful career and for keeping readers around the world waiting for the next Elvis Cole or Joe Pike novel.

CANDACE BUSHNELL
SEX AND THE CITY *AND ASPIRING TO MORE*

Candace Bushnell is a novelist and television producer who, from 1994–1996, wrote a column for the *New York Observer* that was adapted into the bestselling anthology *Sex and the City*. It became the basis for the HBO hit series of the same name.

She followed up with the internationally bestselling novels *4 Blondes*, *Trading Up*, *Lipstick Jungle*, *One Fifth Avenue*, *The Carrie Diaries*, and *Summer and the City*.

Her novels have been successfully adapted for television and films. Candace is the winner of the prestigious 2006 Matrix Award for books (other winners have included Joan Didion and Amy Tan), and she received the Albert Einstein Spirit of Achievement Award. Through her books and television series, Bushnell's work has influenced two generations of women.

Our conversation took place in 2015.

Q. In an interview you said your recent novel, *Killing Monica*, is *not* about Carrie Bradshaw of *Sex and the City* or Sarah Jessica Parker. Will you expand on that?

A. I went online to BookCon, where a reporter was trying to be provocative and made that comparison. It's hilarious to me. When I read this stuff, it's like I'm not reading about myself. We know tabloids make things up. When I read that, I thought, "This must be what it's like to be a celebrity." People like a juicy story, one that's easy but not true. There's just no truth to that allegation.

Q. You said *Killing Monica* is actually about identity. Will you tell us more?

A. *Killing Monica* is truly about identity. Monica is a metaphor for the idea that women have this fantasy of a more perfect version of themselves. We create a persona that works for us in our twenties and thirties, but when we're in our forties, that persona no longer works as well. It's like wearing an itchy sweater. What does a woman do?

Killing Monica is really about rediscovering one's self, and if needed, reinventing the self. It also addresses the issue of having the courage to find your true voice again. I feel so many women lose their real selves when they're younger and rushing to be superwomen, to accomplish everything. For many, part of the *self* gets lost while they're caring for others.

Q. And, of course, your protagonist, Pandy, or PJ, is trying to rediscover herself in the novel.

A. Yes. One reason I laugh when people conclude the novel has something to do with my life is because the novel is a screwball comedy with lots of outlandish things happening. There's mistaken identity, and it's totally madcap. But it's all in the service of the core theme of the book: a woman's search for her true identity.

Q. **So, unlike PJ, you don't have "high literary ambitions"?**

A. [Laughter.] If one didn't have high literary ambitions, there'd be no reason to be a writer. Every writer I know, in every genre, takes writing really seriously, as we should. Writing is hard. It's creative and imaginative, and I have respect for anyone who engages in that process.

Of course, I do aspire, but the reality for me as a writer is simple: I've always had a grating voice—even as a child—and you can never get away from your own voice. And that's what my protagonist Pandy is on the verge of discovering about herself. Although now, after talking with you, I would probably go back and make that moment in the book a bigger one. [More laughter.]

Q. **Last Sunday, in the _New York Times_ column "By the Book," you said you would require every person to read _Demonic Males: Apes and the Origins of Human Violence_. Will you expand on that?**

A. For me, it was a serious and eye-opening book. It's a fascinating scientific examination of human behavior. It addresses male violence toward women and how it's used for power. Part of my thinking in this regard comes from my having grown up in the sixties. There was a revolution in the popular culture that said, "Say no to the _man_." It was a rebellion against corporate America and the homogenization of people. I was thinking about that revolutionary spirit when I answered that question.

Q. **You also mentioned tweaking and rewriting, saying, "Writing is rewriting." Tell us about your writing process.**

A. I'll start a book and get as far as I can—maybe eighty pages into it. Then I go back again and again. I keep revising before I move on to the next section. I break the book into chunks. I write set pieces or little playlets—almost like short stories within the novel—and by going back repeatedly, I eventually integrate all the pieces.

Q. **Your books and films have been viewed as addressing a new paradigm for today's women. Tell us more.**

A. I've always been interested in examining the kinds of lives women lead. I'm fascinated by where we are as a culture and by the age-old questions about feminism and the empowerment of women. I don't have answers, but equality for women is extremely important to me.

Q. **If you weren't a writer and television producer, what would you be doing today?**

A. I'd probably write jingles. [Laughter.]

Q. **You're hosting a dinner party and can invite any five people, living or dead, from any walk of life. Who would they be?**

A. I'd definitely invite Hillary Clinton. Then I'd want Eleanor Roosevelt, Margaret Thatcher, Mother Teresa, and Madonna to be there.

Q. **What would you be talking about?**

A. I could think of a really sappy answer.

Q. **Don't give us sap. Give us Candace.**

A. I'd hope they'd all bring their experiences and insights to making the world a better place for women.

Q. **What's coming next from Candace Bushnell?**

A. I have a line of emojis called Candace Bushnell's EmojiNation. They're geared for women. Hopefully, they'll be available in the app store very soon. I'm also working on my *Killing Monica* theme song for a music video. I have a line of stationery coming out. And there's a *Killing Monica* wine. It's really great. You get a book and a bottle of wine. It's sold online.

It's been great fun talking with you. Congratulations on your many successful career endeavors.

PETER JAMES & IAN RANKIN
SEARCHING FOR THE PERFECT BOOK

Peter James and Ian Rankin are among the foremost writers in the United Kingdom. Internationally acclaimed, their books have been translated into dozens of languages and are regularly on bestseller lists.

Peter James has written twenty-five bestsellers. His most famous character is Brighton-based Detective Roy Grace.

Ian Rankin has written nineteen bestselling Inspector John Rebus novels.

Both authors are also involved in other artistic endeavors.

Peter and Ian collaborated on a story in a book entitled *FaceOff*, a collection of short stories by some of the world's greatest thriller writers.

In 2015, the three of us met at the International Thriller Writers annual meeting, ThrillerFest. Our discussion follows.

Q. **Ian, your first John Rebus novel, *Knots and Crosses*, was classified as genre fiction. I understand you thought it was more in the realm of Robert Louis Stevenson's fiction. Tell us about that and your views of genre fiction.**

I. I was working on a PhD in the Scottish novel and was interested in Scottish writers of the past, many of whom wrote dark psychological novels. One is *The Strange Case of Dr. Jekyll and Mr. Hyde* by Robert Louis Stevenson. Edinburg is still a Jekyll and Hyde city, as are most cities in Scotland. It's one thing to the tourists and something else entirely if you live there. The darker side is just below the surface.

So I wrote a book about this darker side of Edinburgh. I thought a cop would be a good way of exploring the city. When the book was published, it went onto the crime fiction shelves in the local library. I was surprised. I took it off that shelf and put it in the Scottish literature section. The next day I discovered it was back in the crime fiction section. So I started reading crime fiction. It became clear to me I'd written a crime novel by mistake. [Group laughter.]

I must admit I liked the pace and powerful sense of place in crime fiction. I also liked the strong structure—the beginning, middle, and end of those kinds of novels—the crime, the investigation, and the resolution. It all made sense to me. I discovered that everything I wanted to say about the world could be said in a crime novel. So why would I want to write anything else?

Q. **Peter, you've written many Roy Grace books, as well as others. Tell us about your writing process.**

P. I write one Roy Grace novel a year. I try to fit in other things around that. I actually love writing. I'm never happier than when I'm writing. And I love research. Roy Grace is based on a real-life homicide detective. My home was burgled twenty years ago, and I got friendly with the detective on the case. Through him I started meeting police officers. I found the police world utterly fascinating. I'd been writing supernatural and psychological thrillers at the time. One day my publisher asked if I'd ever thought of writing a crime novel.

Frankly, I thought there were far too many good crime writers, like Ian Rankin, who had the market cornered. I also thought that an English crime novelist had to follow in the footsteps of Agatha Christie by writing cozy mysteries. But American writers like early James Patterson, Harlan Coben, Michael Connelly, and others broke that mold. I realized one could write a page-turning police thriller without resorting to that quaint English structure.

Q. **Ian, between 1987 and 2014 you wrote nineteen Inspector Rebus novels and *The Beat Goes On*, a book of short stories. You've also written a stage play, literary criticism, and have made recordings. How do you find the time to do all this, and what's your writing routine?**

I. It helps if you're a workaholic and have no other interests in life. [Group laughter.] My antennae are always twitching, so anything in my life provides material for my next story. I want to rush back to my office and begin writing.

People say to me, "That's a prodigious output," but I'm kind of lazy about writing. I'll do almost anything else. I'll alphabetize my CDs, read the paper, or do the crosswords—anything to put it off. But when I actually start, I write quickly. The first draft usually takes about forty days. I might be mulling it over subconsciously for weeks or months, but the writing itself goes quickly. Then there are many drafts before it sees the light of day. A book a year isn't so great an output. We genre writers laugh at these literary novelists who take ten years to write a novel. No, it took them nine years of sitting around moping and then one year to write the book.

If you become successful as an author, you spend ninety percent of your time *not* writing; your time is consumed by tours and interviews. Sometimes I yearn for the days when I was a student and could spend all day writing, every day. But then, nobody was interested in what I was doing or saying. I was writing for the sheer fun of it. It was the excitement of writing a sentence that had never been written before.

Just like Peter, when I write, it's the most exciting thing in the world because I'm doing something that's never been done. There are twenty-six letters, and you try to pen a sentence that's never been written before. I think that's phenomenal.

P. That's such an important point Ian made about writing a sentence that's never been written before. I think the worst thing for an author is to pen a cliché. I'll agonize over words. If a cloud is scuttling across the sky, I want a new way of describing it—one that hasn't been done thousands of times. We know there are only so many plots in all of literature—I think there are eight—it's really how you *write* that makes the difference.

Q. **Do any of your hobbies or pursuits infiltrate your novels? I ask because, Peter, in your first Roy Grace novel, *Dead Simple*, there's an electrifying car chase.**

P. As a writer, everything I do and everyone I meet become fodder for my writing. I'm a petrol head, which my publisher hates. I've always loved cars and race a 1965 BMW. In my next book, there's going to be a vivid description of a car rolling over because I had a racetrack accident last year. I rolled over at ninety miles an hour. And I'm very interested in the police world. Probably half my social life is with police officers at all levels, from the chief constable of Sussex on down.

Q. **I understand you're also a food critic for a Sussex magazine.**

P. Yes. I travel constantly and eat out quite a bit. The great thing about the publishing world is that on tours, and when dining out with your publisher, you're exposed to fine drink and food. So that makes its way into my novels.

Q. **Ian, do your pursuits seep into the Rebus novels?**

I. I'm a frustrated rock star. I'd much rather have been a rock star than an author. When I invented Rebus, I decided he would be a fan of rock music. He listens to all the bands I do and goes to the concerts I attend. As a result, rock musicians have become great fans of the books. I get emails from Pete Townshend of the Who and members of RDM. Van Morrison contacted me, knowing I'm a fan since Rebus is one. So I've gotten close to being a rock star by being an author. In a sense, I live vicariously through Rebus.

My other hobby—or habit—is drinking beer in the less salubrious bars of Edinburgh. So Rebus drinks in the Oxford bar where there's no food or music. It's just booze and conversation.

Q. **Rebus drinks quite a bit, doesn't he?**

I. He does. And, of course, I have to go to these various pubs to do research. [More group laughter.] So I end up drinking quite a bit there, as well. None of it is tax deductible, by the way. [More laughter.]

Q. Peter, in addition to your prolific novel writing, you've also been involved in twenty-six movies, either as a writer or producer, including 2005's *The Merchant of Venice* starring Al Pacino, Jeremy Irons, and Joseph Fiennes. How did filmdom evolve for you?

P. I came out of film school in 1970 at a time the movie industry was down the toilet. You couldn't get a job in television. I got a job as a gofer on a children's TV show. One day, the producer was in a panic because the writer was sick. He asked me to write that day's show. I was twenty-three years old and began writing. I then met Bob Clark, a young film director, who was working on a low-budget film. My wealthy uncle in Canada backed the film and it did really well. So, I kind of fell into the film business.

Q. Of those films with which you've been involved, which is your proudest achievement?

P. *The Merchant of Venice.* In 2005, when the Roy Grace novels took off, I had to make a decision about my direction. It was a no-brainer. Because when you're making a film, you're dealing with many different egos: three or four producers, the director, the production people, the photographer, the actors, even the distributor. I don't know how Ian feels about the two film adaptations of the Rebus novels.

I. The Rebus books were adapted for television years ago. The actor playing Rebus, John Hannah, was perhaps a bit too young and too soft-looking. Fans didn't feel he was up to it. Another actor took over and the fans were happier. But the TV company decided to reduce the films to one hour per book. That translated to forty-five minutes when you included advertising. Basically, they threw away the story. It was very frustrating. So I got the rights back.

Q. **In the book of short stories** *FaceOff,* **Rebus and Grace work together on a crime that's decades old. How did you collaborate on the short story "In the Nick of Time"?**

P. When I was asked with whom I'd most like to write a story, it was Ian Rankin. I always loved his writing. We met up in Scotland, and Ian came up with the story's idea.

Q. **The irony of the story reminded me of an O. Henry story.**

I. Yes, it's something of a morality tale, isn't it? The problem we had was that Scotland and the south of England are different jurisdictions. How would these cops work together? I thought if we could get a case from the past—a cold case—there was a possibility. Actually, Peter did most of the writing. Of course, we had some differences here and there: things like, "I don't think Rebus would say that."

P. It felt quite strange to write a scene for John Rebus. I wondered if I should be doing this. But it was virtually seamless once we got started.

I. I've spoken with other authors involved in *FaceOff.* Some had difficulty making their characters mesh because they're from very different fictional worlds. But for us, it was fairly easy. When we go to conventions such as ThrillerFest, we end up at a bar and say, "Our characters should get together in a book." But in the cold light of day, you think that's insane.

Q. **Will there be a collaborative novel featuring Roy Grace and John Rebus?**

I. I haven't thought of it. But this short story has introduced our characters to each other's world—Edinburgh and Brighton. So maybe it's a possibility.

Q. And criminals often flee to other jurisdictions.

P. Right. They don't keep office hours, and they don't obey borders. So this could be the seed of something very good.

Q. Did you always want to be a writer? What did you do before you became a full-time writer?

I. As a youngster, I was fascinated by stories. I wrote poetry, short stories, and eventually graduated to novels. I wasn't successful until I was in my forties. I had a lot of day jobs. I was a swineherd in France; I worked in a French vineyard; I was a tax man and a music journalist. I did anything that would pay me and let me write in my spare time.

P. From the age of seven, I knew I wanted to write, make films, and race cars. I lacked confidence as a child. I never thought I'd write something anyone would want to read. When I was fifteen, I did win the school poetry prize, which gave me a little confidence. I wrote three novels in my teens that luckily never got published and never will be. Speaking of confidence, when I was at film school, there was this very posh girl I wanted to take out. I saw an advertisement for a cleaning job, so I took it to have some money to take her out.

I. How did the date go with the girl?

P. It was a disaster. [More laughter.]

Q. What's the most surprising thing you've learned about writing over the years?

I. One thing that's saddened me as I get older is that writing doesn't get easier. When I started, I thought this would be like being a car mechanic. Once you've stripped enough engines and put them back together, you can do it blindfolded. But for a writer, each book is different. It's never the same engine. You want each book to be better than the one before. You want to make this one *the* book. We keep going because none of us has written the perfect book—the distillation of everything you want to say about the world. If we ever wrote that book, we could stop.

P. The big surprise for me is that people want to read what I've written. It amazes me. The big joy for me is that writing is the least ageist of any career. There are writers at the top of the bestseller list in their seventies, eighties, and nineties.

I would totally agree with Ian that it actually gets harder because you have to raise the bar as you go along. The nice surprise is that I get a little more confident with the passing of time. Yet, when I sit down for that first page of the first chapter, I think, "I got away with it last time, and they'll find me out with this one."

Q. **Do you feel you're an imposter? [Group laughter.]**

I. I think all people in the creative arts feel that way. Actors say the same thing: "I can't believe I'm getting paid for this. Eventually, I'll be found out."

Q. **If you could invite any five guests for dinner, either writers or figures from history, dead or alive, who would they be?**

P. I'd like to have Oscar Wilde, Ted Bundy [lots of laughter], the BTK serial killer—Dennis Rader—and the Wichita serial killer. [More laughter.] Albert Einstein would be fun, and going back in time, it would be Aristotle. I think they'd talk about dramatic construction. [Yet more laughter.]

I. I would love to have Robert Louis Stevenson. Bob Dylan would be another guest, but he might be grumpy. So maybe it would be Keith Richards instead. Also, someone like Bessie Smith or Billie Holiday would be fun. I would also love to have the Scottish philosopher David Hume. And finally,

Mary, Queen of Scots because she'd have lots of stories about murders and intrigue. You know, we well-balanced crime fiction writers channel our dark stuff into our books. But, Mark, don't interview romantic novelists. [More laughter.]

Q. **Ian, I must tell you this: I have a dear friend who enjoys your Inspector Rebus books so much, he's named his beloved dog Rebus.**

I. Now, that's the highest compliment I've ever been paid. [More laughter.]

Congratulations to each of you on your successes. And thank you for being multitalented artists whose creativity has provided countless hours of enjoyment to so many people.

MEG GARDINER
PUTTING DEMONS ON THE PAGE

Meg Gardiner is the author of twelve critically acclaimed crime novels, including *China Lake*, which won the Edgar Award.

Raised in Santa Barbara, California, Meg graduated from Stanford University, where she lettered in varsity cross-country and earned a BA in economics. She went on to graduate from Stanford Law School.

She practiced law in Los Angeles and taught in the Writing Program at the University of California Santa Barbara. Later she moved with her husband and three young children to London. There she began writing mysteries set in the California she loves.

In addition to her twelve novels, Meg has published short stories in American and British magazines. She's contributed essays to various anthologies, including *Now Write! Mysteries*, *The Mystery Writers of America Cookbook*, and the Anthony Award–winning *Books to Die For*.

Our conversations took place in 2017.

Q. **I understand you had some terrifying experiences that led to your fascination with unsolved serial murders such as those appearing in your recent thriller *UNSUB*. Will you share those experiences with us?**

A. The first terrifying experience I had was as a child when I saw a police drawing of the Zodiac Killer in my local newspaper. It was a picture of a gunman wearing a black executioner's hood with the Zodiac symbol on its front. Seeing that drawing, I asked my parents what it was, and my father told me it was a picture of the infamous Zodiac Killer, who murdered people for the hell of it. As a little kid, it shocked and rocked me to think someone could do something like that. It kept me awake at night.

Only a few years ago, I found out there had been two double murders in the neighborhood where I grew up—a safe, easygoing suburban area in Santa Barbara, California. At the time, the murders hadn't been linked, and it's only been since the advances in forensic science that investigators determined these murders were committed by that same person: the infamous and still uncaptured serial killer who roamed California. He was first called the Night Stalker and is now called the Golden State Killer.

Learning there was a walking path between where these murders happened and where my brother's family lived—two hundred yards away—freaked me out. The crime scenes were directly across the street from his house.

Simply realizing how close these things can come to you, even when your world seems completely normal and safe—knowing someone is out there masquerading as a normal person who has a job, goes to your local supermarket, and has a nighttime hobby of rape and murder—is very unsettling.

Q. **Do you think that early, fearful experience of the Zodiac Killer has expressed itself in your writing?**

A. I think the idea that someone is *out there* when we would all like our worlds to be orderly and predictable left its mark on me.

Q. **Tell us what characteristics make for a good protagonist.**

A. A really interesting protagonist must have some burning desire—maybe for justice, survival, love, or passion. I want to explore what my main character both wants and fears more than anything else because that will affect everything she does. What is the protagonist afraid of losing beyond all else?

Q. **What makes serial killers such fascinating subjects for crime fiction?**

A. I think the public has a sense that serial killers are clever, their motives are mysterious; they don't kill for money or revenge; they're sneaky and crawl through the cracks while hiding from society. We all want to have a glimpse into the dark side of human nature. We want to try understanding why someone would engage in these kinds of killings.

Q. **You became a commercial litigation attorney and worked in that field before becoming a novelist. Tell us about your journey to becoming an author.**

A. I wanted to write from the time I was a child. I grew up in a family of attorneys with fulfilling careers and love of the law. When I finished college, my father suggested that if I wanted to be a writer, I could write when I was half starving, or I could write when I took a break from my litigation practice.

So I went to law school. It was a fascinating, challenging, and rewarding career. I had three small children and knew I needed a break from going to court, so I took a job teaching legal writing at the University of California. Ultimately, that was my gateway to writing fiction. I eventually escaped from law. [Laughter.] I wrote short stories and magazine pieces while I was teaching, and attempted to write a novel, but had no idea how to do it.

Then my husband was offered a job in London. We moved from Southern California to the UK. I had no job waiting for me and I was the *trailing* spouse [more laughter] as they called it in the expat community. The kids were out of diapers. I'd told myself I was going to write a novel, and I decided it was time to put up or shut up. I wrote a terrible novel, which I put away. Then I wrote another, which was published in the UK. Then a few more were published there.

Q. **So, your novels were published in the UK. How did you become published and well-known in the United States?**

A. I had a British literary agent who was shocked that I was published in the UK and almost everywhere else in the world, but not in the United States. I'd written five books in the Evan Delaney series, but American publishers were uninterested in my fiction.

Then an American author went through his closet looking for a book to read on a flight to England. He found my book *China Lake*, which the publisher had sent him. He probably decided the print was large and easy on the eyes and stuck it in his carry-on. He read it, and when Stephen King got off the plane, he decided he liked my novel. He read the rest of my books and didn't understand why I had no American publisher. He kindly mentioned me on his website, urging people to look for my books. He then wrote a column for *Entertainment Weekly*, again mentioning my books. Strangely, within forty-eight hours of that column being published, fourteen American publishers were interested.

It was all due to the fact that Stephen King is an incredibly gracious and generous person. He supports other writers, artists, and musicians, and he uses his voice to bring attention to other artists. I'm eternally grateful to him.

Q. **You once said, "I put my demons on the page." What did you mean?**

A. If something scares me, upsets or worries me, if it troubles my sleep, it's likely to do the same thing to readers, and I can turn that into compelling fiction. I was once on a conference panel and another author said she writes to exorcise her demons. She felt it was cathartic. She asked me if I felt that way and I said, "I inflict my demons on my readers." [Laughter.] But I try to do it in an entertaining way.

Q. **You said you write crime fiction "because it gets to the heart of the human condition." Tell us more.**

A. Crime novels—whether they're thrillers, suspense books, or mysteries—always feature people facing the greatest challenges of their lives. Some element of evil has invaded their world, and chaos undermines everything they've known, and they must rise to the challenge and put things right. The compelling aspects of the human condition, as I see it, isn't about the English professor trying to suppress his crush on the sophomore coed.

Q. **A well-known critic once said crime writers lack real talent. You had an interesting response to that statement. What was it?**

A. I thought the entire notion of talent was silly. The idea of talent being everything is really pernicious. The idea that if you don't have sufficient talent you might as well just pack it in and give up. As a writer and a parent, I think that outlook can be undermining. Yes, talent is important, but on its own, it's not enough. Hard work, training, dedication, observing the world, and putting in the work—sometimes joyfully, sometimes as a struggle—that's how you get to be good at writing or any other endeavor. I said to the critic, "I once had talent, but I sold it so I could write a crime novel."

Q. Your blog is titled "Lying for a Living." How come?

A. It's labeled that because I get to make things up and get paid to do it. Things come out of my imagination. It's a little bit flip. Actually, I think fiction is the lie that tells the *truth*. The only lies on paper are called nonfiction memoirs. [Lots of laughter.] Fiction is a metaphor for life.

Q. What's the most challenging part of being an author?

A. I think the most challenging part is executing an idea. Ideas are everywhere. It's not only coming up with an idea, but turning it into something in three hundred fifty pages is the challenge.

Q. I understand you were a collegiate cross-country runner and a three-time *Jeopardy!* champion. Will you tell us a few things about your life that readers would find interesting?

A. I have an overdeveloped trivia lobe in my brain. *Jeopardy!* is the most fun you can have standing up. I'll just say that. [Laughter.]

Q. Is it true that your latest novel, *UNSUB,* will also be a CBS TV series?

A. Yes, that's true. It's been bought by the people behind *Justified* and *Masters of Sex.* They are great at developing cool and exciting dramas. I'm thrilled by it.

Q. **Who do you see playing Caitlin Hendrix?**

A. Oh, no. I can't answer that because everybody who reads UNSUB creates the character in their own mind. In a way, every reader is a casting director, and I don't want to take over that job.

Q. **If you could meet any two *fictional* characters in all of literature, who would they be and why?**

A. Dave Robicheaux from James Lee Burke's series, because I'm in love with him. [Laughter.] My husband won't appreciate that. And . . . Kinsey Millhone from Sue Grafton's series because she's from my hometown and would be a great friend. If I ever got in trouble, I'd have her to call.

Q. **Will you complete this sentence: "Writing novels has taught me _____?"**

A. It's taught me perseverance and patience. It's taught me that we all have the possibility to be successful if we take the chance when it's presented to us.

Congratulations on such a successful career. Don Winslow compared your latest novel, *UNSUB*, to *The Silence of the Lambs* for its chilling plot, and about which he said, "The UNSUB, or unknown subject, at the heart of Meg Gardiner's thriller is terrifying." I agree completely.

FREDERICK FORSYTH
A LIFE OF INTRIGUE

Frederick Forsyth wrote some of the world's most acclaimed and successful suspense novels. Beginning with *The Day of the Jackal* and followed by *The Odessa File*, *The Dogs of War*, and twelve others, Frederick Forsyth has mesmerized millions of readers and moviegoers with stories about assassinations, conspiracies, civil wars, the drug trade, mercenaries, and international intrigue.

A former Royal Air Force pilot and reporter for Reuters and the BBC, he won the Diamond Dagger from Britain's Crime Writers' Association in 2012 for a career of sustained excellence.

The Outsider is perhaps his most exciting tale of all—his own. A memoir written in a lucid, conversational style, it tells his personal stories, tales as intriguing as his most thrilling novels.

Our conversation took place in 2015, soon after the publication of his memoir.

Q. **As described in your memoir, *The Outsider*, how did your first novel, *The Day of the Jackal*, come into being?**

A. I had the best reason in the world for writing it: I was absolutely broke. I'd returned from reporting on the war in Nigeria and Biafra. I was in London, but I had no apartment, no car, no job or any prospect of a job, and certainly had no savings. I thought, "What does one do?" and at that point, I came up with the most naive answer in the world: "You write a novel and make some fast money."

Well, you *don't*. [Laughter.]

If you make any money at all by writing, it's a miracle. And it is slow. But I didn't know that. I know now if you want to make money, do anything, but *don't* write a novel.

Anyway, I sat down and wrote the only story I could really *think* of, which was something I'd seen personally seven years earlier, working for Reuters Agency in Paris in 1962–1963. It involved the repeated attempts by the OAS to assassinate Charles de Gaulle. I saw them try and fail over and over again.

I concluded they would fail unless they came up with an outsider unknown to the French authorities—someone with no face, no name, no passport, but with a gun. And that was what I sat down and wrote. And that's how the Jackal came into being.

Q. **Is it true you wrote the novel in thirty-five days?**

A. Right. It's true. But I had nothing else to *do*. [Laughter.] I was lounging on a friend's couch. He went off to work mornings, so I took my typewriter and five hundred sheets of paper to the kitchen table, rolled the first sheet in, and began to type off the top of my head. I had virtually no notes. It was all there in my memory, along with some imagination. I invented things that *didn't* happen, but I decided to write what *would have* happened. I was writing about twelve pages a day, and thirty-five days later, there was the novel.

Q. **When I read *The Day of the Jackal*, even though I knew de Gaulle was never assassinated, I kept turning the pages to find out what would happen.**

A. I tried to persuade the first four publishers who rejected it that it wasn't about whether de Gaulle lived or died. It was about how close to happening it would be in the man-on-man duel between the Jackal and the French detective on his trail.

Q. **I'm aware the movie version of your novel *The Odessa File* led to the capture of a Nazi war criminal. Will you share that story with us?**

A. The inspiration behind using this man, Eduard Roschmann, the "Butcher of Riga," was Simon Wiesenthal himself. I visited him in Vienna and told him I was trying to write a story that mirrored the capture of Adolf Eichmann in Argentina by the Israeli Secret Service. But in the prospective novel, he would be discovered inside Germany, using false papers. Wiesenthal asked me what kind of character I was thinking about, and I said, "Maybe a concentration camp commandant. A man of singular cruelty. I'll have to invent one."

Wiesenthal waved toward a stacked shelf and said, "Why invent one? I have twelve right there. Which one would you like?" So I settled on Eduard Roschmann, the Butcher of Riga. The book was published, and the movie was made.

Then, somewhere in a little, flea-bitten cinema south of Buenos Aires, a man was watching the movie and said, "I know that man. He lives down the street from me."

He went to the police. It was during one of those brief

windows of democracy in Argentina—between generals—and the government arrested Roschmann.

Some magistrate, with right-wing leanings, gave the man bail, and Roschmann decided to flee to Paraguay, a safe haven for Nazis back then. He was actually on a ferry going across the Paraguay River when he had a massive heart attack and died. The Paraguayans didn't want him, but the ferryman said, "He already paid his fare." [Laughter.] So the body remained there, and the ferry went back and forth with the body on the foredeck—until he began to *stink*.

Eventually, they got him off on the Paraguayan side, where Viennese police officers were waiting. They identified him with photographs and fingerprints. They also knew Roschmann had two missing toes from frostbite. The police knew that from reading *The Odessa File*. So he's buried in a gravel bank somewhere on the northern side of the Paraguay River.

Q. **Wanting to be a pilot more than anything else, you were an RAF fighter pilot at nineteen. You then became a reporter and then a novelist. How did you make the transition from reporting to writing fiction?**

A. I was a foreign correspondent and then worked for the BBC. I had a serious disagreement with the BBC about how the Nigerian-Biafra War should be reported. They said it shouldn't be reported at all. I said, "You can't ignore a *war*." They said they could avoid covering a war.

I did not become a journalist to participate in managed news for any government department, so I walked away.

I went back into the African forest for two years and covered the war. Eventually, the good guys were crushed. I got out on the third-to-last plane. I returned to London and asked myself the question, "What the hell should I do now?" And that's when *The Day of the Jackal* got written.

After that, the editor wanted to sign me up for two more novels. It was a real body blow. I thought I would only do one novel. I didn't know if *The Jackal* would even sell; nor did the editor. In fact, they only printed five thousand copies. The last count as of recently was around ten million copies sold, but never mind. I didn't see myself as having the capacity to tell stories. I asked myself, "What the hell do I know about?"

Well, I knew about Germany. I'd heard about this bizarre pro-Nazi self-help organization called ODESSA. I also knew about West Africa, since I'd been there with the mercenaries. I told the editor about it and he said, "Okay, Nazis first, mercenaries second, and I want the first one by the end of the year." So, they became *The Odessa File* and *The Dogs of War* respectively.

Q.   Your memoir details some of your near-death experiences. Tell us about them.

A.   I'm not a danger freak, and I don't want to give you that impression. I never deliberately walked into perilous situations because I wanted to experience the danger. But I was born with an extra-large bundle of curiosity. There are instances in the book where, looking back, they're funny, but at the time, they were scary.

I'm seventy-seven and still around. I took those risks and I'm still here.

Q.   What was the scariest incident you recall?

A.   When I was coming out of East Germany one night, I had a packet of documents I was to deliver to British foreign intelligence. I was in a deserted area, about to store the packet under the car's battery, when suddenly the whole area was illuminated in a wash of white light. I recognized the car: it was the People's Police of East Germany. I said to myself, "I think I am done for." But, by the grace of the big gentleman in the sky, it didn't happen. The reason they swept into the area was the fact that one of them wanted to relieve himself in the undergrowth. I was nearly discovered but was saved by a bursting bladder. [Laughter.]

Q. **What made you choose the title *The Outsider* for your memoir?**

A. I really never wanted to be part of the herd or run with the mass. If you join in, you lose your autonomy. You have to abide by other people's rules, which just wasn't what I wanted to do. I always preferred to stay outside the mainstream and perch like a bird on a rail to watch the game. The air force was a meritocracy. You didn't get your wings by succumbing to office politics.

Reuters was also a meritocracy.

The BBC was governed by politics and coteries, with everyone vying for promotion.

So, at the end of the day, I felt like an outsider.

Q. **Do you have a favorite of all your novels?**

A. I have to remain grateful to *The Jackal*. It gave me my break. Had it been turned down any more times, I'd have put it in a drawer and gone back to journalism. So the book set me on a new road. That apart, I think possibly *The Fist of God* might be my favorite. It's the story of the first Iraq war. I began to ferret out things that were true, but we hadn't been told about them.

Q. **Is there a single crucial lesson you've learned about writing?**

A. The most important lesson is this: keep it simple.

We all write in different ways. Some writers use flowery language and have beautiful prose. I write like a journalist. There are no frills. I keep it *understandable*. The guy on the commuter train doesn't have time to admire beautiful Brontë-esque prose. He wants the story. If I were to divide a novel into parts, it would be like this: 20 percent would be characterization, descriptive passages, dialogue, and prose style, and 80 percent would be plot.

The truth be told, I'm basically a storyteller, and I keep it simple.

Q. **Do you have any advice for writers starting out?**

A. My advice is also quite simple: Writing is one of the hardest professions of all. It's probably as difficult as starting out as a young actor. You need a break, and the way to get that break is determined only by perseverance. A beginning writer must keep trying, no matter what happens. A new writer will be rebuffed, as are actors in auditions. There will be a drawer full of rejection slips.

But those who made it did so by just refusing to take no for an answer. And also by believing they had some kind of talent. And they kept trying. It's brutal advice, but it's true. I was incredibly lucky that my first novel was accepted.

Ken Follett wrote twelve novels before *Eye of the Needle* was accepted for publication. J. K. Rowling had to hawk her first novel around and around. Nobody wanted to know about a little boy with a wand.

Q. **Is there another novel coming from Frederick Forsyth?**

A. I'm afraid not. I'm an old codger now, and I'm best off sitting in the garden and playing with the grandchildren. Of course, I said the same thing two novels ago, but I think the memoir is my last writing project.

Congratulations on a lifetime of work and on writing *The Outsider*, a riveting memoir filled with intrigue and every bit as exciting as your novels.

FAYE KELLERMAN
THE WRITER AND THE DENTIST

Faye Kellerman is the bestselling author of twenty-seven novels, twenty-three of which feature the husband-and-wife team of Peter Decker and Rina Lazarus. Faye and her husband, Jonathan Kellerman, are the only married couple ever to appear on the *New York Times* bestseller list simultaneously for two different novels.

Faye earned a BA in mathematics and a doctorate in dentistry at UCLA. Her first novel, *The Ritual Bath*, was published in 1986 to wide critical and commercial acclaim. That book won the Macavity Award for the Best First Novel from the Mystery Readers of America. *The Ritual Bath* introduced readers to Peter Decker and Rina Lazarus, and Faye has continued writing about this couple.

Our conversations took place between 2015 and 2017.

Q. You have a degree in mathematics and received a doctorate in dental surgery. At the age of thirty-four, your first novel, *The Ritual Bath*, was published. As a mathematician and dentist, how did you discover the writer within you?

A. I was always a kid with a vivid imagination. I made up stories in my head and played them out. I would walk around talking to myself to the point where my grandmother asked my mother, "Is this child normal?" And my mother said, "She's just playing her games." I had all these little stories and was also very good at math. I went into math because I had a hard time learning to read. I was phonetically dyslexic. I was a math major and became a dentist.

After graduating from dental school, I took time off before going into dentistry to be with my son, Jesse. At that point, all the stories began coming back, because for the first time in twenty-five years, I didn't have to use my brain to advance my education. I realized something then: imagination never goes away.

At that time, Jonathan and I had been married for six years. He was always an avid writer. I said to myself, "He's doing the same thing I'm doing, making up stories, except he's writing them down." It took many years—seven or eight years—before I had something worth publishing.

Jonathan's success encouraged me, and he himself encouraged me. I felt somewhat embarrassed about it, feeling I was making up stories when I should be drilling teeth.

Eventually, I got published. Once that happened, there was no turning back. I knew from my husband's experience that you don't write to become a bestselling novelist. It's a fluke if it happens. And a fluke happened to me.

Q. **It's clear from reading your novels that you write very detailed detective fiction. What kind of research do you do?**

A. Over the years I've done a great deal of research. I love doing it. I used to go into the library stacks to do research, but now, of course, we have the Internet. Even with the Internet, you still have to read books to get all the details you want.

When I write a novel, I try to write something that's coherent and entertaining. I spend the most time on building characters. I try to write something with richness, but above all, the reader deserves characters who seem to jump off the page.

Trying to get that character depth, I've visited police stations. I read science and books on forensics. I look things up and try to make the novel as accurate as possible. For details about bodies, as a dental student, we had gross anatomy, so I know a body from the inside out. I do take a bit of literary license. If I don't know certain exact details, I'll make an approximation for the novel.

Q. **Your physical descriptions of characters are quite elaborate. How do you balance creating that richness while maintaining a novel's narrative drive?**

A. I think of a character's description as something akin to scene setting or stage setting. It's not there for the sake of simply providing details. We're not Sherlock Holmes. We don't need to know about the dangling button. I want to give the reader an idea of where a scene is taking place, who the main characters are, and what they look like. I like to leave a little bit to the reader's imagination. But if you set the scene, what follows is not distracting. Once the scene is there, the characters take over with their dialogue, but they are placed in position for the reader.

Q. **What do you feel makes Peter Decker and Rina Lazarus so appealing to the reading public?**

A. I think they're appealing because they're full, fleshed-out characters.

I like that Peter is a great family man and is passionate about his work. To him, solving each crime becomes a personal mission. I like characters who care about what they're doing and who are concerned about the victims. I think readers also like that.

Rena and Peter have a very good marriage, but it's a realistic one. Sometimes they fight, and I think lots of people can identify with that. She's also a good homemaker and enjoys cooking her kugel and brisket, but she contributes to Peter's investigations whenever she feels it's necessary to join in.

Part of why I moved them to a small town in upstate New York and away from Los Angeles was to allow Rena to play a larger role in the investigations. With the LAPD, there was no way she could have access to the material Peter shares with her now. The LAPD is a huge, monolithic bureaucracy, but in a small town, there are fewer resources, so she can become involved.

Q. **As the Deckers have grown older, are you concerned they might no longer appeal to younger readers?**

A. I try to make the characters as universal as possible. That was a consideration when I wrote *Murder 101*. I moved the Deckers to a small college town to keep the story fresh and young. The introduction of a younger police detective who doesn't know the ropes was done to infuse the story with some youth. As a writer, I want my books to appeal to as many people as possible. If my main characters are in an older age group, I try to balance them with someone younger.

Q. **Peter Decker's interrogation tactics are quite impressive. Have you studied interrogation techniques?**

A. I haven't studied interrogation techniques as a field of endeavor, but I've seen interrogations moving away from the old concept of "good cop / bad cop."

In my books, Peter and the interviewee simply talk. If you get a person talking, he or she will tell you all sorts of things. I think to be a good interrogator, you must be a very good listener. If you get guilty people talking, they will inevitably come out with a contradiction to a lie they've told. A good interrogator must engage in active listening, and that's what Peter does.

Q. **Over twenty-eight years the Deckers' lives have evolved. Writers often borrow from their own lives. Are there parallels between the Deckers and the Kellermans?**

A. I'm sure there are, but not on a one-to-one ratio. As Jonathan and I grow and experience things, so do the Deckers. As we have experiences, they do, too. In my personal life, I have children and grandchildren, so I'm forced—in order to keep up with them in conversation—to be exposed to their interests and activities. You have to learn to use whatever resources are around you, and it keeps you fresh and young.

Q. **As a writing couple, what's a typical day like in your household? Are you and Jonathan on different schedules? Write in different places?**

A. Dentistry and mathematics taught me the necessity of being focused and organized. Things are easier now because the kids are out of the house. We wake up when we want to as opposed to when we had children at home. We begin writing at about nine thirty or ten o'clock. We write at roughly the same time, most often in the mornings because we both feel fresher at that time. We spend about two to three hours writing, and then come all the details of running your life. There's a lot of juggling with the books: promotion, writing, dealing with the business of writing. At first I found it stressful, but now I have fun with it.

After about five in the afternoon, I try not to go to my computer. I want to relax, read a book, go out for dinner, or see a movie.

Q. **Do you ever brainstorm with Jonathan for plot ideas or twists?**

A. We don't really brainstorm. I'll come up with the root of an idea, and I might mention it to him. Sometimes I show him a finished book. Many times I give him the first fifty pages and ask him what he thinks.

I tend to do a lot of walking to stimulate my imagination. I love to walk and think about what might make an interesting story that will provide readers with a few hours of entertainment and relaxation.

Q. **Which question do you get asked more often than any other?**

A. The question I'm asked most often is "How do you come up with ideas?"

The thing is, I never know what's going to become an integral part of a novel, but it all derives from some part of my life experience or imagination.

I write well-fleshed-out characters, and—you know this better than I do—inevitably, more ideas spring from my subconscious. They all have a little bit of me in them. It's very hard to figure out in advance how a story will unfold, but after having written so many novels, I feel more comfortable letting the ideas come up from somewhere in my own subconscious.

Writing is much easier now because that sense of panic I used to experience doesn't set in as I begin a new book.

Q. What moves you most in a novel?

A. I'm most moved by very interesting characters.

Occasionally, I'll find a novel that's so cleverly plotted, it grabs me. But mostly I want to follow a person in whatever journey he or she is taking, if that character is likable and identifiable. And I try to impart that in my own novels. I always ask myself: how does the crime affect the people involved?

Q. If you could reexperience reading one novel as though for the first time, which one would it be?

A. Wow. That's a tough one. [Laughter.] Leaving my husband's books aside, and my son Jesse's, I'll pick *Jane Eyre*. It's a very personal story of a girl who becomes a woman. I'd also say *The Count of Monte Cristo*. That's a novel of world adventure and a swashbuckling account of extreme revenge.

Both books moved me as a teenager and opened my eyes to a world far beyond my very confined one.

Q. Dentists usually have manual dexterity, and their hobbies often involve using their hands. How about you?

A. I've done a lot of sewing. I crochet. I really love gardening. If I have any spare time, I love to prune and plant. I love the aesthetics of it, and it's so rewarding. I sometimes play the mandolin and the guitar; so yes, I enjoy using my hands.

Q. As a successful novelist since 1986, what has surprised you most about writing?

A. The biggest surprise is it doesn't get easier. With most tasks, the more you perform them, the more rote they become. With writing, you can never, ever sit back and have it come easily. It's always a struggle. It's a joy, but you're always thinking. Writing always gives me a headache. [Laughter.] The more you write, the harder it gets because you've used up plots; you've used up characters; you've used up words. You wonder how you're going to keep this book fresh and new—especially in a series.

You know, with genre novels, there's an expectation. You don't want your fans to lose that sense of anticipation. You want each book to be satisfying to you and you want it to be fresh. That's one of the major reasons why I moved the Deckers from LA to Greenbury, New York. I wanted them to be in a new place with a different atmosphere, and I wanted them to face new challenges.

Q. **What does being a writer mean to you?**

A. It means freedom to let my mind wander. I love the ability to let my mind explore whatever it wants. When you write it down, it has to be informed and make sense. But if you have an imagination, you can go everywhere. I love that—the inception—having a germ of an idea and building upon it. You can do whatever you want with it. Many writers would say you can play God.

Q. **If you could have dinner with any five people, living or dead, from any walk of life, who would they be?**

A. One of them would be Moses. I'd have a lot of questions for him. I'd love to have my literary idols there. Ross Macdonald would be at the table, along with Raymond Chandler, James M. Cain, Billy Wilder, and Chaim Potok. I've been rereading Jane Austin and realize she basically wrote *Downton Abbey*. I'd love to have her join us. F. Scott Fitzgerald would be another guest. And, of course, there's Abe Lincoln. I realize I now have way more than five guests. [Laughter.]

I'm really interested in people who did something revolutionary. I'd want to have a huge banquet with all these people.

Congratulations on your long-standing success with a series that has captured and held a wide-reading audience for more than thirty years.

JONATHAN KELLERMAN
UNDERSTANDING PEOPLE, PLAYING GOD

Jonathan Kellerman, the bestselling author of more than forty crime novels, is known to mystery lovers everywhere. With a doctorate in psychology, Jonathan has applied his knowledge not only to his novels, but to those he has co-written with his wife, Faye, and son, Jesse. All three are bestselling authors. Additionally, he wrote two children's books and several nonfiction works, including *Savage Spawn: Reflections on Violent Children*, and *With Strings Attached: The Art and Beauty of Vintage Guitars*.

He's won the Samuel Goldwyn Writing Award, Edgar and Anthony Awards, and has been nominated for a Shamus Award. Along with Sue Grafton's Alphabet series, Jonathan's acclaimed Alex Delaware series is one of the longest running on the literary landscape.

Our conversations took place in 2016 and 2017.

Q. **You have a doctorate in psychology and practiced clinical psychology. What made you turn to writing fiction?**

A. I've been writing fiction since the age of nine. However, I never saw writing as a job. I was also attracted to science—and music and art, which I continue to pursue. In college, I got a gig as an editorial cartoonist for the campus newspaper. That led to opportunities to write for the paper—columns, reviews, and straight reporting. I ended up as an editor and, essentially, had a dual identity: journalist and student of psychology. In my senior year, I won a literary prize and got an agent.

But that didn't end my desire to become a child psychologist. While in grad school, I continued to write, publishing scientific articles, nonfiction, a short story, and my doctoral dissertation. At the same time, I was writing novels at night in my garage. Eventually, my first novel was published in 1985.

I had a practice in child clinical psychology that I loved and was reluctant to give up. So I continued to write and treat patients. I published five bestselling novels while in full-time practice, but eventually working two jobs became untenable. In 1990, I became a full-time novelist.

Q. **How did this enormous change in your work impact your life?**

A. As a psychologist, my life was extremely structured—I worked by the hour. I could look at my appointment book and know what I would be doing months in advance. Even with three associates, it became tougher and tougher to go on vacation, travel, and do other things. Still, I enjoyed it immensely.

As a full-time writer, my life became unstructured. For some people, the lack of parameters can be tough. Fortunately,

I love what I do and have never felt the need to be self-disciplined or live a highly regimented life. I've been privileged to work two great jobs.

Q. **You once said, "Psychology and fiction are actually quite synchronous." Tell us more about that.**

A. I think both involve attempts to better understand people. As a psychologist, I love my work because I learn about people and what drives them. But as a writer, I get to play God by creating characters, and then I get to see how they react to difficult situations. What unifies psychology and fiction is they are both avenues to explore more about the human condition.

Q. **Alex Delaware has evolved over the years. Tell us a bit about that evolution.**

A. It's funny because it wasn't a conscious decision to have Alex evolve over time. People reading the earlier books are in a better position than I am to see the changes in him. I rarely read my earlier books unless I'm doing research for accuracy. My son, Jesse, said the earlier books are a bit more literary. There's more verbiage and description in them than in the later novels.

While I don't age Alex in real time, he's mellowed out over the years. Maybe you're a better judge than I am. Maybe he's mellowing as I've mellowed over time. [Laughter.] I must say, I don't want him to lose his edge. I still want him to be compulsively driven because that's what drives a crime novel forward. I don't think there's anything more boring than a crime novel in which the protagonist is really laid-back.

Q. **Jonathan, will you talk a bit about writing dialogue?**

A. It took me a long time to get published as a novelist. I felt dialogue was a weakness of mine, so I really paid attention to it. The key is to create dialogue in fiction that resembles what readers sense people sound like when they talk.

I look at some of the best writers of dialogue—Elmore Leonard and others—and my wife, Faye. From her very first novel, she was able to nail dialogue. She's a great mimic. She could have gone onstage and been the female Rich Little. She can imitate almost anyone, has perfect pitch, and has a golden ear for dialogue. I really paid attention and learned from her. As a psychologist, I got to do a lot of listening, which helped me pick up the nuances of speech.

Q. **The dialogue in your books is edgy and quite realistic.**

A. I learned to write dialogue from my wife. Even her first novel had superb dialogue. The thing with dialogue is it has to sound like people talking, but, of course, it can't because the way people *really* talk is boring, repetitive, circular, and filled with *um*s and *ah*s.

A novel's dialogue is an artifice in which you construct a false reality. I learned to keep it snappy and to open my ears to what people say and how they say it. The rhythm of dialogue came easily to me because I'm a musician and understand cadence and timing.

There's one other thing I realized: in addition to writing, I paint. It's what I'm naturally best at. I realize that both painting and writing are forms of trickery. In painting, I'm simulating three dimensions using two. It's the same with writing. It's a form of trompe l'oeil.

Q. **Your novels not only tell a story but serve as a vehicle for commentary about life. Tell us about that.**

A. I think that's just naturally the way I see the world. You as a psychiatrist and I as a psychologist must acknowledge we got into this field because we see things in multiple dimensions.

I never set out to write a "message book," but things concern me, and by dealing with larger issues, I hope to elevate the story beyond it being just a good crime novel. And I call what I write a crime novel rather than a mystery because the story is always *propelled* by the crime.

Of course, my experience as a psychologist informs my writing. For example, I worked with children in oncology. An event like a terrible cancer diagnosis can become a catalyst for unlocking many other issues. That awareness colors my writing in the sense that a specific crime can open up a Pandora's box of reactions. Every crime impacts people, and trauma can bring out the best or worst in them, whether in a novel or in real life.

Q. **Alex Delaware had a difficult childhood. As psychologists, both he and you know the indelible effects of the past on current functioning. How does Alex's past affect his present life?**

A. Alex evolved as I got to know him better by writing books about him. When I wrote the first one, *When the Bough Breaks*, which was published in 1985, I never thought I'd get it published, let alone that it would become the first book in a successful series. I learned about Alex along with my readers, and things began falling into place.

I parcel out his childhood and his personal history very judiciously. In some novels, he's a protagonist; in others, he's a consulting psychologist. Of course, his past has impacted his interest in psychology and his wanting to set certain things right.

Q. **I'm sure you've been asked this question before, but how much of Jonathan Kellerman exists in Alex Delaware?**

A. I think the author is in *every* character.

It took five years for an Alex Delaware novel to be published, and I realized I'd be best off writing about what I knew, which was clinical child psychiatry. So there are career parallels. But Alex is younger than I am; he's thinner, more athletic, and much braver than I am. I'm a coward, which describes many crime writers. We write about things that frighten us.

I'm married with four kids; he's single with no kids. He's free to engage in high-risk behavior while I'm not. There's a lot of me in him and in Milo, and in the bad guys, too. In a sense, all fiction is autobiography.

Q. **What has surprised you about writing fiction?**

A. The surprise to me is that I've been able to make a living at it. I was trained in psychology and was heavily into academic medicine and saw my identity as such. I loved to write, but never saw it as a way to make a living. But *When the Bough Breaks* became a bestseller, and it changed everything. Now I've been writing professionally for thirty-five years, far longer than my involvement in psychology. I think it's the greatest job in the world. People sometimes like to think of the "tortured writer," but that's not the case with me. I've never been depressed in my life. I've been very lucky not to have the mood issues some creative people have.

The more books you write, the tougher it gets. With every book, I do the same thing I did with the first one: I sit down and try to write the best book possible. That *does* make it tougher. I have to have enough in the book that people are comfortable with because it's the same character, but I want to be original all over again.

Q. What do you love about being a writer?

A. It beats honest labor. [Laughter.] My life as a psychologist was very structured. As a writer, I have the freedom to make my own day and create something.

Q. If you could read any one novel again as though reading it for the first time, which one would it be?

A. I've never been asked that question. [Laughter.] That's a tough one. *The Count of Monte Cristo* was the seminal novel in my life. I read it as a youngster. It struck me as an amazing book. There was so much going on: adventure, camaraderie, relationships, and revenge.

Q. If you could meet any two fictional characters from all of literature, who would they be?

A. I'd love to meet Edmond Dantès of *The Count of Monte Cristo* because he was so interesting. He evolved from the depths of despair to triumph. I'd also love to meet Watson from the Sherlock Holmes stories. I don't think Sherlock would be very good company, but Watson was a doctor and highly intelligent. I think I could relate to him better than I could to Sherlock Holmes.

Q. If you could have dinner with any four or five people, writers or historical figures, living or dead, who would they be?

A. I think King Solomon is a very interesting guy. I would love to meet Freud. I'd want to have dinner with anyone who changed the world in a landmark way. Lord Byron's daughter would be a guest. She invented the computer back in the 1800s. She was a brilliant mathematician, but because she was a woman, she really wasn't heard from. I spent a little time with Gorbachev, who was very interesting. I'd like to spend more time with him.

Congratulations on penning the Alex Delaware series. The novels are compelling psychological crime novels with deeply imagined characters, and they're told in a literary style.

KATHY REICHS
WHEN BONES SPEAK

Kathy Reichs is a forensic anthropologist and a professor of anthropology at the University of North Carolina at Charlotte. She's the author of the bestselling series featuring Temperance Brennan, who is also a forensic anthropologist. Kathy's the producer of the hit TV series *Bones*, based on her work and novels.

Dr. Reichs served on the board of directors and as vice president of the American Academy of Forensic Sciences and on the American Board of Forensic Anthropology.

Our conversation took place in 2015 at the ThrillerFest convention in New York City.

Q. For those who may not know, what exactly is forensic anthropology?

A. Forensic anthropology is a specialty area within physical anthropology. It relies on knowledge about the human skeleton. The term *forensic* means it's in a legal context. We work for medical examiners, coroners, law enforcement, and the military. We primarily address questions such as the identification of remains, and we analyze bone to figure out what happened to the person. Was it a homicide or a suicide? Was the lethal injury caused by a sharp or blunt instrument? How long has the victim been dead? What happened to the body after the victim died?

Q. As a forensic anthropologist, you've been involved in some very high-profile cases, haven't you?

A. Yes. I was involved in identifying remains of recovered victims after 9/11. I've been retained to work on a number of Canadian cases. In fact, my first book, *Déjà Dead*, was based on a case involving a serial killer named Serge Archambault. I helped identify and did a detailed analysis of the bones of his first victim to determine the pattern of dismemberment. It ended up as crucial testimony in the trial and helped lead to his conviction.

I also testified in the Casey Anthony trial and at the United Nations tribunal on genocide in Rwanda.

Q. I understand you've also helped identify bodies from World War II, Korea, and other conflicts.

A. Yes. That's through JPAC, the Joint POW/MIA Accounting Command. Whenever remains are found, there are multiple levels of expertise required to make an identification, and one of those must be at the civilian level.

Q. **How did you decide to become a forensic anthropologist?**

A. I didn't really make the decision; forensic anthropology came looking for me. I was trained to do bioarcheology and was focusing on ancient skeletons. The police began bringing me cases, asking for my help. That was back in the days before board certification and when law enforcement wasn't very sophisticated about expert qualifications. Having expertise in bones, I was a sensible choice.

We now have a much more sophisticated process of guaranteeing expertise: there are peer review processes, board certification, and examinations.

Q. **The medical and forensic issues in your books are detailed in so many areas, not just descriptions of bones. Will you talk about that?**

A. I use a lot of medical details. I work closely with pathologists, so when I have a question, I direct it to the appropriate expert. I don't want every book to be driven only by bones. I try to bring different kinds of forensic science into each story—whether it's blood-spatter pattern analysis, gunshot wounds, trajectory analysis, toxicology, or DNA analysis. I double-check all those facts to make sure I'm getting them right.

Q. **Temperance and Detective Andrew Ryan have had a long-standing relationship. Do you have plans for their future?**

A. I definitely have plans for Temperance's and Ryan's future. Am I going to reveal what they are? No, probably not. [Laughter.] There's a surprising turn of events in my latest book, *Speaking in Bones*, and we'll see how that goes.

Q.   **How and when did you decide to become a novelist?**

A.   I became a full professor at the university, and that left me with some free time to explore new challenges. I'd written academic books, but I wanted to try something different. I had a colleague who was writing fiction. After reading one of her books, I thought, "Maybe I can do this." It was during the nineties, and forensic science was in the public's mind. People had seen the O. J. trial, and they'd heard about blood-spatter analysis. I wanted to create a strong female heroine. And I'd just finished working on a very interesting serial murder case. It all came together, and having the freedom to try something new, I wrote my first novel.

Q.   **You really exemplify the old adage "Write what you know," and then of course, you expand upon it.**

A.   I decided to write what I know because I figured it was easier than doing research and making something up about being a private detective or some other profession. Because I worked in a full-spectrum medical, legal, and crime lab, I had the advantage of all my colleagues being around me.

Q.   **And the cases kept rolling in, didn't they?**

A.   Yes. That's one of the intriguing things about working in that context. People often ask, "What's a typical day?" There isn't one. Each day is different. One day, I might go to the lab and it turns out someone found moose bones, and not knowing what they were, called the police. Or, on another day, an investigation might open into a serial murder case.

Q.   **Is there anything about being a successful author that has been unexpected?**

A.   Yes. I never expected to be involved in all the touring and promotion authors must do. I was totally unaware of that.

I had the classic vision of the writer sitting alone, just writing away on a book. I never thought about going from city to city to bookstores and giving public presentations. It isn't so much a requirement to promote the books, but I think my readers get so much out of having personal interactions, and frankly, I feel I owe that to them and also to the booksellers. I feel a loyalty, especially to the small bookstores, which seem to be disappearing faster than some species.

Q. **Are there any issues or problems you face when writing a series of eighteen novels with the same cast of characters?**

A. Yes, there are. In some ways, it gets easier as you continue to write a series with the same core characters. You get to know them better as you go along writing about them. But it also gets harder because when someone picks up a Temperance Brennan book for the first time, you have to introduce the main premise and the core characters.

But on the other hand, it may be the eighteenth book someone else is reading, so you don't want to bore that reader with repetitious details. It's a balancing act between informing the newcomer and not boring someone who's read the previous books.

Q. **Do you have a favorite among all your novels?**

A. I really like *Bones to Ashes*. It incorporates the Acadian culture of New Brunswick into the story. I spent a lot of time with the Acadians. I loved learning about their culture . . . and eating lobster. [Laughter.] I'd also just learned about the extensive problem of child pornography on the internet, which I brought into the book. I'd worked on a case of a small skeleton found near the New Brunswick-Quebec border. I managed to bring those three elements into the book, and that makes *Bones to Ashes* very special to me.

But, in a way, each of my books resonates personally for me. I never write about a place where I haven't visited, whether it's Guatemala or northern Canada.

Q. **Do any of your readers ever "confuse" you with Temperance Brennan?**

A. Yes. I'm often confused with Tempe. Readers will come to a signing and say, "I really didn't like it when you did this or that." I have to remind them, "That wasn't me. That was Tempe who did that." We do kind of merge in some people's minds. I'm sure readers of the books and viewers of the TV show also blend the two characters. I'm often asked why they're different from each other.

Q. **So, some readers blur reality and fantasy?**

A. Yes, they do. I did base Tempe in certain ways on myself, although she's got her own quirks and flaws, which are strictly hers, not mine. [Laughter.]

Q. **You're hosting a dinner party and can invite any five people, living or dead, from any walk of life. Who are they?**

A. The thing is, if you're making a guest list, you'd put a lot of thought into it. It's tough just coming up with the names off the top of my head.

I think I'd like to invite Woody Allen. I've got a lot of questions for him. I think I'd like to include Jesus. I've got a lot of questions for him, too. I'd like to see the two of them interact because they might have a lot of questions for each other. I'd very much like to meet Queen Elizabeth I. She was a tough lady. Let's throw Hillary in there because right now there are some things I'd like to have her clear up. I'd also invite Douglas Adams, who wrote *The Hitchhiker's Guide to the Galaxy*. He was an amazing wit and would add a lot to the gathering.

Congratulations on writing a compelling series of novels that blends science, forensics, anthropology, medicine, relationships, and psychology in a seamlessly suspenseful way.

CLIVE CUSSLER
OVERNIGHT SUCCESS IN ELEVEN YEARS

Clive Cussler is an adventure novelist and marine archaeologist. His thrillers have reached the *New York Times* bestseller list more than twenty times. His books have been published in forty languages in more than one hundred countries. He is the founder and chairman of the National Underwater and Marine Agency (NUMA), which has discovered more than sixty shipwreck sites.

After his discharge from the military, he worked in advertising, first as a copywriter and later as a creative director. He produced radio and television commercials, many of which won international awards. He began writing fiction in 1965 and is the sole or lead author of more than sixty books.

After a prolific career, Clive Cussler died on February 24, 2020. He worked productively until the end.

Our conversation occurred in 2015.

Q. I understand you first began writing fiction just to fill your time. Will you tell us about that?

A. Well, it all started when my wife found a job working nights as a secretary and dispatcher at the local police department. After work, I'd come home, fix dinner for the kids, put them to bed, and then wander around the house. There wasn't much to do. I said to myself, "Well, I think I'll write a book." I then researched all the heroes and villains in the Sherlock Holmes, James Bond, and Travis McGee books. When I finished, I asked myself what I could do that would be different. Since I was very familiar with the sea, I thought I'd put my hero in and around water. That's how Dirk Pitt was born.

Q. Which was the first book you had published?

A. The first published was *The Mediterranean Caper*, although the first one I actually wrote was *Pacific Vortex!* When I carried it into my agent's office, he didn't think it was very good. So, he sold the second one, *The Mediterranean Caper*. It took three years to get sold, and the first one never got sold in its original form.

Six years later, while having lunch with my new editor, I mentioned *Pacific Vortex!* He said, "You mean there's another Dirk Pitt book out there?" I said, "Yes. There's one that was never published."

He asked to see it. I spent three months revising it and gave it to him. Then it was published. On the publication date, my agent called and said he was going to Jamaica for a vacation. He didn't want to be around when the book came out. [Laughter.] He was staying at some hotel in Jamaica. I got the number and called him. I said, "*Pacific Vortex!* just went to number one on the *New York Times* bestseller list."

Q. **So, even the first one you ever wrote made it to the best-seller list?**

A. Yes, eventually. After eleven years of writing books, *Raise the Titanic!* was my breakthrough book. So, after that happened, people said, "Congratulations on this *overnight success*." I guess writing four books over eleven years made me an instant success. [More laughter.]

After eleven years of my writing books, my wife was still working. As she walked out the door one day, I said to her, "When *Raise the Titanic!* sells two hundred fifty thousand copies, you can stop working." We both laughed.

Later that day, I called her and said, "Now you can quit."

Q. **In your novels, places and settings are described beautifully and have enormous verisimilitude. Tell us about your research.**

A. I love doing research, as does Justin Scott, my coauthor. We'll approach the research from different directions and meet somewhere down the line. I've always found research to be the most enjoyable part of writing. Writing can be a pain. I collect vintage cars, so you always find them in my books. I try to make the books fun for me to write.

Q. **After more than sixty books, is it difficult to come up with fresh ideas?**

A. Yes, it is. I use a basic concept: I ask myself, "What if?" For instance, what if they raised the *Titanic*? Why did it sink? Was something on board that could have caused the ship to sink? That's the way I start a book, and it spreads out from there. I have the beginning and end of the book in mind, but I rarely have the middle.

Q. **So you don't plot the story out chapter by chapter.**

A. No. I can't do that. As I start writing, I come up with more ideas, and the book grows as I go along.

Q. **If you had not been writing novels, what would you have been doing over the years?**

A. My wife and I have always laughed about that. I'd probably have had a small advertising agency down in Newport Beach, California. But I was tired of advertising, and I'm very glad things worked out the way they did.

Q. **Is there anything about the writing life that's been a surprise to you?**

A. I get up in the morning, get to the office, and write until about six o'clock in the evening. Then I share a bottle of wine with my wife. I would have to say, the only real surprise has been the success. That's really been quite unexpected.

Q. **What's your favorite part of the writing life?**

A. I love doing the research for the novels. For me, the writing is hard work. I enjoy doing the Isaac Bell series because I love going back to the early twentieth century. Who were the Gibson girls? What was the Knickerbocker Hotel like?

I usually spend about three months on the research for a book. My favorite era is the twenties, partly because of the classic cars of the twenties and thirties. We did one Isaac Bell book that took place in 1919, at the time of Prohibition. I've gone back and forth with him—in one book Isaac is in his forties, and in the next he's back in his twenties. It's your own universe, so you can do what you want.

In a way, I don't really see myself as an author. I feel I'm more an entertainer than anything else. It's my job to entertain the readers so when they reach the end of the book, they feel they've gotten their money's worth.

Q. **Do you have any advice for novice writers?**

A. If you have some natural talent and really want to write, you should read the books of someone who's very successful in your genre. You don't want to plagiarize, but you want to learn from that author. You study the structure, style, and characterizations he employs. Hemingway always said he studied Dostoyevsky.

There's a great story about Thomas Wolfe when he was in the merchant marines. He came ashore, went to an old bookstore, and bought James Joyce's *Ulysses*, which is about the size of a telephone book. He went back to the ship, and over the next few months, copied *Ulysses* down in a notebook, word for word. When he finished, he threw the notebook off the ship's stern. His shipmates couldn't believe what he'd done after spending months copying the book. They asked why he'd thrown it overboard. His answer was "Because now I know how to write a book."

Q. **If you could have dinner with any five people from any walk of life, living or dead, who would they be?**

A. For me, I'd love to have the great heroes of our country. They would be George Washington and Abraham Lincoln. Albert Einstein would be great to invite, also. And then there's Jim Thorpe. One more would be General Patton. If I had to pick one writer, it would be Hemingway.

Congratulations on a prolific and successful career during which you've entertained millions and millions of people.

KEN FOLLETT
FROM EYE OF THE NEEDLE *TO THE CENTURY TRILOGY*

Ken Follett's books have sold more than 130 million copies worldwide.

His website notes that he became a reporter with his hometown newspaper the *South Wales Echo* and later with the *London Evening News*. While working at the *Evening News*, he wrote his first novel, which was published but did not become a bestseller. He then went to work for a small London publishing house and continued to write novels in his spare time.

In 1978, *Eye of the Needle*, his *eleventh* book, was his first major success. It was a thriller that won the Edgar Award and became a film starring Kate Nelligan and Donald Sutherland. After writing spy and thriller novels, Ken switched gears and began penning *The Pillars of the Earth*, followed by *World Without End*. Then came the Century Trilogy, which opened with *Fall of Giants* in 2010, followed by *Winter of the World* in 2012. The last novel in the trilogy is *Edge of Eternity*, which covers the time period from the 1960s through the 1980s.

Our conversation took place in 2016, when *Edge of Eternity* was published.

Q. You grew up in a home where watching movies or television was prohibited. How did that affect you?

A. At the time, I was absolutely outraged. At the age of eight, all my friends went to the movies on Saturday mornings. I would have loved to go with them. Of course, it did mean that I read more, and in the long run, that probably wasn't a bad thing.

Q. In college, you majored in philosophy. What led you to make that decision?

A. That was also a consequence of my family. By the time I applied to college, I had grave doubts about my parents' religion. I had arguments with my father about theology. Philosophy is, in part, a study of what is a good argument and what is not, what is evidence and what is fake evidence. So, my interest in philosophy stemmed from the agonizing conflict I had over whether or not I believed in my parents' religion. In the end, I completely rejected it.

I'm not a religious person. I'm an atheist. I ended up being the absolute opposite of my parents. It was a process that took some years, and studying philosophy was part of that process.

Q. Nearly every reader alive knows your breakthrough novel was the immensely popular *Eye of the Needle* in 1978. That was followed by other bestselling espionage thrillers. Yet with *The Pillars of the Earth*, you began writing historical fiction. What made you change direction?

A. It was mainly my interest in the Middle Ages, and in particular, the building of the Gothic cathedrals. Most people who stand before a medieval cathedral wonder why it's here. They ask themselves, "Why did medieval people want one of these so badly that they went to the enormous trouble and expense of building it? What compelled them to do this?"

That question is really the driving force of *The Pillars of the Earth*. The novel is my answer to that question, and it helps shed light on the importance of these magnificent cathedrals.

Q. **The Century Trilogy has a sprawling historical perspective. Talk a bit about the time frame, from your idea for a story to the completed novel.**

A. I realized the twentieth century was the most dramatic period in our history. We had the First World War, which was the most terrible one the human race had ever experienced. Then, came World War II, which was even worse. And ultimately, we had the Cold War, which if it had turned into a hot war, would probably have wiped out the entire human race. There, basically, is the terrible drama of the twentieth century.

But it's also our story—mine and yours. We were born in the twentieth century, and its history is the story of what we, our parents, and grandparents experienced. It's very immediate to us. So I decided to write a historical novel about the twentieth century.

As for time frame, the complete project took me seven years. It's about one million words total for the entire trilogy. I spent the first six months mapping it. Early on in the process, I realized it was not one book, but three. I looked at a book called *Age of Extremes* by Eric Hobsbawm, which gives a brief history of the twentieth century. It struck me that the period beginning with the First World War and ending with the fall of the Berlin Wall was the period about which to write. I realized it needed to be three books, each one based on a different war.

I began with a six-month study of the century, during which time I mapped out each book in a very rough way. Then I concentrated on book one, *Fall of Giants*, which is about the First World War and the Russian Revolution. It took two and a half years to write.

It took two years for each of the other two books, *Winter of the World* and *Edge of Eternity*. In each case, the writing of the book divided roughly into three equal parts: the planning and research, which involved a detailed outline of each chapter. That came to sixty or seventy densely typed pages, which was as long as some of my earliest novels.

When I was happy with that, I wrote a first draft. The completed draft went to quite a few people—editors, some family members, and I always hired experts to check my research. After getting notes from these readers, my rewrite was a lengthy process, which really improved the story. For *Edge of Eternity*, it was eight months for each of the three stages.

Q. **You once said, "I want to tell a story that makes the reader always want to see what will happen next." Will you talk about that?**

A. I think this is what popular fiction is all about. We get involved in the story. We identify with the characters. We love some and hate others. We share their hopes and fears. We have an emotional response to them in the context of the story. This is what we want from popular fiction. If you feel anxious about what will happen to the characters, or if you feel sad or hopeful, or happy for them, then you're into the story and you keep turning the pages.

I think the immersion in the story, the feeling that what's happening in the story is more important than what's happening in real life, is what we want from literature. That's the joy of it. You know you're enjoying a book when the plane lands and you think, "Oh darn, now I've got to stop reading."

Q. You also said, "For me, the words should be like a pane of glass that you look through, not at." This has always been evident in your novels. Will you talk a bit more about your writing style?

A. We enjoy the way some writers put words together. For example, P. G. Wodehouse or Philip Roth does so, each in his own way. Part of our enjoyment of their books is their linguistic style.

I'm not that kind of writer. The important thing in my books is the story. I want the reader to see the story. When you're reading one of my books, I don't want you thinking about a sentence or marveling at a vivid image. Or exclaiming, "What a clever alliteration." I don't want you thinking about my prose. I want you to focus on the story. To illustrate that, I've said, "My style is like a window. You look through it and see the story. You don't pay attention to the pane of glass."

Q. You've written thirty novels over the years. Over that period of time have you faced any difficulties with writing?

A. That's difficult to answer. Even as a child, that was what I was good at in school—using my imagination and writing my fantasies. It always seemed natural for me. From time to time, when I'm writing a scene, tears come to my eyes. I think to myself, "Don't be a fool, Follett. You're making this up." [Laughter.]

Q. It's the power of your story. You've sucked yourself in.

A. [More laughter.] I suppose so. My imagination has gotten the better of me.

Q. What do you love most of all about being a writer?

A. I love the complete immersion it requires. Writing a book people will devour doesn't get easier as the years go by. I have an approach I know works, but each time I begin a novel,

I wonder if this one will work. I ask myself, "Will they like this one?" The effort absorbs and uses up everything I've got. It uses all my intelligence and knowledge of the world and people. Absolutely everything goes into the novel. It's the most all-consuming thing imaginable. It's that complete engagement in a challenging task I love so much.

Q. **If you could have dinner with any five people, either living or dead, who would they be?**

A. Because of my absorption in the sixties when writing *Edge of Eternity*, I would be very curious to meet President Kennedy. It would be great, wouldn't it, to have a sixties dinner party? Bobby Kennedy is a terrifically interesting character. Martin Luther King Jr. is probably the biggest hero of the twentieth century, so I'd love to have him there. Let's liven up this dinner party by throwing in Nikita Khrushchev. Oh, and maybe Fidel Castro. [Laughter.] They'd be arguing about politics, that's for sure. Oh, I nearly left someone out. I'd also invite Marilyn Monroe, an icon of that era.

Q. **What would they all be talking about?**

A. Why, they'd be talking about Marilyn Monroe, of course. [More laughter.]

Congratulations on an enormous and successful body of work and for having completed the Century Trilogy, which has taken millions of readers on a fantastic historical journey through the entire twentieth century.

WALTER MOSLEY
THE COLOR PURPLE, *POLITICS,* AND *STORYTELLING*

Walter Mosley was born in California. When he was twelve years old, his family moved from South Central to a more affluent West LA neighborhood. Although racial conflicts flared throughout Los Angeles at the time, his family was nonpolitical. He later became more politicized and outspoken about racial inequality in the United States, which continues to inform much of his fiction.

He earned a political science degree at Johnson State College, then abandoned a doctorate program in political theory and began working in computer programming. While working for Mobil Oil, and after being inspired by Alice Walker's novel, *The Color Purple*, he took a writing course at New York's City College.

He began writing at thirty-four and has continued ever since, having penned fifty books in different fiction genres including mystery and Afrofuturist science fiction. He has also written nonfiction, screenplays, and stage plays.

In 1990, *Devil in a Blue Dress* was published. It featured the iconic character Ezekiel "Easy" Rawlins. The book was adapted into a 1995 movie starring Denzel Washington, Jennifer Beals, Tom Sizemore, Maury Chaykin, and Don Cheadle.

His works have been translated into twenty-one languages. He's won many awards and has served on the board of directors of the National Book Awards.

Our discussion took place at ThrillerFest in 2017.

Q. **You once said your writing imagination was due to "an emptiness in my childhood that I filled up with fantasies." Will you tell us more about that?**

A. I was an only child. My mother was an only child and my father was an orphan. There was a lack of interaction between and among us. I was alone a lot. That being the case, I had to fill up time, so I made up stories. And I think that has stayed with me all these years.

Q. **Were your parents profound influences on you in relation to reading and storytelling?**

A. My parents were extremely sophisticated. I was reading comic books and my father said to my mother, "He's not reading. What're we gonna do?" My mother said, "The house is filled with books. You and I are always reading, so if there's any possibility of him turning out to be a reader, he will be."

That was the most they ever said about it. And it's true: books were everywhere. I was looking at them, thinking about them, and I learned to revere them in certain ways.

I wasn't told to read one book or another. My parents left it up to me to discover reading.

Q. **You once described your father as a deep thinker and storyteller, a "Black Socrates." Will you elaborate a bit?**

A. If you were poor and white, you might have claimed Socrates as an inspiration.

If you were poor and Chinese, maybe you would have said Confucius.

But if you were poor and Black, there was nobody from your race you could claim.

Maybe you'd look up to someone, but that person wasn't from your race or ethnicity.

My paternal grandfather was the only Black man in New Iberia, Louisiana, who could read. Everyone brought him their contracts, letters, or whatever else required a written response.

My father, like his father and like Socrates, was first and foremost an educator. To me, my dad was a "Black Socrates."

Q. **What inspired you to begin writing fiction?**

A. I was in a political theory program at UMass Amherst. One day, I was sitting in class and listening to a revered professor of political theory—a man who studied Thucydides, the Greek historian, physician, and general—and though I was really interested in the subject, I was incredibly bored by his lecture.

It was at that moment I realized I'd never be happy or truly successful as a teacher.

So I walked away from pursuing my doctorate and went back to working in computer programming. Some years later, while still working in programming, I started to write.

Q. **You were thirty-four years old and attended a writing course. I understand you were inspired by Alice Walker's *The Color Purple*. What about the book inspired you?**

A. I don't know that I was *inspired* by *The Color Purple*, but when I read the book, I thought, "I could write like this." Not that I thought I was as good a writer as she was, but I knew I could use dialect and the Black experience and make it into fiction.

I hadn't had that realization before, even though I had read Richard Wright and other Black writers.

Q. **I also read that a mentor at City College encouraged you by saying, "You're Black, Jewish, with a poor upbringing: there are riches therein." How did that affect you?**

A. That was Edna O'Brien. I think she's the greatest living writer of English prose. She was teaching at City College.

Yes, she said that to me, but I already knew it. However, what Edna did do—which was much more important—one day, while reading something I had written, she said, "Walter, you should write a novel."

I went, "Wow!" This was Edna O'Brien, a brilliant person, who was also unbelievably beautiful. I would look at her and fall in love. And six weeks later I'd written a novel—because Edna had told me to do it.

I don't think she understood the impact she had on me.

Q. **Six weeks, first draft?**

A. Yes. *Gone Fishin'* was my first work of fiction.

Q. **Easy Rawlins is your most famous character. At the end of the 2007 novel *Blonde Faith*, you had him die. Or so it seemed. Will you talk about that?**

A. I'd gotten to the end of the book. Easy was brokenhearted and drunk, driving a car barefooted on the Pacific Coast Highway. He would pass cars and finally, he sped up and passed another one. A truck was coming from the opposite direction and he was forced onto the shoulder. Then the shoulder ended.

Now, I was simply writing this . . . I wasn't really thinking. I was just writing. I wasn't sure if I should have him go down the embankment. Then, I thought, "That's what you wrote. You must have had a reason to write it, so leave it that way."

And I did. I left it that he drove off the side of the mountain.

Now, it's a first-person narrative, so obviously, he *can't* be dead, because in a first-person narrative, *he's* telling the story to the reader. So it's impossible for him to be dead. But everybody else thought he was dead. That was fine with me because I didn't know if I could write about Easy anymore.

Q. **What made you feel you didn't know if you could write anymore about Easy?**

A. I couldn't think of anything new or anything different. Some years later, I realized the reason for that was I had been writing about my father and *his* world, but at that moment in time, I was entering *my* world. When I began writing from my own point of view, I could inform Easy from that perspective, and that's when I wrote *Little Green*.

Q. **Yes, after *Blonde Faith*, you turned to writing novels about a New York–based private eye, Leonid McGill. But in 2013, you brought Easy Rawlins back in the novel *Little Green*. So, you rethought his disappearance?**

A. Yes. I never thought of him as being dead. As I said, in the first person, he knew he'd gone off the cliff.

Q. **So, where was he for six years? [Laughter.]**

A. He was nowhere.

I wasn't writing about him for six years because I didn't think I could. But then I realized I'd write about him from my own vantage point.

I told myself, "Okay, let's do it."

So I resumed writing about Easy Rawlins in *Little Green*,

which begins a few days after the accident in which he survived going down the embankment.

Q. **There have been debates in academic literary circles about whether your work should be considered Jewish literature, or if you should be viewed as a Black author. What are your thoughts about being thus classified, and how do you view your work?**

A. Well, let's talk about generations.

My mother's generation would say, "He's a Jewish writer. He's one of us."

Their children would say, "Oh, Walter's writing stories."

Historically, the thing about being Jewish has been assimilation. You like to think of yourself as being part of the dominant culture. For example, you identify as being German because you were a heroic soldier in World War I. You think of yourself as a good German until the day you realize the dominant culture doesn't want you anymore.

In America, you identify as being white. You think you're assimilated until the day you're not wanted because you're a Jew.

A lot of people would say, "He's *not* a Jewish writer." I mean, Philip Roth wrote a novel about a Black university professor having sex with one of his students, and yet he was still Philip Roth, a Jewish writer.

Bernard Malamud wrote about Roy Hobbs in *The Natural*, but Roy Hobbs wasn't Jewish.

So, the idea of excluding me from being a Jewish writer and just seeing me as a Black writer is an act of racism.

Q. **So obviously, you consider yourself simply a writer.**

A. My mother's Jewish. That means I'm Jewish. And so, I'm Jewish, and I'm a writer . . . so I'm a Jewish writer.

I'm also a Black writer in America.

And beyond all that, I'm a *writer*. Period. The fact that people argue about it is wonderful. I enjoy that. [Laughter.]

Q. **It's nice to be argued about, isn't it?**

A. Absolutely. [More laughter.]

Q. **You once said your first love is the genre of science fiction. What about it do you love so much?**

A. It's hard to say. It's like being asked what you love about your children. Or, what do you love about the ocean? But science fiction is wonderful because it opens your imagination to all kinds of possibilities. Children's stories are really science fiction or alternative fiction of some sort. I mean, think about *Jack and the Beanstalk* or *Alice's Adventures in Wonderland* or *Winnie-the-Pooh*. They all involve an alternative reality.

Also, if you're Black in America, science fiction is one way to overcome your own history. If you write, "In 1832, there was a Black president," that's science fiction; it didn't happen, but by writing that, you've created an alternative history, which is science fiction.

I didn't think about that element at the time I began reading science fiction. I just enjoyed the genre.

Q. **You've written stage plays in addition to novels. You've also written screenplays. How did you learn these crafts, and how do you approach them as compared to writing novels?**

A. I could spend a long time talking about that. I'm not sure I studied the craft that much. To me, art is an unconscious activity. People's desire to make it conscious—to explore and pick apart the craft of it—baffles me. I don't know much about the craft or how to consciously write these things. I've been teaching screenplay writing at Sundance for twenty years. Every time I teach, I expect they won't ask me back. And then they call and ask me to come back to teach some more. If that's what they want, okay, I'll do it. [Laughter.] Each genre of writing has its own avenues and its own limitations. I like playing with that. It's true about nonfiction, too. It's really true about all art and especially true about poetry. I don't think much about the craft or the means by which I write. I just write. It flows.

Q. Speaking of poetry, David Mamet says rap music is the operative poetry of our time.

A. Mamet's a brilliant guy, and I really like him. Yes, rap music certainly has poetic elements in its use of language and cadence. So do pop songs. So does good oration. It's all over the place.

Q. Is it true that you've written virtually every day since 1986?

A. Yeah.

Q. You never take a day off?

A. Maybe if I have a plane trip, or if I'm sick. Before I came down here to meet you, I was writing.

Q. What's a typical writing day like for you?

A. I get up and I write for three hours. That's it.

Q. You've been outspoken about racism in the publishing industry. What do you think can be done about it?

A. The publishing industry has become more and more corporate. Everything it publishes—from children's books to pornography—is catering to different types of readers: Native

Americans, so-called Hispanics, so-called Black and white and Asian people.

I think it would behoove publishers to have people from all these groups as editors—not necessarily editing just the books from their race or culture. To have a Native American edit a book for, let's say, Scandinavians, would be very interesting. I think the writers and the readers would learn something.

Art is unconscious, and so is racism. There are those people who are afraid of others whom they don't understand. And there are people who think they are *right* because other people think the way they think. And there are people who think they're smarter than those in another group.

Q. **One of the things I love about the Easy Rawlins character is that he sees racial issues even in their most subtle forms.**

A. He has to deal with racism all the time. When the waitress at the diner is afraid to take his order, he has to deal with it. So it becomes a very practical matter.

Q. **In his own mind, Easy always describes people he meets as having various shades and tones of skin color. He's very aware of racial differences.**

A. Yes. It's done in very practical ways. He'll think so-and-so has very good-looking skin. It's white, or pink, or olive colored, or black, or bronze, or shiny.

The idea of defining race by color is idiotic.

I don't believe in the existence of a "white" race. I mean, there are people we call white, but the differences between and among them can be startling: one person is tall and beefy, has pink skin and red hair and blue eyes, while another you're calling white is short and thin, has ivory-toned skin, black hair, and dark brown eyes, with totally different features, and speaks a different language. What makes them the same?

I think the thing that makes them the "same" was colonization. So-called white people came here and felt they had to kill the so-called red man and enslave the so-called Black men and women. So the people who did the killing and enslaving decided they needed to have a color, too, and they became "white." If you call something white, it should be white, like the whites of your eyes, right? [Laughter.]

Q. **Who are the authors you enjoy reading most these days?**

A. They're probably the same authors as years ago. I reread books a lot. I reread Márquez all the time. Even though I don't like his politics, I reread Eliot. I read a lot of science fiction. I'm almost positive that other writers don't influence me. I write about the world I experience.

Q. **If you could read any single novel again as though reading it for the first time, which one would it be and why?**

A. It has to be *The Stranger* by Camus. It's an extraordinary book that speaks so much to the modern world. It speaks to the issue of humanity, which is dealing with our instincts and our passions.

Q. **What, if anything, keeps you awake at night?**

A. Nothing. [Lots of laughter.] I think it's because I'm old enough that I could have been dead for a long time by now. And I live in America and have my arms and legs. I'm in pretty good health. And as far as I'm concerned, I've had enough success. If there's anything I could get upset about, it pales in comparison to the troubles of people living in Mosul. It's extraordinary to think about how lucky *I* am to have the life I have. Something really *bad* has to happen for me not to sleep.

Q. **So, you don't let "first-world problems" eat away at you?**

A. I don't let *my* "first-world problems" eat at me. I mean, 2.8 million people in America are in prison. Two million of those fall within the definition of people of color. Those people have trouble in the first world. If I were about to go to trial tomorrow for something that might send me to prison, I wouldn't sleep tonight. [More laughter.]

Congratulations on such a diverse and successful career. It's been a pleasure talking with you.

TESS GERRITSEN
MEDICINE, MUSIC, AND MURDER

Tess Gerritsen is a physician and board-certified internist who turned her considerable talents to writing. The Rizzoli and Isles series, featuring a Boston homicide detective and Boston's medical examiner, propelled Tess to the status of an internationally bestselling author and is the foundation for the popular television series of the same name.

Success didn't occur overnight for Tess. She wrote two romance novels before her third one, *Call After Midnight*, was accepted by Harlequin. Her first bestseller came almost a decade and eight romance novels later. With her background as a physician, she turned to combining medicine and crime and moved to Maine with her husband, also a physician. After four stand-alone medical thrillers, Tess created the Jane Rizzoli and Maura Isles series, which sent her popularity into the stratosphere.

Tess has written stand-alone medical and crime thrillers, and her books have been published in forty countries.

Our conversations took place in 2016 and 2017.

Q. **As a physician practicing internal medicine, how did you make the transition to writing novels?**

A. Maternity leave. [Laughter.] I always knew I wanted to be a writer. I went to medical school because my parents were very conservative about what their children would do for a living. That's why so many of us Asian-Americans end up in medical school. But I always wrote. I'd been writing stories since I was a child. I was writing through medical school and my residency. So I became a doctor, but when I went on maternity leave, I went back to writing. By the time I'd sold my first book, I knew that was what I really should be doing.

Q. **Was there a time when you were practicing medicine *and* writing successfully?**

A. Yes. I was working part-time, for perhaps five hours a day. I'd go home, and when my kids were put to bed, I would write at night.

Q. **I understand your novel *Playing with Fire* was born out of a true experience while you were traveling in Italy. Tell us about that.**

A. I was in Venice for my birthday and had a nightmare. I dreamed I was playing my violin while a baby sat next to me. While I was playing this dark and disturbing music, the baby's eyes glowed red and she turned into a monster. I woke up questioning what this was about. I knew there was a story there: something about the power of music.

We talk about music soothing the savage beast, but what if it *awakens* the beast in us? I walked around Venice and had no idea where the story would go, but I kept thinking about it. I wandered into the old Jewish quarter and saw the memorials to the two hundred forty-six Venetian Jews who were deported during World War II.

And then the whole story came to me. This had never before happened, that a story so full-blown and complete came to me in a dream.

Q. **Not until I read *Playing with Fire* did I realize that in addition to being a writer, you're also a composer.**

A. I didn't know it either. [Laughter.] I'm an amateur musician—violin and piano—but I have enough of a background to be able to compose what I hear in my head. I composed a waltz for my son's wedding. Most of my musical experiences have been with Celtic music, but I've studied enough classical and Gypsy music to understand what would work in that particular genre.

Q. **The prose in many of your books is beautiful and has a literary quality. How do you feel about being labeled a genre writer?**

A. I think how you're labeled depends on what voice you're using for your story. For the most part, I am a genre writer. I accept that label because that's what I write about—crime. Crime novels can be literary, but they're still *crime*. There's a large readership for genre fiction. I'm certainly not going to turn up my nose at readers. [Laughter.] You know, it doesn't really matter what the label is. I think all that matters is that you *touch* people. It's important that what you write makes a difference to the readers.

Q. **I know you have thoughts about a novel's first draft. Will you share them with us?**

A. It wasn't always simple for me, but it is now: I've learned to be accepting of a bad first draft. [More laughter.] I've learned you can't be perfect. I've learned to accept that the first draft of a novel is going to be horrible. I've also learned not to edit while working on that first draft. I just let it pour out and keep going forward. It took me a while to learn to let the first draft play out in its own way.

Q. **You're someone who relishes your own curiosity. Tell us about that.**

A. Yes, I love being able to indulge my curiosity. Many of my stories come about because I want to know more about a particular subject. I get a chance, for a while, to be somebody else. I've written about the NASA space program; I spent two years pretending I was an astronaut. I wrote a book about Egyptology and got to explore archaeology. Writing *Playing with Fire*, I got to explore World War II Italy.

Q. **Do you ever find yourself procrastinating?**

A. All the time. It's human nature. I write and stick to my schedule because I have a contract. If I didn't have a book under contract, I would take my time with it. You know, there are so many distractions for a novelist, especially for those of us who are pulled in many directions by multiple passions. I could spend an entire year doing nothing but learning fiddle tunes.

Q. **Have you ever suffered from writer's block?**

A. Yes, with almost every book. But I will tell you that *Playing with Fire* didn't give me writer's block.

Because I write crime fiction, I start out with an idea that excites me. But I don't know where it's going. Most of the time, I don't even know who the bad guy is. About halfway through the first draft, I have to stop writing because I don't know what will happen next. I might call it *plot block* as opposed to writer's block.

My strategy for getting past that point is going for a long walk or lying on the couch and staring at the ceiling. But the number one thing that helps me is driving the car. I can work out a lot of stuff while I'm behind the wheel by myself, on a long, boring drive. I guess it has to do with where your brain is when you're semifocused on something else. It allows my subconscious to work on the plot issues. It's almost like being in a dream state. It's a very creative place for my imagination to be stirred.

Q. **Will you complete this sentence: Writing novels has taught me_____?**

A. It's taught me to pay attention to my emotions. For me, what keeps a book going forward is the fact that characters aren't settled. There's something distressing about whatever situation they're in. In order to write a well-paced novel, you must be cognizant of what's bothering these people. Or, if I were in that situation—what would be bothering me? What would make me want to fix something?

In order to be in touch with my characters' emotions, I have to be in touch with my own.

Q. **What advice would you give to writers starting out?**

A. Beyond allowing one's self to have a bad first draft and not editing that draft, persistence is the key. A writer can't give up just because the book keeps getting turned down by agents and publishers. It took me three books to get something sold.

Also, I can't start a book until I hear a character talking to me, until I hear a voice. I get a feeling for a book by the way that voice sounds. If you get that voice inside your head, it makes the writing so much easier.

And finally, I always say the best books start with the most *emotional* ideas. So I wait for what I call the *punch in the gut*. I wait for that idea that makes me think, "What happens next?" It can happen anywhere at any time. Perhaps I'll overhear a conversation that will strike me as being the kernel of a great idea for a novel. Then I sit down and let the story take me where it will. I enjoy being surprised by how a story evolves, and I think it preserves the surprise for my readers as well.

Q. **You're hosting a dinner party and can invite any five people, living or dead, from any walk of life. Who would they be?**

A. I know I would ask Cleopatra. She's a fascinating character in history. We don't know how much about these legendary people is true, but Cleopatra could purportedly twist men around with her intellect. You know who else I'd invite? Margaret Mead. And then I'd ask Amelia Earhart. I'm really interested in accomplished and interesting women. [Laughter.] The funny thing is I don't find writers all that interesting. We writers live in such a world of imagination, we're too busy to go out and do things ourselves. I'm most interested in people who've *done* things. I would also like to have the young King Tut at the dinner. And last, but certainly not least, I'd invite Genghis Khan.

Congratulations on your career as a physician, musician, and novelist whose books are read all over the world.

JAMES ROLLINS
LICENSED TO KILL

James Rollins is the *New York Times* bestselling author of the Sigma Force series and other novels. His books have been praised as "enormously engrossing" (NPR) and "smart, entertaining adventure fiction" (*New York Journal of Books*). His fiction takes readers to unknown worlds and across eons of time, and his work is reminiscent of books by Michael Crichton, H. G. Wells, and Isaac Asimov.

But he's far more than a thriller author. He's a veterinarian, a man of science, and writes bestselling novels with a uniquely imaginative flavor of their own. They combine elements of history, scientific fact, and speculation, with military suspense and threats of global destruction. His books transcend all genres.

Our conversations took place on a number of occasions between 2014 and 2017.

Q. **Your medical background as a veterinarian is clear in many of your novels. The Associated Press said of your books, "The science reads like the best of Michael Crichton." In that context, what inspired you to begin writing fiction?**

A. I always wanted to be a veterinarian—as early as the third grade, long before I could even spell the word. I loved animals and science. As a kid, I was dragging injured animals and stray dogs home. I also read avidly and spent a lot of time in the library. My mom was a voracious reader, and through her example I learned to love books. I read constantly, whether it was Edgar Rice Burroughs and the Tarzan novels or *The Black Stallion*, and then on to science fiction, either H. G. Wells, Jules Verne, Robert Heinlein, or Isaac Asimov.

I thought one day it would be really cool to write. My brothers and sisters were the early targets for my storytelling. My goal was to see if I could get them to believe the things I made up. I guess seeing a novel I wrote on a bookstore shelf was something of a pipe dream for me. I was on a clear track toward becoming a veterinarian.

I became a veterinarian and started my practice, but I still had this notion of writing. So I joined a writing club in Sacramento and went to meetings. Different authors spoke there, and I eventually joined a critique group. I still have a connection to them, and right now they're reading a book I've just written and I'm sure they'll tear it apart and help me make it better. I wrote a bunch of short stories that were never published. I then wrote a novel and was lucky enough to have that first one sell.

Q. **And now you write full-time?**

A. Yes, although I still do some volunteer work. I spend one Sunday a month doing veterinary work, and my great claim to fame is not that I'm on the bestseller list, but that I can still neuter a cat in thirty seconds. [Laughter.] And don't forget that as a licensed veterinarian, I have a license to kill. [More laughter.]

Q. **In a sense, many of your novels could be called historical thrillers. Are you a history buff?**

A. I am. In the third grade, I wanted to be either a veterinarian or an archaeologist. That was career option number two. I've always loved history and science. I've always been something of an armchair archaeologist. I often put my characters in caves looking for something that's been hidden for centuries. In fact, the first book I wrote, *Subterranean*, dealt with a cavern far below the earth's surface.

Q. **At the beginning of your novel *The 6th Extinction*, you have a section called "Notes from the Scientific Record." In it you say, "Life on this planet has always been a balancing act—a complex web of interconnectivity that's surprisingly fragile. Remove or even alter enough key components and that web begins to fray and fall apart." Talk a bit about this.**

A. According to most scientific thought, we're currently involved in what will be the sixth mass extinction on our planet. We are now seeing an extinction rate of species about a thousandfold higher than the rate of extinction since the arrival of mankind on the planet. This is a unique extinction because it's the hand of man driving it as opposed to volcanic eruptions, meteor strikes, or other cataclysms that caused previous extinctions.

My goal in writing *The 6th Extinction* was to help determine, if through human genius and imagination, we can extricate ourselves from this forthcoming fate. This drove me to do research about conservation efforts and the work of synthetic biologists. The more I read, the more fascinated and horrified I was regarding our ability to reengineer and modify many organisms, which could lead to our ultimate destruction.

Q.   **Your novels often address scientific processes, genetics, altering life forms, and ecoterrorism. Will you comment on these issues?**

A.   One of the fascinating things I discovered is that there has been a democratization of the scientific process. We're now seeing genetic labs popping up not only at the university or military level, but in backyards, garages, and small private centers. Because the costs of setting up such a lab have dropped dramatically, someone can now build a genetics laboratory in a garage. People are patenting life forms right now. Most of it involves activity with no oversight. Only recently, at the NIH, a vial of smallpox virus was found in someone's closet. This raises enormous concern for the potential of some lethal organism being let loose in the population. It could be the result of terrorism or an accidental occurrence.

Q.   **Do you think people will eventually be able to hack into genetic codes the way they can hack into computers?**

A.   There's a very active biopunk movement, which is a spinoff of the old cyberpunk days. Cyberpunks of the past are the biopunks of today. I've talked with some of these people. They've actually patented some of their creations. It's a burgeoning industry.

Q. Some of your novels deal with the implications of genetic modification to existing life forms. Will you discuss that?

A. This field is changing so rapidly, I had to edit the novel within months of it going to press. As an example, in May 2014, the Scripps Institute produced living, replicating bacteria with two new nucleotides from the genetic alphabet inserted into them. They were added to the standard four that compose the DNA of all life on this planet. That very genetic modification—the introduction of foreign nucleotides into DNA—occurs in the novel. While writing the book, I thought I was brushing beyond the fringes of science, but each time I manage to step beyond that edge, science catches up with me. The implications of this are enormous. Some life forms could be altered and become dangerous, while others could be altered so they can better survive in the face of ongoing extinction.

Q. As a man of science, how do you decide where to draw the line between fantasy and biological fact in your novels?

A. It's a challenge to keep ahead of the curve of what I thought was fantastical but really is not. I love taking my readers into the realm of what's truly going on in the world today. I then extrapolate and look beyond the horizon to where that might lead us. I love doing this in all my novels.

I enjoy harkening back to some of the themes I addressed at the beginning of my career, such as creating strange biospheres that while not real, are supported by science as being quite possible.

Q. **I know your novel *The Bone Labyrinth* started out as an exploration of the origins of human intelligence. Can you tell us more about what's termed the "Great Leap Forward"?**

A. For two hundred thousand years, human brains haven't changed much; they're basically the same size and shape. But for some reason, about fifty thousand years ago, there was an explosion of art, ingenuity, and civilization. That moment has been called the "Great Leap Forward."

No one has conclusively determined the cause for that sudden burst of ingenuity and intelligence. One commonly accepted theory is around that time, mankind began migrating out of Africa and was exposed to new threats and challenges, requiring innovation in order to find new ways to survive. There have been other theories, including ones involving changes in diet, and various speculations. At that time, the Neanderthal tribes of Europe and the Middle East began interbreeding with early mankind, and we began to see the influx of Neanderthal DNA into our genome.

When you cross breeds of animals or people you have *hybridization*, resulting in increased intelligence and vigor in the offspring. Anthropologists tell us when hominin DNA entered our genome, it was beneficial. It remains in our DNA even after thousands of years.

If this hybridization actually happened, I wondered if I could build a story around that phenomenon.

Parenthetically, it was recently discovered that another two hominins probably contributed to our DNA. In fact, as I was writing this novel, because of new discoveries, I was forced to tweak the story as more information emerged.

Q. So new revelations about the human genome emerged even as you were writing the novel.

A. Yes. One of the fun things about writing a novel is I get so immersed in research while writing. I always have my ear tuned to the newest findings, so new developments become incorporated into the novel.

Q. Many of your books delve into archaeology, genetics, paleontology, ancient civilizations, astronomy, history, the kabbalah, faith, myth, and legend. Your research must have been incredibly extensive.

A. To me that's one of the joys of writing a novel. And it's a trap I have to avoid. When I was writing the book *Sandstorm*, I kept researching more and more and finally realized I wasn't writing. I enjoyed the research, but I wasn't being productive.

So now I limit myself to researching for only ninety days. During that time, I build the spine of my story. On the ninety-first day, I begin putting words on paper. For this book, it wasn't only a matter of interviewing different paleontologists and reading current journal articles, but I also traveled to China, since part of the book takes place there. I like doing that—blending historical mystery with cutting-edge science and determining if there's a story to be told.

Q. When not working with a co-author, how do you approach the process, from doing research to producing the completed project?

A. Typically, I'll spend ninety days researching the history or science to be included in the novel. I'll also look at locations for the novel's setting. At the same time, I build a skeletal plot to the story. By the ninety-first day, I have a rough outline and the major points of the novel are researched.

I then begin to write, though with each day more things come up requiring research—some minutiae or facts to fill in certain blanks. It takes about six to seven months to complete the first draft and then another month or two to do a final polish. I can write for five hours a day before feeling burned out. I typically produce five double-spaced pages daily. Then off it goes to the editor.

Q. **You're an enormously prolific author. Do you ever procrastinate?**

A. Oh yeah. [Laughter.]

Q. **Given it's a common human tendency, how do you deal with it?**

A. I've always written two books a year. It's a pattern I established and try to maintain. I realized I had to set a goal. I had to have an inherent commitment to myself about my writing. When I was a full-time practicing veterinarian, I committed to writing three double-spaced pages a day. I thought if I ever gave up my day job, I'd be much more productive. And I am.

I write five double-spaced pages a day. Over time, I've learned that after those pages, I hit a wall. I'm a slow writer. It takes me about an hour to write one double-spaced page. Five pages of fresh writing take five hours. The rest of the day involves editing, polishing, researching, or double-checking facts. Of course, Facebook and Twitter require a certain amount of commitment, too.

I work from a skeletal outline, which I view as the main tent poles of a novel, but I don't stick to an outline. To me one of the joys of writing a novel is the discovery element of that novel as I'm writing it. Sometimes I may write my characters into a corner and I get stuck, but that's really a good jam to be in.

If the author can't figure how to get them out of that trap, the readers won't either. It may take me a day or two of extreme frustration to figure how to get them out of that corner, but when they're on the right track, it feels so satisfying.

Q. What do you read for enjoyment?

A. I have a bevy of authors where each time one of their books comes out, I read it. I don't just read thrillers. I still read science fiction, modern thrillers, and historical mysteries. I have different favorites in different genres: George R. R. Martin, whom I've been following for almost thirty years, Steve Berry, Clive Cussler, Tom Clancy, and some others.

Q. You produce books at an incredible pace. Do you ever struggle with a tendency to ease off or take it easy?

A. You know, I still belong to a creative writing group. It's the same one I joined before I was ever published. One of the things I've learned is although writing is a solitary profession, eventually, you bring your writing to the world. Something I've become aware of is this: it's always good to have someone watching your back. I've got twelve first readers who come from very different aspects of life, and I lean on them to learn how they receive and interpret what I've written. They keep me honest.

Sometimes I'm a little lazy and think, "Well, this is good enough. It's satisfactory." If I give the work to the group, they'll rake me over the coals. They detect that I'm skimming a bit, and they call me on it. They still remember me from when I was writing lousy short stories, now buried in my backyard, which will hopefully never see the light of day. [Laughter.]

Q. **Your books have sold millions of copies. Your photograph is on the flap of each one. Has your life changed since you began writing novels?**

A. Not particularly. Once in a blue moon, someone will recognize me, which is startling. Once someone called my name in an airport. I was shocked he actually recognized me. [Laughter.] That's happened only three times, which is sort of a nice thing about being a writer—you have anonymity. Most people don't really recognize an author they've been reading, even if it's their favorite one.

Q. **You're an immensely popular bestselling author. Do you ever have doubts about a book while you're writing?**

A. When I first started writing, my goal was to write one novel. I just wanted to be able to walk into a bookstore and see my book on the shelf. Now, thirty-two books into this career, I find that every novel is still a struggle. Whenever I get to the middle of writing a novel, I'm sure the book is awful, that I've lost all talent and don't know what I'm doing.

Then I get to a certain point where the train seems to be back on the track and I'm very happy with the novel. I keep thinking, "Well, with the next novel, I won't fall into that trap." But I'm in the middle of my next novel—thirty-two novels later—and I'm there again. It never gets easier. [Laughter.]

Q. **Is there a level of anticipation or excitement as you begin a new book or as you come close to completing one?**

A. Nothing gets me more excited than writing. Each morning I cannot get to my chair fast enough. Overnight I'll have a new idea, maybe from reading another author, or something just popped into my head. I have a bedside pad for jotting things down. To me one of the joys is simply being able to tell good stories. Writing is so much fun, even though on some days it's like pulling teeth.

Q. **What advice would you give to a beginning writer?**

A. There's the old adage saying you should write every day. The rule of thumb is to expect to write a million words before you will ever be published. It's not a craft where a neophyte sits down and there's a burst of skill.

So my advice is to write every day—if not three pages, then one page, or even a paragraph—just write every day.

I'd add to that: besides writing every day, a writer should read every night. As an avid reader, I see little tricks authors do, and I like to see if I can do something similar in my next book.

When I began writing my first novel, *Subterranean*, a copy of Michael Crichton's *Jurassic Park* sat on a shelf above my desk. Rather than reinventing the wheel, I patterned my first novel after the pacing of *Jurassic Park*.

When I'm having trouble writing on a given day, if I read another author that night, the little knot in the back of my head begins to untie. My writerly eye sees what the other author did, and it can be a clue about where to go in my writing.

I listen to audiobooks when I'm driving, and I have a book on my bedside table. Because of reading, I'm always finding a new tool for my writerly toolbox. I try to incorporate that new tool as soon as I discover it in another author's work. I challenge myself.

Q. **If you could have any six people over for dinner, writers or figures from history—living or dead—who would they be?**

A. I would love to sit down with Michael Crichton. I'd love to meet Howard Carter, the archaeologist who discovered the tomb of Tutankhamun. Mark Twain would make for some very entertaining conversation. It's a poorly kept secret that I've written fantasy novels under the pen name of James Clemens. Plato or Socrates would round things out and we'd have a great mix of people.

Congratulations on a stellar writing career in which you blend history, archaeology, science, and compelling storytelling into genre-bending novels enjoyed by millions of people the world over.

JAYNE ANN KRENTZ
ROMANTIC SUSPENSE AND FAMILY BONDS

Under seven different pseudonyms, Jayne Ann Krentz has written more than 120 romance and romantic suspense novels. Many have been bestsellers. Now she uses only three names: Jayne Ann Krentz when writing contemporary romantic suspense, Amanda Quick for historical romantic suspense, and Jayne Castle when penning paranormal romantic suspense. Her books have sold more than thirty-five million copies in various countries.

Our conversations occurred between 2015 and 2017.

Q. **Tell us about your path to becoming a published author.**

A. There was only one reason why I became a writer—I wanted to tell my story my way. I needed to tell that story even if no one wanted to read it. I couldn't stop myself. I'm convinced that every author has a core story and that he or she will spend a lifetime exploring it. That core story has nothing to do with fictional landscapes. Big-city noir, small-town community, para-normal, historical, fantasy—it doesn't matter. The setting is only the vehicle. The core story is defined by the emotional conflicts, themes, and world views that compel and fascinate the author.

Q. **I understand that for six years, while working at Duke University, you wrote and mailed many proposals for new novels and were consistently rejected. Now you're a *New York Times* bestselling author of romantic suspense novels with more than fifty books making the bestseller list. Tell our readers about dedication and persistence.**

A. I have never considered myself dedicated or persistent. The simple truth is that I can't stop writing. It's a compulsion, an addiction. And, like any good addiction, it's got a light side and a dark side. It's all too easy to turn off the rest of my life when I'm into a story.

Q. **You're an outspoken advocate for the romance and romantic suspense genres. What are your thoughts about these genres and their standing?**

A. The romance genre is slammed with the same critiques applied to all popular fiction. I think it's because people tend to take popular fiction for granted. They don't appre-ciate that romance novels, and all popular fiction, transmit our culture's core values to the next generation. Romance novels convey values especially important to women. Most crucial is the belief in the healing power of love. In popular fiction—romance included—the values we see preserved are ones everyone recognizes: an appreciation of honor, the healing power of love, doing the right thing when the chips are down, and the issue of good versus evil. The romance genre—along with other forms of popular fiction—affirms those values. They really derive from ancient heroic literary traditions.

I also find the romantic suspense novel to be a very American genre. It captures the essence of two strong characters facing a dangerous situation in which they must work together to survive. It's an American story with its roots in the old Wild West. As Americans, it's really our story.

Q. Do these elements make romance novels so enduring?

A. While the healing power of love is probably the core value, there are other factors that account for the enduring power of the genre. Romance novels affirm the importance of nurturing and of loving protectiveness. The foundation of "family" is at the center of the story. It's not about sex, nor about romance, per se. It's all centered on family. I think that's why the appeal of romance novels is so enduring. Most women, and many men, too, have an appreciation for family. That's the key to the romance story. Rather than calling the ending a "happy ending," the ending of a romance novel is actually the formation of a new family.

Q. Many of your novels combine romance and suspense. What makes *romantic suspense* such a compelling genre?

A. As far as I'm concerned, romantic suspense is the most compelling of all genres because it combines two of the most compelling forces in fiction—an intense relationship and serious danger. The definition of romantic suspense (as opposed to suspense with a romantic element) is that every twist in the suspense must result in a twist in the relationship and vice versa. One element drives the other. Each raises the stakes in the other.

Q. Do you see your audience as being primarily women?

A. I write a story to satisfy myself. I don't really focus on the audience. I think about what the story needs in order to be satisfying to me. Statistically, yes, most readers of romance are women. But keep in mind, the majority of all fiction is read by women. I think the suspense and thriller genres tend to appeal more to men because they're the warrior stories. But one of the most popular male writers among women is Lee Child. I understand in his latest Jack Reacher novel, Reacher learns he has a son. And that's important because if you don't have a family, you don't have a future.

Q. From your oeuvre of works, it's clear you've written two, three, and sometimes four novels a year. Tell us about your writing schedule and routines.

A. Nowadays I think you'll see many more mystery and thriller writers doing more than one novel a year. Robert B. Parker was writing three a year. John Sandford is doing two. It's always been a marketing consideration. I wrote a good number of novels each year at the beginning of my career, but I don't do it anymore.

I've always been a disciplined writer. Most successful writers I know are very disciplined. I'm at the computer at seven in the morning. I work until about noon; after that any creativity I may have is pretty well shot for the day. Then life gets in the way and I go shopping. [Laughter.]

Q. **Is there a reason you've used so many pen names over the years?**

A. It was always a business decision. There were times when I was writing for two or three different publishing houses and they each demanded a different name. They wanted to tie up a particular name.

Q. **Your birth name was Jayne Castle. There's an interesting story of why you had to give up using that name for ten years. Will you tell us about that?**

A. Ah, yes. The story of how I lost my birth name dates back to the early days of my career, when I decided I didn't really need an agent. Let's just say I signed some very bad contracts. I finally got my name back, but these days, whenever I speak to aspiring writers, I encourage them to join writers' organizations and educate themselves on best practices in the business. Like it or not, this is a business on several levels.

Q. **You're still using three different names for your novels.**

A. Yes, I've been using those three names for three years. The market changes from season to season. One season the Amanda Quick name works better, and the next season Jayne Castle takes off. I want to leave one or two names behind, but as long as they work, I'll keep using them. They allow me to take my core stories into three different landscapes or subgenres. I find it refreshing to move among my three worlds.

Q. **Your erotic scenes are done very artfully. Will you talk about writing them?**

A. To an extent, it's like writing violent scenes. The trick is to remember that what happens physically isn't the important thing. What matters most is the emotional element. It's crucial to depict the emotions with which the characters enter the scene and those they have at its conclusion.

The erotic scene should be a life-changing event. It should add to the progress of the romance itself in the same way an act of violence must trigger the next step in a thriller novel. In order to rise above the level of prurience, the erotic scene must demonstrate growth—in either character development or the novel's plot.

Q. You've had such writing success for years. What about the writing life has surprised you?

A. What surprises me is the fact that today authors get stuck with so much of the marketing end of publishing. It wasn't the case when I started out. I think it's because of the chaos in the industry now. Publishers used to get your book into bookstores and they did the marketing. But today, with so much happening online, the reality is that most writers are forced to do a great deal of their own marketing.

Q. What do you find intriguing about the writing life?

A. I just love seeing a scene come together on the page. I live from scene to scene. If I actually sat down and thought about the fact that I've got five hundred pages to go, I'd be doomed before I started. Each scene, for me, is a little story unto itself. When I get that scene just right, I feel so good.

Q. You were formerly a librarian and now are known to give generously to libraries. What thoughts do you have about the importance of libraries?

A. No civilization can be called civilized unless it possesses libraries. They are the fortresses that stand between humans and the raw forces of chaos. Libraries look different from one era to the next, but their function remains the same. They connect us to our past and help us imagine the future.

Q. **Are there any authors who influenced you as a writer?**

A. Robert B. Parker will always be one of my idols.

Q. **Which authors do you enjoy reading these days?**

A. I'll read anything by Christina Dodd, Susan Elizabeth Phillips, Beatriz Williams, and Deanna Raybourn. In addition, I love John Sandford's Virgil Flowers series and Gregg Hurwitz's Orphan X novels.

Q. **If you could have dinner with any five people from history or literature, living or dead, who would they be?**

A. Any five from the stable of writers who wrote the Carolyn Keene Nancy Drew books, my favorite and formative series.

Congratulations on a prolific and immensely successful literary career.

C. J. BOX

SHANE, HIGH NOON, *AND THE MODERN WESTERN*

C. J. Box is the bestselling author of eighteen Joe Pickett novels, four stand-alones, and a collection of short stories called *Shots Fired*. He's won multiple awards, including the Edgar, the Anthony, the Gumshoe, and the Barry. His books have been translated into twenty-seven languages.

He lives with his family outside Cheyenne, Wyoming.

Joe Pickett, the protagonist in the series, is a Wyoming game warden who often finds himself embroiled in situations dangerous for him and his family.

Our talks took place on different occasions between 2015 and 2017.

Q. How and why did you begin writing fiction?

A. I always had an interest in writing. All through high school and college, I was associated with the student newspapers. My first job was working for a small weekly newspaper in Wyoming. That's when I really started thinking about writing fiction. My first novel, which later became *Open Season*, was hatched while I was a newspaper reporter, covering a story about creatures in Wyoming called black-footed ferrets. They were thought to have been extinct but were discovered at that time. That story played out in a fascinating way, and I used it as the subject matter for my first book.

Q. Who were your earliest reading influences as a youngster?

A. The first books I can remember reading were Encyclopedia Brown books, a series featuring a boy detective named Leroy Brown. I would go to my local library in Casper, Wyoming, and the librarians would locate those books for me from all over the state. Later on, *Catch-22* was one of the first huge books I ever read, and I loved it so much, I read it four times.

Q. I've learned that until recently you had a day job, even though your Joe Picket novels have been international bestsellers. Tell us about that.

A. My wife and I co-owned an international tourism marketing company. We had contracts with state government tourism departments in the West, and we marketed five states in the Rocky Mountains to Europe and Australia. We had seven offices overseas. We were extensions of state tourism offices. We operated the business for twenty-four years, and I wrote fiction on a part-time basis.

Q. **At what point over those years did you write and get your first novel published?**

A. I was writing the entire time we worked in marketing. It took twenty years from my first conceiving a novel to having *Open Season* published. I had hoped to have the novel published someday but was busy running the business. It took five years after I'd completed the novel to get it published.

Q. **So you were no stranger to rejections?**

A. I had some very weird experiences. My first agent had the manuscript—this was in the pre-internet days. I sent him the entire printed manuscript by snail mail. He had it for four years and said he couldn't sell it. I even stopped calling him since nothing was happening. I went to a writing conference and learned, to my astonishment, that my agent had been dead for six months. I had no idea it had happened. To this very day I've never met an editor who saw that original manuscript. So now I tell people to make sure their agent is young and vibrant. Anyway, I got another agent and the book was sold very soon afterward.

Q. **You've mentioned your "first readers" in the acknowledgments at the end of your novels. Tell us who they are and the role they play in your writing.**

A. The very first reader is my wife, Laurie. She's really a good editor and doesn't pull any punches. She does primarily conceptual editing and tells me where I may have gone astray. I bought my three daughters Kindles, so I could email the manuscripts to them. They provide input, too. They're particularly good when it comes to commenting on child and girl characters. They keep me on track and will tell me something like, "The kid wouldn't say it like that; she'd say it like this . . ."

In one book, my youngest daughter straightened out the text messages I wrote. They also do continuity editing. They'll say, "You used that phrase in the last book." So, all told, the entire family participates, and it's very valuable.

Q. **One can't help but notice Joe Pickett and his wife have three daughters, as do you. Any additional similarities between you and Joe?**

A. Not a lot, other than my having been a state employee for a while, as is Joe. I'm familiar with government bureaucracy and how difficult it is at times to do your job. I'm familiar writing about Joe's family situation, dealing with three daughters. [Laughter.]

Q. **Unlike many contemporary thriller protagonists, Joe is happily married, is a good father, doesn't have a dark past, works hard, and is very honest. What do you feel makes him such a beloved fictional character?**

A. I think it's because he's real and he's also flawed. Therefore the reader has empathy for him. The reader knows he can screw things up and something bad can happen to him and his family. I hope it draws the reader in more because it's easy to see one's self in his situation. A reader can easily identify with Joe.

Q. **What do you think makes Joe Picket so appealing even to people unfamiliar with life in the West?**

A. I like to think it's his fallibility. He's a very real guy who makes mistakes. He's not a superman, by any means. His biggest attribute is tenacity. When he gets into something, he doesn't let it go. He's like a bulldog. But he's also a family man and a state employee. Readers can relate to him, which makes him kind of unusual in the mystery genre.

Q. **Joe Picket has been on the mystery-thriller scene for seventeen books. How has he evolved over the years?**

A. He's definitely evolved. Part of the reason is the books take place in real time. He gets a year older with each novel. He has a much harder view of things now than he did in the first books, when he was kind of naive. He's been in so many difficult situations and has experienced so many betrayals, he's become a bit more cynical as time has gone by.

As a reader, I don't like when a series seems frozen in time. You've got to suspend disbelief for a series to work in the first place, but when a character doesn't age and change, it tips things over the top. It loses credibility. I like the fact that everyone ages a year with each book and reflects the experiences they had in the previous one.

Q. **What are the most enjoyable parts of the writing life?**

A. I love working with the people in publishing. They're intelligent and very literate. I enjoy meeting readers who are really into the books. As a writer, I'm something of an entrepreneur. I can create my own work habits, my own hours. I love writing the first draft of a novel. It's exhilarating.

Q. **What about writing that first draft do you love?**

A. What I love about writing the first draft is that it's done with pure joy and with all the creative juices flowing. Characters are coming alive and things are happening right in front of me. It must be like what a songwriter feels when a catchy hook comes into his head. He knows he must build a whole song around it, but that initial rush must be wonderful.

Q. **What about rewriting and revising?**

A. Editing, revising, and copyreading aren't nearly as much fun as writing the first draft. There's something inspirational about getting the basic story written.

Q. **You write one novel a year, and every other year you write two novels. How do you keep up this pace?**

A. Honestly, I don't know how I do it. [Laughter.] I don't have any co-writers; I don't hire anyone to do research; I just keep at it every day. I don't take extended time off—except when the time is right, you can find me fly-fishing. [Laughter.] I write my thousand or fifteen hundred words a day and generally produce a book and a half a year.

Q. **In light of that, do you ever procrastinate?**

A. I really don't. I think that comes from my having been a journalist. Even though it's been a long time since I was one, if you're covering events for a daily or weekly newspaper, you can't procrastinate. You've got to produce the piece and you must do it on deadline. You can't wait for inspiration; you just have to do it. On those days when I don't really feel like writing, I just do it, and if necessary, I go back later to make it better.

Q. **Do you find it easier or more difficult to write a stand-alone as opposed to writing books in the Joe Pickett series?**

A. It's sometimes harder to do a stand-alone, but it's very rewarding. I can go outside of Joe's world into different states, plots, and characters. Then, when I return to the Joe Pickett series, it feels fresher.

Q. **Your novels have various thematic elements, one of them being revenge for perceived wrongs. Is this a classic Western theme?**

A. I think revenge is one of the three or four classic Western themes. The bad guy comes back to town and the good guy must stand up to him. You see that in a classic movie such as *High Noon* and many others. I think it's somewhat nuanced in *Vicious Circle*. Joe has some empathy toward Dallas Cates, the bad guy who's coming back. Joe feels that as a law enforcement officer, he participated in overcharging the man and feels he did it in a way that wasn't completely ethical. Joe is willing to drop the feud if Dallas will just stop in his quest.

Q. **Would you characterize the Joe Pickett novels as thrillers, Westerns, or both?**

A. I think they're both. I like to think of them as contemporary Westerns. There are mystery elements, thriller elements, but mainly they're adventurous tales. I don't sit down and wonder if I'm going to write a mystery or a thriller. Almost all the books are Westerns to some degree. I recall talking to George Pelecanos, whose books are mostly set in the mean streets of Baltimore. He considers his books to be Westerns.

Q. **The prose in your novels is elegant, yet straightforward and easily readable. How would you describe your writing style?**

A. I try not to show off. I want to simply communicate as effectively as I can to tell a story. I think that comes from my background as a journalist and from what I enjoy reading. I pare things back. If I write a purple prose paragraph describing scenery, I'll go back and try to cut it down to its essence, so the reader gets a good sense of what it looks and smells like, but it doesn't go on and on.

Q. **Speaking of what you enjoy reading, who are your literary influences?**

A. My favorite author of all times is Thomas McGuane. I also enjoy reading books by Jim Harrison. I'm a big fan of Cormac McCarthy. They all write contemporary Westerns in a straightforward style. And they all have a great sense of place.

Q. **After writing so many Joe Pickett novels, do you face any challenges when writing about him and his family?**

A. I think the biggest challenge is to keep the writing fresh and not fall into being formulaic. There are sixteen books in the series, but because they're written in real time, where Joe Picket, his wife, and his children are all getting older, the characters and situations stay fresh for me.

I think readers are very perceptive. They can tell when an author is starting to get tired of his own material. I know, as a reader, I can tell when that happens with an author. I don't want that to ever happen with my novels. I try to change things up by including topics in the news and controversial themes and subject matters in the novels. I think that keeps things fresh for both me and the reader. Life demands that we adapt, so our characters must also adapt to changing circumstances.

Q. **You're such a well-known author. Which question are you asked most frequently?**

A. It's either, "Is Joe Pickett based on someone you know?" Many people can't quite conceive of creating characters out of fictional cloth. They feel the characters must be based on real people. The other question that comes up frequently is, "Why don't you turn this series into a movie or a TV series?"

Q. **If you could have dinner with five people from any walk of life, living or dead, who would they be?**

A. I know I would want to sit down with Theodore Roosevelt. Another would be Joseph Heller. Then I'd invite Raymond Chandler. Winston Churchill would be there. He had a strangely similar life path to Theodore Roosevelt's. And then there would be the rodeo cowboy Bill Pickett. He's the man for whom Joe Pickett is named. He was the first all-around champion of the Cheyenne Frontier Days rodeo.

It's been a pleasure talking with you about Joe Pickett, writing, and your books. which *Publishers Weekly* described as "world-class." I've found each Joe Pickett novel to be suspenseful, beautifully written, and I could easily relate to all the characters.

KARIN SLAUGHTER
TAKING US TO DARK PLACES

Karin Slaughter's first book, *Blindsighted*, became an international success published in thirty languages, and made the Crime Writers' Association's Dagger Award shortlist for Best Thriller Debut of 2001.

Karin has over 35 million books in print in over 38 territories, she has debuted at number one in the US, the UK, the Netherlands, Belgium, Germany, Ireland, New Zealand, Australia, and Canada. Her stand-alone novel, *Pieces of Her*, is coming to Netflix and stars Toni Collette.

Our conversations took place in 2016 and 2017.

Q. Some people have pointed out that your books are very dark and the crimes are often motivated by sexual perversion. Will you talk about that?

A. The sorts of crimes I tend to write about are generally marked by some sort of sexual perversion, but I think that ignores the true motivating factor for those crimes, which is control. If you look at the perpetrator in the novel *Pretty Girls*, there's not a sexual release component. He wants to dominate his victims in every way. The same goes for the killer in *Cop Town*, who feels that the world is changing and leaving him behind.

I think all murders can be viewed through the lens of control—either the need to have it or the fear of losing it—whether I'm writing about gang members shooting one another in the street or a serial killer abducting women.

Q. Tess Gerritsen once said Karin Slaughter "takes us to the deep, dark places other novelists don't dare to go." What did she mean?

A. I can't speak for Tess, but I think what she means is that I like to explore the psychology of the crime—to get inside the heads of both the investigators and perpetrators. Every author has to make a decision within a story about how far they are going to push the suspension of disbelief.

I tend to write about crimes I've heard about from agents or police officers, and I try to write about them as realistically as possible. I also want to be careful because, if you choose to go down this road, you can fall into a sort of unrelenting darkness.

So, I anchor everything in the humanity of the characters. For instance, in *Pretty Girls*, Claire and Lydia have complementary moral compasses. Will Trent is always going to try to point true north. I think there's a great deal of humor in my stories. There always has to be some light to balance out the dark.

Q. You were once asked which fictional character you would like to meet. You answered, "Scarlett O'Hara." What about her is so fascinating?

A. I was twelve years old and reading crap like *Flowers in the Attic*, which I thought was a beautiful love story, and a discerning librarian put *Gone with the Wind* in my hands. I instantly fell in love with the storytelling. Scarlett, like me, was a Southerner who didn't want to follow the hard-and-fast rules laid down for women of her time. Neither did Margaret Mitchell, for that matter. To be a young girl growing up in a small town where girls were told not to run or jump or make a lot of noise or—worse—be too clever, reading about Scarlett O'Hara doing all of these things and more was a revelation.

Q. Your recent novel, *Pretty Girls*, focuses on the psychological devastation experienced by *families* of crime victims. This seems to be a different area of concentration for you.

A. Yes, it absolutely is. It was a very conscious departure on my part. For years I've written about Will Trent, a cop, and my other narrators have been either cops or doctors specializing in forensic medicine. I wanted to tell a story revealing the toll crime takes on victims and their families—what crime leaves behind and how it can tear families apart. I think that's an important element of crime stories that's often ignored.

Q. What struck me is how the main characters evolved over the course of the story.

A. I wanted to do that. I made a purposeful choice that the characters you meet in the first few chapters would undergo some sort of evolution. They wouldn't be the same people they were at the beginning of the book. I think that's another important aspect of crime—people change because of it. I wanted very much to include that in the arc of the story.

Q. **You're very well known for the Grant County and Will Trent series. How does writing a stand-alone novel differ from penning a novel in a series?**

A. It's somewhat easier for me to write a series. I have firsthand experience with the characters and know who they are. In a stand-alone novel, I have to create all the characters from the start.

In a stand-alone, a writer has to do a bit more work, which is very rewarding. And you don't have to pull any punches. You can have the characters deeply affected by the events in the book, knowing you don't have to continue with them on their journey after this horrible thing happened. As opposed to writing a series, in a stand-alone novel I can take risks with the characters and their development.

Q. **Speaking of horrible things, I'm sure you agree the hallmark of a good story is conflict.**

A. Oh, absolutely. That's why I love crime novels so much. When I write a crime novel, the conflict is already built in. A crime creates an immense challenge for the protagonist and those around him or her.

Q. **What thoughts do you have about being labeled a genre writer?**

A. I don't have a chip on my shoulder about that. I think it's all literature. As for genres, I write in the bestselling genre in every Western country. If that's the ghetto, then I'm in the top-selling ghetto. [Laughter.] Also, I think it's just a matter of interpretation.

I know Gillian Flynn was upset that people said *Gone Girl* wasn't in the crime/thriller genre. That's because some people who find themselves reading and enjoying a crime novel end up saying, "I only read *literature*. I don't read commercial fiction." They give themselves permission to enjoy something like *Gone Girl* by saying, "The book transcends the crime genre and isn't part of it."

But look at *Gone with the Wind* with a brutal murder, or *The Great Gatsby* and its murder, or *To Kill a Mockingbird* with tense courtroom drama and allegations of rape. Or, for that matter, look at *Crime and Punishment*. In a real sense, they're all crime novels.

Crime is really a great way to tell a story. I think a hundred years from now, the novels remembered will be crime novels.

Q. **After sixteen novels and other works, what's the most important lesson you learned about writing?**

A. For me, the most important lesson is simple: I want to be a better writer. I want to learn and grow, to know how to tell stories in a different and more challenging way. I've learned it doesn't get easier each time. It actually gets harder. I always want to make sure the book I'm writing is the best book I can deliver. I've learned in each book that I always want to say something new. I've grown as a writer, and my characters have evolved. The benchmark of success for me is to be able to feel I've accomplished those goals.

Q. **What would you be doing if you weren't a writer?**

A. I love puzzles. I always wanted to learn how to make watches. I'd be a watchmaker. People always say something's just a cog in a machine. But if you understand watches, every single cog is vitally important.

Q. **This question isn't related to writing, but as a former baseball player, I have to ask. Is it true you're related to the great right fielder and Hall of Famer Enos Slaughter?**

A. Yes. He was my grandfather's brother, so he was my great-uncle. My grandfather was a ne'er-do-well, and he and Enos didn't get along. In addition to being a terrific athlete, Enos was very smart and driven. My grandfather wasn't, so there was a rift in their relationship. I think there may have been a woman involved in their feud, because with the male Slaughters, there's usually a woman in the picture.

Q. **What, if anything, keeps you awake at night?**

A. Not a lot. I'm a really good sleeper, which is great when you travel as much as I do. I do worry about political things. I really worry a great deal about the income inequality gap and fear it's not going to be adequately addressed no matter who wins the [2016] election. One person can't do it. There has to be a societal shift for that change to occur.

I think we need more people to understand the seriousness of the problem and to become engaged in solving it. Nothing changes in that regard until something like the Great Depression comes along. Or something like 9/11 happens. They people pull together.

Q. **Do you ever worry about writing-related issues?**

A. I do. I work out most of what I'm going to write in my head before I sit down and actually write it. If, when I sit down to write, it still doesn't come to me, I think it's not ready to be written. Some people call that writer's block. I just give myself the excuse to take more naps, watch television, or read. It's sort of like what happens if you're looking for your keys. The minute you stop looking is when you find them. So, by doing something else, the plotline or story comes to me.

Q. You're hosting a dinner party and can invite any five people, living or dead, from any walk of life. Who would they be?

A. To begin, I'd invite Flannery O'Connor. Then I'd have Margaret Mitchell and Truman Capote, two Southern writers. I'd invite Bill and Hillary Clinton because they could get any one of those other guests to talk and be interesting, even if some of them had a little too much to drink or if they were typically shy writers. I've met both Clintons. Bill has an amazing mind, and Hillary really has it together. It's incredibly impressive when you're a woman and meet another woman who has so much to offer. It may be hard for a man to understand, but I was even more impressed by Hillary than by Bill Clinton.

Congratulations on your success. Gillian Flynn said, "Karin Slaughter's eye for detail and truth is unmatched . . . I'd follow her anywhere." And congratulations on the fact that your Will Trent series, Grant County series, and your novel *Cop Town* are in development for film and television.

JOSEPH FINDER
THE MASTER OF CONSPIRACIES

Joseph Finder has a background every thriller novelist would love to have. His plan was to become a spy for the CIA. Or maybe a professor of Russian history. Instead, he became a bestselling thriller writer and winner of the Strand Critics Award for Best Novel for *Buried Secrets*, winner of the International Thriller Writers Award for Best Novel for *Killer Instinct*, and winner of the Barry and Gumshoe Awards for Best Thriller for his novel *Company Man*.

He spent his early childhood living around the world. He majored in Russian studies at Yale, where he was Phi Beta Kappa, completed a master's degree at the Harvard Russian Research Center, and then taught at Harvard University. He was actively recruited by the CIA but decided he preferred writing.

His first book was published when he was only twenty-four, and he's gone on to write critically acclaimed thrillers such as *Extraordinary Powers*, *The Zero Hour*, and *High Crimes*, which went on to Hollywood filmdom. He's won nearly all the awards a thriller writer can.

Our conversations took place a number of times between 2015 and 2017.

Q. **Your first novel, *The Moscow Club*, was published when you were twenty-three years old and still a student at Harvard. I know there's an interesting story behind it. Will you share it with us?**

A. *The Moscow Club* began as a nonfiction book. I'd learned Armand Hammer, the CEO of Occidental Petroleum, had connections with Russia's KGB. But there were things I couldn't put in a nonfiction book because I couldn't completely nail down the facts. So instead, I decided to write a novel in which an Armand Hammer–like character was featured. In fiction I could say whatever I wanted.

Armand Hammer was very unhappy about the book. His lawyer, Louis Nizer, published an op-ed piece in the *New York Times* threatening a libel lawsuit against the publisher. But Hammer couldn't sue because he would never want to go through the discovery process. Instead, he contacted Harvard and tried to have me expelled. He really went after me. It was very scary.

When the book came out, Hammer bought as many copies as he could to take the book off the market. So, thanks to him, in the end, the book sold very well. [Laughter.]

Q. **I've read many of your novels. What's made you so interested in corporate corruption, greed, and conspiracy?**

A. The corporate world, just like the legal world and, frankly, the academic world, is filled with corruption. In the corporate world, you're dealing with vast sums of money. So the conspiracies can be quite large—even all-encompassing. And they can have major ramifications.

Q. **Many of your novels occur within a corporate setting, yet your biography doesn't suggest a business background. Do you do a good deal of research?**

A. Not having a corporate background makes me feel like an anthropologist—Margaret Mead going to Fiji—where, when I go to the corporate world to do research, it all seems so alien to me. I notice things one wouldn't necessarily notice working in that environment. Even though I don't have a corporate background, I'm trying to interpret that world and create dramatic scenes from the standpoint of an ordinary person who doesn't really know much about it. It's something of an advantage.

I just gravitate toward scenarios in which ordinary people face extraordinary circumstances. It's really a Hitchcock formula. All his thrillers involve precisely that: ordinary people getting caught up in something bigger than they are. And readers can relate to that because the protagonist isn't a superhero.

Q. **Do you have a specific method of constructing a thriller?**

A. Yes. I start off thinking of a thriller novel as if it were a movie trailer. You know, a movie trailer gives you all the best parts. I imagine the dramatic high points of a story. Once I've figured that out—once I have the "trailer" in my head—I know how to create the story. I spend time brainstorming the plot. Then I do research. When I know how the book is going to end, I start the writing process.

Q. **So you always know the ending of a thriller before you begin writing it?**

A. Yes. Before I start, I must know how it ends. It seems important for me to understand the entire story before I actually begin writing it. I don't really quite know exactly how I'm going to get to the end. The fun of writing is the journey of discovering things yourself. I discover them as I go along and the scenes unfold in an unpredictable way. I basically create what's called in the screenwriting business a beat sheet. It contains the major plot points. How I get from one plot point to the next is completely up to me. It's part of the creative process.

Q. **The first sentence of your novel *Suspicion* is, "Sometimes the smallest decision can change your life forever." Of course, this is an indelible truth for that novel. Generally, do you feel a small incident or decision mushrooming into something far larger is a good model for a thriller?**

A. That's the sort of thriller I most enjoy. I want the reader to go on a wild ride—a roller coaster. As a reader, I identify most with the everyday decisions we make and how one small choice can change your life. It's the sort of story arc I'm interested in. It's not the only way to write a thriller, but when a huge transformation derives from a seemingly minor decision, a reader can identify very closely with it. I fully admit I steal from Hitchcock. [Laughter.] I love when an ordinary man makes a small decision and his life is turned upside down.

Q. **Has the explosion of technology been a help, a hindrance, or both to thriller writers?**

A. I think it's a help, not a hindrance. Writers can agonize over the fact that with cell phones, no one is out of reach. In the old days, you had to get to a phone booth. I think it's a matter of playing with the technology we have. We've all had cell phones that ran out of juice or have been in dead zones. Or we've lost our phones. There are great possibilities with technology.

Q. **Do you take elements of your own life, your experiences, and combine them with your imagination and let them become part of your novels?**

A. Yes, I do. The hero in *Suspicion* is a writer—a biographer. He could have been me in another life. He lives in Boston, as do I. He has a teenage daughter in high school, as I did until only a few years ago. So, many elements of Danny's life are intimately familiar to me—even mirror some aspects of my own life. That familiarity enables me to render the scenes and situations plausible and realistic.

Q. **Which do you prefer—writing a series or stand-alone novels?**

A. With a stand-alone novel, you can take a character on a dramatic arc where his or her world is turned upside down. You can't do that in a series. The flip side in a series is you can feel intimate about your character. I felt I got to know Nick Heller and his family and the rest of the group of characters. When I begin the next Nick Heller book, I know who he is. I've figured out his voice. So there are advantages to each—whether it's a stand-alone novel or a series.

Q. **Your novel, *The Fixer*, involves a son discovering something of his father's in the attic of the house where they lived. It's an intriguing premise. How did that come to you?**

A. The initial premise was a story about a guy down on his luck who discovers a huge pile of cash in the old family house. While I was writing the book, my father died. He was nearly ninety-seven. It changed my life in ways I'd never expected. I realized all I knew about my father was what I saw in the family. There are aspects of your parents you never know. They had lives before they had kids.

The Fixer began to change direction on its own; it turned into a story about a son discovering what his father's life was really about. That's what I was going through myself. It's unusual for my personal life to intrude on my fiction, but it happened in this one. This is why I consider *The Fixer* the most personal book I've ever written.

Q.   **In many of your books, your protagonist changes during the course of the story. Is it important for a character to evolve in a novel?**

A.   It depends on the kind of novel you're writing. When you write a stand-alone as opposed to a series novel, the protagonist has to be transformed by the story. If that doesn't happen, the book isn't really interesting. My stand-alones are always about my characters facing something that completely changes the meaning of their lives. It was important to me for the reader to initially see Rick as someone who'd lost touch with his values and then to appreciate the dramatic transformation he makes over the course of the novel.

Q.   **In the Nick Heller novel *Guilty Minds*, you draw from actual instances of scandals involving prominent government officials. Were these events part of the inspiration for writing the novel?**

A.   Yes. I'm fascinated by websites like Gawker and TMZ. They're irresistible to me. Everyone reads them. Yet the standard of proof is very low. We're reading no more than allegations, and people often believe what they read.

I love stories about Washington scandals, such as the one about Wilbur Mills and his dalliance with an Argentinian stripper, Fanne Foxe. Some of the most powerful politicians have been brought down, completely derailed, by dalliances.

A website focused on politics provides so much potential for both abuse and discovery of scandal.

Q. **What's your writing day like?**

A. I'm very routinized. I have an office a few blocks away from my home. I usually get there by eight in the morning and write until midday. I take a break to work out or have lunch with someone. In the afternoons, I tend to do the more business-oriented aspects of my job. Usually, in the late afternoon, I go back to writing.

Q. **What does being a writer mean to you?**

A. It means getting paid to make stuff up. It's a great job, and it's a hard one. It's one I feel really fortunate to get to do. There are people who have really hard jobs. Being a writer is relatively cushy. The stresses of the writing life are all internal: the pressure to produce a book comes from within yourself; you don't have anyone telling you what to do, and you're your own boss. I really like that part of it.

So, being a writer, to me, is having the freedom and ability to make things up, to live in my head, to be creative, and basically, to tell stories.

I don't really have hobbies. Many writers I know don't have hobbies, either. Writing a book is so creative and takes so much out of you, it can consume you. I love coming home at the end of the day feeling blissful after having written well. Somehow, I got through it; I did it.

I also love being my own boss. I don't think I'd have worked well as a company man in a hierarchy. I really appreciate the autonomy that comes with writing. I love being an entrepreneur. I make my own business decisions: Will I convert my website to a mobile-friendly website? Will I send out newsletters? And there are many other decisions. I get to make them all.

Q. **If you weren't a writer, what would you be doing?**

A. I would probably be some sort of movie producer. I would have to do something in the entertainment business, which is actually what I do now.

Q. **What advice would you give to beginning writers?**

A. I would give them the advice I got and in many ways ignored. Just write. These days, with so much self-publishing going on, where there's a great deal of self-promotion, writers spend a great deal of time on publicity and marketing. That time should be spent writing books and articles. That's what we're best at.

I believe the most successful writers are not necessarily the most talented but are the most stubborn. They're the ones most willing to endure rejection and negotiate the rigors of the publishing process. They keep coming back again and again. If you don't have that mind-set, you're not going to make it as a writer. The world is not set up to give you the opportunity to become a published writer. You have to go out and fight for it.

Q. **I get different perspectives from different authors when I ask about writing.**

A. One of the things I love about authors is that nobody taught us how to do this. Ultimately, we learned about writing fiction on our own. We do some things in similar ways and some things differently. Lee Child never prepares an outline. He starts out with a basic idea in mind and just writes. I'm a little too insecure to do that. I need to have a net. I think of this as driving with a map versus driving with a navigation system. If you overly outline a novel, it's like having the nav system on as you drive across the country. It can drive you crazy. But if you have a map, it helps you know where you're going while still allowing you to take a detour off the road.

Writers have different approaches and come from different places. There's no famous writers' school. We all basically decided to do this thing and be stubborn about it until we were successful.

Q. **As a successful novelist, what thoughts do you have about the publishing industry today?**

A. The publishing industry has gone through incredible turmoil in the last few years. There's been the rise of e-publishing and self-publishing. In some ways, it's taken the power out of publishers' hands, but I want to be in business with a publisher. I think publishers are learning how to deal with the digital market. I also think e-books are somewhat exaggerated in importance. I suspect that in the end, maybe 25 percent of published books will be digital. Regular old dead-tree books—paper—will probably continue to be 75 percent of the market.

My last publisher made my book a *New York Times* best-seller. My new publisher is putting an enormous amount of resources behind me. I owe a great deal to the publishing business.

Q. **What's surprised you about the writing life?**

A. Many things have surprised me. One is how much I like my fellow writers. When I entered this field, I thought it would be very competitive. But I found, especially with the

International Thriller Writers, my fellow writers are really supportive. They're great friends.

I'm surprised by the fact with every book I start, I feel like it's the first one I've ever written. As I begin each novel, it's as if I'm back at the beginning of my career. I often agonize at the early stages of a new book: Do I really know how to do this? What am I doing? I'll say to my wife, "I just don't qualify. I don't know what I'm doing anymore." And she says, "This happens with every new book."

But eventually, something kicks in and I'm able to go. The bottom line is: it doesn't get easier. I think as you progress in your career, your standards get higher. You expect more from yourself. Maybe it's necessary to make sure you're doing your very best work.

Q. **Do you ever read your earlier novels? If so, how do they strike you?**

A. I enjoy looking back over what I've done, and those books represent a sort of photograph of where I was at that point in my career. Some of my earlier books are international conspiracy novels, but I don't write those kinds of thrillers any longer.

Now I'm interested in different things. We grow and evolve as writers. Looking back on some of my earlier books, I have mixed feelings about them. But they were the best I could do at that time.

Even today when I reread a book shortly after it's been published, I usually find something I could have done differently. In fact, with every book, you should be more demanding of yourself. If we're not getting better at our craft, something is wrong. Actually, that can make writing new novels harder. Because our critical faculties are more highly developed, we become less tolerant of mistakes.

Q. **Do you have a favorite among all your own novels?**

A. I have a couple. One is *Extraordinary Powers*, the novel that did the worst in the marketplace. I've always felt a connection to that book and have been very protective of it. It's quite different from the rest of my fiction and involves mind reading. The other is *Paranoia*, my first *New York Times* hardcover bestseller. It was a breakthrough novel for me and was as close to my real voice as possible. I appreciate different things about each book.

Q. **If you could read and experience one book again as though reading it for the first time, which would it be?**

A. It would probably be *A Wrinkle in Time* by Madeleine L'Engle. I read it as a kid and it blew me away. E L. Doctorow's *Ragtime* would be another, along with William Styron's *Sophie's Choice*. These were books in which I was completely immersed.

Q. **If you were hosting a dinner party with any five or six figures from history or literature—living or dead—who would they be and why?**

A. I'd like to have Poe there. He was such an interesting man—a terrifically talented writer who, by the way, was very entrepreneurial. I think he was basically the first professional writer. Also Charles Dickens. He is another one of my heroes. He was a fantastic writer and a great storyteller. This may sound weird, but I've always been interested in Harry Truman. I read all the biographies about him. He was a fascinating, plainspoken politician, and very clever. I think Franklin Roosevelt was just as clever. He was a genius of a politician.

I know this is a weird combination, but I think it would make for some interesting conversation. And then there's Jesus. He was a charismatic rabbi who clearly had the ability to create a following and had a message of peace and love. Jesus would be a great dinner guest. And to top it all off, I think Mark Twain would be a great addition to the guest list.

Congratulations on your many successes and for being an author the *Boston Globe* called "A master of the modern thriller" and about whom Harlan Coben said, "Joseph Finder has catapulted himself into the front ranks of contemporary writers."

REED FARREL COLEMAN
THE POET OF NOIR

Reed Farrel Coleman, known to thriller lovers everywhere, is the author of the *New York Times* bestselling Robert B. Parker books featuring Chief Jesse Stone. He's written twenty-two other novels. Because of his writing style, he's been dubbed a "hard-boiled poet" and the "noir poet laureate."

He's received the Shamus Award three times for best detective novel of the year and has also won the Barry Award and the Anthony Award, in addition to being a three-time Edgar Award nominee. His books include nine novels in the Moe Prager series. His new series features Gus Murphy, a retired cop who does freelance work.

Our conversations took place on many occasions in 2016 and 2017.

Q. Your writing has been praised by Pat Conroy, Michael Connelly, Jeffery Deaver, C. J. Box, and Nelson DeMille, among others. Who are your writing influences?

A. *Everything* I read influences me. I'll never stop being influenced by what I read. If I had to pick a few authors who've influenced me, I would say they've been Dashiell Hammett and Raymond Chandler, and my more modern influences include Peter Spiegelman, Daniel Woodrell, Megan Abbott, Philip Kerr, Dennis Lehane, George Pelecanos, and Lawrence Block. But I can just as easily read a book by a first-time author and find it influences me. I must repeat, for me, the list of influences is never long enough.

Q. You've been called a "hard-boiled poet" and the "noir poet laureate" by various critics. What about your writing has resulted in these characterizations?

A. Bribery. [Laughter.] I started as a poet when I was thirteen, and it's evolved into prose, but I've never lost my love for the sound of language. I'm not conscious of it while working, but when I reread my writing, I see a certain lyricism and know I've never lost the love of the sound of words.

Q. The first book in your new Gus Murphy series is *Where It Hurts*. Gus is in a terrible place: his son has died, his wife betrayed him and they're now divorced, and his daughter has serious problems. What made you begin a new series with the protagonist in such a dark place?

A. I think the darker the place a novel starts, the more interesting the possibilities for the series.

Q. **Did Gus's predicament affect you as you were writing about his troubles?**

A. Every protagonist about whom I write affects me because I'm living his plight emotionally. I think that's why people respond to my work.

Q. **How much of Reed Farrel Coleman is embodied in Gus Murphy?**

A. Actually, unlike Moe Prager—who is very much like me—Gus is a better-looking, less intelligent, and braver person than I am. Gus isn't me at all. People think only someone who has suffered tragedy could write such a book, with Gus having lost his son. That kind of tragedy hasn't befallen me. I'm grateful *not* to be Gus. I'm enjoying *imagining* someone in that situation and seeing how he goes on with his life.

Q. **I must say the voices of your protagonists are very authentic.**

A. Thank you. I take that as high praise. I've been told I have a very strong authorial voice. That comes from the fact that I don't separate myself from my protagonists. I invest myself emotionally in their lives. The emotions they feel are mine. Many other authors write differently, but that's the only way I know how to do it.

Q. **It's difficult to imagine you having written about Gus Murphy without having been deeply affected.**

A. Yes. I can't read the first three pages of the first Gus Murphy book without crying. The only way I can write well is by putting myself in my characters' shoes. Not only in a protagonist's, but in the antagonist's, too. It's quite draining, but I wouldn't trade it for anything.

Q.   **You certainly had your finger on the pulse of grief.**

A.   Many people who've read *Where It Hurts* have asked if I've had tragedy in my life. While my parents died at ages we would now consider fairly young, fortunately I've not suffered the kind of tragedy Gus has.

I think a writer's job is to be an observer and a sponge. I've been around people who have suffered all sorts of tragedies. So I absorb those experiences of other people and pour those feelings onto the page. "Writing as art" is often dismissed for genre writers. The assumption is if it's a mystery or thriller, it's formulaic; it's fluff. I defy anyone who reads this book to conclude it's fluff.

Q.   **Will you talk about a character's evolution through the course of a novel and within a series?**

A.   Oh, absolutely. I was influenced by the classic private-eye novels: Philip Marlowe, Sam Spade, and others. But the flaw I found in those characters was they were static. They didn't evolve. They remained who they were. One happy client walked out of the PI's office and the next one walked in.

That worked in 1940, but it doesn't work for me. What interests me as a reader and writer is the *evolution* of a character. In the Moe Prager series, the first book takes place in 1978 and the last book in 2013. Through the course of nine books, Moe ages, gets sick, divorces, and has different businesses. None of us stay the same as time moves on, so I love watching my characters change over the course of time.

Q.   **One of the things I love about your novels is that the protagonist comments to himself about the human condition. How does this relate to crime novels?**

A.   Let's think about where a PI or detective operates. It's in the arena of crime and its aftermath—the worst and most emotionally trying area possible. It's one reason why people are drawn to war movies: the characters are operating in the most emotionally heightened conditions possible.

Murder does the same thing. You deal with people who are in the most extreme situations, which exposes them for who they really are. In day-to-day life, we all do a great deal of covering up about who and what we are, but when we're stressed and pushed, that's when our true selves are revealed. It's a great arena for the protagonist to be an observer of the human condition.

I contend that mystery or crime fiction is perhaps the best platform to explore the human condition. Crime is essential to this genre, and when there's been a violent crime, people are at a heightened level of humanity—either good or bad. It's like wartime. That's why war novels are often great reflections of humanity.

Q. **Let's talk about your Robert B. Parker books. He was the author of seventy books and was considered the dean of American crime fiction. After his death, you were chosen by his estate to keep the Chief Jesse Stone series alive. What was it like to take over a series written by such a writer?**

A. It was an interesting challenge because I felt like a psychologist might feel stepping into Sigmund Freud's shoes. [Laughter.] It's not like I took over some minor writer's character . . I tried not to worry about that reality and decided not to try to live up to Bob's legacy. I think writing is difficult enough without throwing more hurdles in front of myself than already exist. I realized how momentous a task it was, but my approach was to simply write the best book I could.

Q. **Do you feel you had to adhere to Robert Parker's voice for Jesse, or were you tempted to take him in a slightly different direction?**

A. When I was offered the opportunity, one of the first people I called was my friend Tom Schreck. He's an author, a New York State boxing judge, a drug counselor, and a huge Robert B. Parker fan. I wanted his advice about how to go about writing these books. He said something that crystallized my approach to this series.

Tom is an avid Elvis Presley fan. He said, "I've seen all the best Elvis impersonators, but no matter how good they are, there are two things you can never get past: number one is, you're aware it's an imitation, and number two is, the impersonator can never do anything new. He's *trapped* in the Elvis persona."

His words were like an explosion in my head. I determined not to try imitating Bob because I could never escape the fact that readers would see it as imitation. Imitation—no matter how good—is never as good as the original. And I could never do anything new if I was going to mimic what Bob did.

I decided I'd be true to the character—Jesse Stone would act as he had in the past, but the reader would see different aspects of Jesse emerge, and the town of Paradise would evolve. So, in a sense, I use the same camera Bob did, but my focus is different.

Q. **How do you go about formulating various protagonists for different series?**

A. My own series are easier because the best place to look for new characters is to look in the mirror. Somewhat like method acting for writing, I try to come up with some aspect of a character that I feel within myself—a flaw, an emotion, an incident—something that happened to me, and it becomes the basis for a character. It's far more challenging to find a way into somebody else's character. My way into Jesse was his baseball career because I've always been an avid baseball fan and consider myself a jock. That was my route into Jesse.

Q. **Has your writing process changed over the years?**

A. I'm not sure my process has changed, but I've changed as a writer. I've never stopped being influenced by other writers. My writing has become slightly more refined. For me, the more I write, the better I get at it. When I no longer feel I'm getting better as a writer, that's when I'll stop. For example, I once had an idea for a novel, but I wasn't yet a good enough writer to tackle it. It took me five years to complete *Gun Church* because it took me that long to develop the skills.

Q. **Looking back on your career, is there anything about your own journey as a writer you would change or do differently, if you could?**

A. I have some regrets, but I know enough about how things work that if I changed anything in the past, I wouldn't be where I am today. And I'm in such a good place now, I would be a fool to want to change a thing.

Q. **Do you ever procrastinate?**

A. It's against my religion. [Laughter.] Even as an undisciplined kid, I never procrastinated. I was always the first kid in class to give a speech when no one wanted to do it. I always felt waiting caused me more anxiety than doing something I didn't want to do. I'm still that way.

Q. **If you could read any one novel again as though it's the first time you're reading it, which one would it be?**

A. That's pretty easy for me to answer. It would be *The Long Goodbye* by Raymond Chandler. It has its flaws, but it's the kind of writing I wish I could do. There are others, like *Slaughterhouse-Five*, that come close to it, but that would be the one.

Q. **If you weren't a writer, what would you be doing?**

A. [Laughter.] That's a difficult question because I've had many jobs. My favorites . . . I'd either be working in the cargo area at Kennedy Airport or driving a home heating oil delivery truck.

Q. **Why those two?**

A. I worked in the cargo area at Kennedy for five years, and I'm sure you saw *Goodfellas*. I worked with those guys. It was like working in the Wild West. And I loved driving an oil truck. It gave me some of the same things writing gives me: I was alone and had time to think. No boss was bothering me, and I could measure myself as a person and as a man.

Q. **What's the most important lesson you learned about writing?**

A. The most important lesson is there's no such thing as wasted writing. The more I do—even at this stage of my life—the better I get.

Q. **What do you love about the writing life?**

A. I love the independence. I love not having a boss. I love the discipline of it. Growing up, I was an undisciplined quitter. I love the discipline of having to write every single day. I write seven days a week, and if I can, three hundred sixty-five days a year.

Q. **What's the biggest challenge you face as a writer?**

A. I think the biggest challenge is the realization of how hard it is to write novels. As much as I love writing, the fact is it's hard work. Even if I don't feel well, I sit down and write. If I had another job, I might call in sick, but the job of writing is always there, right in front of me. I always tell people who say they would like to write, if it's not a calling and you earn a living doing something else, keep doing that something else. It has to be a labor of love to write.

Q. **You're hosting a dinner party and can invite any five people, living or dead, from any walk of life. Who would they be?**

A. I'd invite Moses, Jesus of Nazareth, Marilyn Monroe, T. S. Eliot, even though he'd hate being with so many Jews. [Laughter.] And then I'd invite my grandfather. He apparently loved me, but I don't remember him. He died when I was very young.

Congratulations on writing beautifully crafted crime novels whose complexities and observations about life elevate the novel beyond its genre. And it's a pleasure to have Robert B. Parker's Jesse Stone still alive and fighting crime.

CATHERINE COULTER
FLYING BY THE SEAT OF MY PANTS

Catherine Coulter has written seventy-three novels in various genres and has topped the *New York Times* bestseller list sixty-seven times. She's written historical romance novels, contemporary romance, and FBI suspense thrillers. Her new series, *A Brit in the FBI*, features Nicholas Drummond, a British citizen who works with the FBI. The second installment in this series is *The Lost Key*, coauthored with J. T. Ellison.

Our talk took place in 2014.

Q. **I heard a fascinating story about how you came to write your first novel. Will you share it with us?**

A. My husband was in medical school and I was working as a speechwriter on Wall Street. I was reading about ten books a week because my husband was so busy. I'd see him at dinner and that would be it. One night, I was reading this awful book. I got so bored, I just threw it across the room and said to my husband, "I could do better." He picked up the book and said, "Why not go for it?"

So I began writing. It was a Regency romance novel. I picked that genre because I grew up reading Georgette Heyer and just loved those books. My master's degree was in the Napoleonic era of England and France. Novel writing was new for me, and I figured by picking a setting and time period I knew very well, I would limit the unknowns. Instinctively, I knew to write what I would love to read. I hired a freelance editor and we plotted the book.

The editor had connections to the three-top publishing houses doing Regency romance novels. I submitted the manuscript, and after three days, an editor called me, took me to lunch, and offered me a three-book contract. I was extraordinarily lucky.

I must say, the years during which I've written were the golden age for *publishers*. But the publishing world has changed. Now is a wonderful time for *writers* because there are so many more options than there were in those days.

Back when I started, book tours were fun. I still enjoy them, but it's getting harder to wear three-inch heels eight hours a day. [Laughter.] Today, Amazon and social media are what's driving books sales.

Q. After having written so many novels, what made you decide to collaborate with J. T. Ellison on the Nicholas Drummond series?

A. By February 2012, I realized I was getting bored. It was the same old, same old. I thought of my friend Clive Cussler, so I called him and said I'd like to write a book with somebody. He told me exactly what he did to get a co-writer. I basically followed his model.

My husband and I each read about twenty suspense thrillers, trying to see which potential co-writer would work well with me. We took our time because I knew this person would become very important in my life. Of all the people we read, we both independently picked J. T. Ellison. I didn't know who she was, and I'd never read her books before. I had no idea how the collaboration would work out.

I called JT and went through the same process Clive did. It turned out so well because both JT and I are Type A personalities. We're both very disciplined, and she's got a wonderful personality. You know, you have to have a bus driver, and she knew I drove the bus. I had the idea for the first Nicholas Drummond book, *The Final Cut*.

We were able to get on the same page about the characters and the novel's direction. In this series, I always write the scenes about Lacey Sherlock and Dillon Savich, because these are two characters from my earlier books, and I know them very well.

It was really interesting because I'm very heavy on dialogue, whereas JT calls herself "an introspective navel-gazer." So JT had to make lots of writing style changes in the Nicholas Drummond books to copy my style of writing. But every sentence in both *The Final Cut* and *The Lost Key* has my toes, fingers, and feet on it.

Q. **You've written novels in many genres. How do you manage to shift from one to another?**

A. Until a couple of years ago, I was writing one FBI thriller and one historical romance each year. I'll tell you, it really keeps you from getting writer's block because it unconstipates your brain. [Laughter.] They're two such disparate genres, and now, doing two FBI thrillers each year is not as much fun. So I'm writing my very first novella. It's a historical story and it's getting my synapses hopping around again.

Q. **After seventy-three novels, what has been your biggest surprise about writing?**

A. I must preface this by saying, I've always written without an outline. I've flown by the proverbial seat of my pants. JT has always written that way, too. We sat down across from each other when we began working on *The Final Cut* and realized that collaborating on a novel meant we had to do things differently because, when it came to devising a plot, we were wandering all over the place. We were forced to become more organized to come up with a more cohesive narrative thread. So, we went chapter by chapter and plotted each one in the book. It turned out very well.

I always thought that if you outline a novel, you lose the spontaneity. But to my surprise, that didn't happen. By outlining, we could see, for instance, that we needed another character here or an action scene there. I was amazed to see that outlining a novel opened up a whole different part of my brain. It was a huge surprise for me, but I'm not sure it would work when I'm writing without a co-author.

The other big surprise for me about writing over all these years is that it doesn't get easier. Each book is so different from every other one. And each one presents a new challenge.

Q.   What are the most appealing things about being a writer?

A.   I love the fact that there's always a reason for me to put my feet on the floor in the morning. Because there's something I'm going to do. I look forward to it every day. I also love that if I have a jerk-face of a boss, it's because *I'm* a jerk-face. I'm my own boss, so it doesn't matter.

And there's something else I recognized from the very beginning: no other person except a writer has this—I never know what's coming in the mail. It could be a new contract for an audiobook or a letter from a reader forwarded to me by the publisher. You have this strange relationship with the postman. [Laughter.]

Q.   What advice would you give to writers starting out today?

A.   Read everything you can get your hands on. Memorize Strunk and White's *Elements of Style.* Buy two copies of it, one for under your pillow and one to sit by your computer. And plant your butt in your chair every day at the same time. If you're not disciplined, hang it up. If it's a hobby, you're not a real writer. You've got to have these basic attributes to be a success in anything.

Q.   If you could have dinner with any five people, living or dead, from any walk of life, who would they be?

A.   Georgette Heyer, a British author who died in 1972. She's the one who invented a subgenre called the Regency romance. It would be wonderful to dine with her. She was an absolutely brilliant writer. Then I'd love to invite Agatha Christie to dinner. I would love to have dinner with Charles II. And I'd want to meet the modern Plato—the same philosopher but brought into contemporary times. And then maybe Edward I. He's very much alive in my books—he's a character for me—and I'd just love to ask him questions about how he deals with my other characters. He lives on in my own private little realm of ideas.

Congratulations on such a successful career and on being a best-selling multi-genre author.

GREG ILES
DOING IT HIS WAY

Greg Iles is known to readers everywhere. His first novel *Spandau Phoenix* was published in 1993 and became a bestseller. He has since had many chart toppers. In his fourth novel, *The Quiet Game*, he created Penn Cage and placed him in Natchez, the oldest city on the Mississippi River.

Greg's novels have been made into films, translated into more than twenty languages, and published in more than thirty-five countries.

He broke the formula adhered to by most commercial novelists when he began to write in a variety of genres. Despite not being pigeonholed into a single genre, most of his books have been on the bestseller lists.

Greg wrote the Natchez Burning trilogy featuring Penn Cage. The first two novels are *Natchez Burning* and *The Bone Tree*. *Mississippi Blood* is the last volume in the trilogy.

Our talk took place in 2017.

Q. *Mississippi Blood* features a compellingly suspenseful murder trial at the heart of the novel. How did you learn so much about courtroom procedures and tactics?

A. I'm not an attorney and don't have any formal knowledge of courtroom procedures. I've attended a few murder trials, but most of what I learned about trial tactics and routines can be attributed to my attorney buddy who read the first draft and made many corrections. My guides for writing convincing trial scenes came from my having read Robert Traver's *Anatomy of a Murder* and Scott Turow's *Presumed Innocent*. Those books gave me plenty of information.

As you know, an actual trial is a drama acted out in real life.

For a novelist writing a trial scene, the trick is to eliminate all the tedious elements found in an actual trial while retaining the very essence of the conflict that is at the crux of every trial. That conflict of competing narratives between prosecution and defense is the dramatic force, whether in an actual courtroom trial or one within the pages of a book.

If your narrative is convincing, your trial tactics will work, whether to a jury or to the readers of your novel.

Q. I found Penn Cage to be a fascinating character. How has he evolved over the course of the trilogy?

A. It was never my intention for Penn to be a series character. I thought his story would be explored in a stand-alone novel, but as I returned to Mississippi more and more in my fiction, Penn evolved from being an observer to an *actor* in the drama of the novels. His evolution involved his becoming more and more morally challenged with each book, which forced him to compromise with his own values as he went forward. As with us all, the more we see of life and surmount challenges, the more we must make certain compromises.

Q. *Mississippi Blood* is the third book in the trilogy, and while I hadn't read the earlier two, I was easily able to follow everything. How did you handle giving enough backstory in each successive novel without repeating too much of the contents of the earlier books?

A. It's a temptation to make the worst mistake possible by providing exposition for the reader who came late to the trilogy. I had to trust that a new reader could be dropped into this story in medias res, and I felt the power of the story would clutch the reader through to the end. I avoided giving too much backstory beyond just using a few compressing devices early in the book—a newspaper summary—which I felt would suffice. I had to trust the story would carry itself.

Q. I understand in 2011, you sustained life-threatening injuries in an automobile accident and found new motivation by reentering the world of Penn Cage, the realm of Natchez, and the secrets of the town. Will you tell us about that?

A. I was driving when a car going seventy miles an hour T-boned me and hit my driver's-side door. I sustained a torn aorta, many broken bones, and lost half my right leg. I was in a medically induced coma for a week. When I came out of that situation missing a leg, my entire attitude toward writing changed. I realized I'd been compromising with myself.

What I mean is this: I originally conceived of the Natchez Burning story as *one* book, which I was on the verge of completing when the accident occurred. But I had been short-changing myself because I couldn't properly address important issues such as race, family, and the South in a single novel.

When I came out of that coma, I realized I didn't care how long the story had to be. I no longer cared who would get angry at me, and I told myself if I was going to be a Southern writer, I had to be unflinching in my commitment to the truth. It didn't matter what the consequences might be.

The accident altered my life. I undertook a quest to write what I felt I *needed* to write. I decided to write a trilogy instead of writing this story in one book. I lost my publisher and changed agents. I had no idea how everything would turn out, but I knew what I needed to do. There are very few trilogies in mainstream trade publishing. Generally, it's considered commercial suicide. The accident took me from being perceived as a thriller writer to being seen as a fiction writer dealing with very serious issues. And I'm gratified to have made that transition.

Q. **Speaking of Southern writers, your writing has been compared to that of Pat Conroy, Thomas Wolfe, and William Faulkner. How would you describe your style?**

A. I would not compare myself with those writers. Like so many of us, I was inspired by them. I was fortunate enough to meet Pat Conroy a year before he died. I also got to meet William Styron and James Dickey.

I recall something Faulkner said: "We look at our heroes, and on the deepest level, we're trying to be them." I would never presume to compare myself with those writers. But I look at the place and time when they were writing and the subjects they chose, and I jumped into the water in *my* time. I feel I've got to do the best I can.

What separates me from them is I'm a commercial novelist. I have to make a living by writing. Even though I write what I want to, I still have to sell enough books so the publishing industry will pay me. That's a difficult compromise to make. Throughout my career, I have had to make that compromise to a greater or lesser degree. With this trilogy, I've compromised to the least degree possible. The writers you mentioned were commercial novelists, but while writing, they threw monetary interests to the wind much more than I can.

We both know this as writers: when writing a novel, we're looking for resonance. I feel resonance is achieved by providing the reader with emotional insight that's gained only through *suffering*. In a good commercial novel, we find two or three such insights in the book. What separates a good commercial novelist from a Faulkner or Tolstoy is this: those great novels have profound insights on almost every page or chapter. They distill the human condition in ways most commercial novels never can.

Q. **I understand Sony Pictures is developing a cable television series based on the Natchez Burning trilogy. Tell us about that.**

A. It's in development right now, but these things take a very long time. So I'm just waiting to see what happens.

Q. **What do you love about the writing life?**

A. I'll tell you something I learned as a musician and playing with the Rock Bottom Remainders. [Greg is a member of a rock group comprised of literary luminaries such as Stephen King, Dave Barry, Scott Turow, Amy Tan, James McBride, Mitch Albom, and others]. It applies to being a writer, as well: no matter how much you love something, when you begin doing it for a living, it changes things. In a way, the thing you love doing the most is inevitably compromised.

What do I love about the writing life? I love the *freedom* of it. If you're fortunate enough to make a living from writing, you probably have more freedom than in almost any other career. When you get over that initial hump of attaining success, you have a great deal of freedom. You're on your own. That's what I love.

Q. **You're having a dinner party and can invite any five guests, living or dead, from any walk of life. Who would they be?**

A. That's a great question. I really have to think about it. [Reflection for a while.] I'd love to invite Carl Jung, along with Robert Oppenheimer, to hear them discuss science and psychology. It would be fascinating to have Friedrich Nietzsche there, along with the great Greek playwright Euripides. They could add a great deal of insight about what it means to be human. And I think Marie Curie would add to the mix. Can you imagine the conversation these five people would have?

Congratulations on a writing career that has spanned genres and has received abundant praise from *Publishers Weekly*, *Kirkus*, Steven King, Scott Turow, Jodi Picoult, and many others.

SCOTT TUROW
THE ROAD NOT TAKEN

Scott Turow, the bestselling author of *Presumed Innocent, The Burden of Proof, Innocent,* and other novels, is often said to have invented the modern legal thriller. Certainly, he's among the tradition's finest and most popular practitioners. His books have sold more than forty million copies worldwide and once earned him a spot on the cover of *Time* magazine, not to mention numerous awards.

Despite his literary successes, he remains a practicing attorney. From 1978 to 1986 he was an assistant United States attorney in Chicago, serving as lead prosecutor in several high-visibility federal trials investigating corruption in the Illinois judiciary. Today he is a partner in an international law firm, where he takes on pro bono cases and has a special interest in the rights and opportunities of former felons.

Over the course of his thirty-year writing career, Scott Turow has taken readers inside courtrooms in the fictional Kindle County, Illinois, a hotbed of corruption and legal controversy.

Q. **Did you always want to be a novelist?**

A. Always. At the age of six, my dream was to play shortstop for the Chicago Cubs, but once reality set in, I recognized I'd have to take on occupational responsibilities like the adults around me. The real desire to write came to me at the age of ten, when I read *The Count of Monte Cristo*. It was during one of my willed absences from school. I was lucky enough to have had tonsillitis and told my mother I was too sick to go to school. As a former teacher, she was wise enough not to fight me on that but insisted that I use the time off productively. She handed me *The Count of Monte Cristo*. I was absolutely captivated by it. Somehow, the idea came to me that if a book could be that exciting to read, how much more exciting must it have been for the author to live with the idea and imagine the events in the book? That was the formative moment for me. From about twelve on, if you'd asked me what I wanted to be, I'd have said "I want to be a writer."

Q. **Given what you've just said, what made you choose to go to law school?**

A. My real ambition was to be a novelist. I began writing fiction and was lucky enough to have some short fiction published while I was in college. I won a couple of writing fellowships that took me to Stanford. For five years, I was a writing fellow and a lecturer in the English department. I was prescient enough to realize that I was headed for a career as an English professor—a great career—but I was doing it as a way to support myself as a writer. I realized I had to have a job because writing wasn't going to provide a livelihood at the age of twenty-five.

I had friends who were writers, but I also had friends who were lawyers. I loved what they were doing. I was fascinated by the legal work and especially by the people who were on one side or the other in criminal cases. I made what seemed like a daring decision: to go to law school even though I had an offer from the University of Rochester to be an assistant professor. I felt I had a calling to the law. I applied to law school, got accepted, and for me, it was a great decision. I don't think I'd have been anywhere near as happy as a professor as I am as a lawyer.

Q. **It's something like the road not taken, isn't it?**

A. Yes, it is. And I'm very glad I chose the road I've been on.

Q. **The law is replete with stories, isn't it?**

A. Absolutely, but the narrative element of the law was not as consciously apparent to me when I was in law school. I'd give Gerry Spence, the renowned trial lawyer who never lost a case, credit for demonstrating the crucial importance of the narrative element in presenting a case to a jury.

Whether he represented the defense or the prosecution, he was a genius at figuring out the story line of every trial. He turned every case into a compelling story.

You're right: if you don't have a story to tell in the courtroom, you'll be out of luck.

Q. **How did your very first novel, *Presumed Innocent*, change your life?**

A. When I was about sixteen, I read an essay written by the lawyer who wrote the screenplay for *Bullitt*. He said, "*Bullitt* changed my life." I thought it was amazing to be able to say, "I wrote something that changed my life." I never had the notion that could happen to me, but *Presumed Innocent* did it.

It gave me recognition as a writer, which I'd long sought,

and it gave me a certain amount of financial security. My second novel, *The Burden of Proof*, along with *Presumed Innocent*, gave me the confidence and exhilaration that come from knowing I wrote something that used everything within me in an incredibly productive way. If it weren't for *Presumed Innocent*, you and I wouldn't be having this conversation.

Q. **That's probably true. Some people would say you invented the legal thriller.**

A. Some people are kind enough to say that, but it's probably an exaggeration if you think about *The Merchant of Venice* and the trial of Socrates. In terms of the contemporary approach of having a lawyer as a flawed protagonist, *Presumed Innocent* was the first novel to go down that pathway. I often think of the monk Dom Pérignon, who "invented" champagne. He had no idea what he was doing when he drank this bottle of accidentally fermented wine. By legend, he fell down the stairs. [Laughter.] I sort of fell down the stairs.

Q. **But in a good way.**

A. Yes, absolutely. [More laughter.]

Q. **You once said, "I'm a big believer in the fact that all authors really write only one book." What did you mean?**

A. This comment is sometimes attributed to Hemingway or to Graham Greene. I admire both of them enormously. It turns out that most writers have a universal obsession they're working out through their novels. In my case, I think it's about the use and abuse of power and the notion of justice found in the law. I don't use it as an excuse for repeating myself in my books. For twenty years I avoided writing again about Rusty Sabich because I didn't want to write the same book again. But thematically, there's no doubt the same leitmotif runs through all my books.

We all have a "home" for a reason. Most people enjoy having familiar signposts in their lives—places and things they can call their own and with which they can measure their own lives. That's true imaginatively as well, and that's why every author's book tends to resemble the books they've already written.

Q. **You're still a practicing attorney. How do you find the time to work in the law and write full-length novels?**

A. Since 1991, I've been a part-time lawyer. Initially, I was still trying lots of cases, but over the years my caseload has diminished, and now my principle work is pro bono.

I'm on a quest to enhance the lives of and employment opportunities for people who've been released from prison and have been law-abiding for a long time.

Q. **What's a typical day like for you?**

A. Usually, by about ten o'clock in the morning, I'm in front of a computer, writing. I'll sit for three to five hours a day and write. I don't know of any author who writes for sixty minutes of each hour. I never have. I'm terribly distractible. My good friend Richard Russo says, "Every author experiences the temptation of finding his or her head inside the refrigerator and wondering what am I doing here? I'm not really hungry." [Laughter.] The reason is, of course, it's the farthest point in the house from where the computer is. I use email to distract myself.

If I have to deal with something at the law firm, I do it. I'm perfectly capable of picking up the phone, talking at length to a client, then putting down the phone and going back to finish the sentence I was in the middle of writing.

In the afternoon, I turn my attention to the more mundane things in life at the office.

Q. **What do you enjoy doing in your spare time?**

A. My number one pursuit, aside from spending time with my wife, is spending time with our grandchildren. I have four grandchildren who all live elsewhere, so we spend a lot of time traveling. Everyone says the same thing about being a grandparent—it's the one thing in life that lives up to its advanced billing. It's very fulfilling.

I also play golf when I can.

Q. **I know you belong to a particular music group. Tell us about the Rock Bottom Remainders.**

A. My participation is a way for the other members to prove that they don't take themselves seriously. If they had any real musical ambitions, they wouldn't let me near the group. [Laughter.] I'm the least talented member of the group. I love it but have no right to be anywhere near a stage. I fell into the group by accident. I can't make any meaningful sound out of an instrument and I sing in the key of *H*. [Laughter.] I've been in the group for fifteen years, and the other members are Stephen King, Dave Barry, Amy Tan, Mitch Albom, Greg Iles, and James McBride. These people are among the closest friends I have in the world, and as long as we're not all in wheelchairs, I think we'll keep on doing this. [More laughter.]

Q. **If you could meet any two fictional characters in real life, who would they be?**

A. I would love to meet Anna Karenina. She's an amazingly brave and compelling woman. Among men, I'd like to meet George Smiley, though he's pretty circumspect and I'm not sure I'd get much out of him. It might be really interesting to talk to Moses Herzog, Saul Bellow's character.

Q.   **Will you complete this sentence: Writing novels has taught me_____?**

A.   It's taught me *everything*. If I can go on, it's taught me about psychological process. I've learned that you can't ever really escape from yourself, which goes back to the notion of a writer really writing only one book. No matter how stuck or frustrated a writer may be, inevitably the obsession will take the writer to where he or she was meant to go. So writing novels has taught me—or rather, has made me aware—of my own psychological processes.

Congratulations on a stellar career both as an attorney and a best-selling novelist. It's been a pleasure talking with you.

MARY KUBICA
WHEN SOMEONE GOES MISSING

Mary Kubica is the *New York Times*, *USA Today*, and internationally bestselling author of four novels, including *The Good Girl*, *Pretty Baby*, *Don't You Cry*, and *Every Last Lie*. A former high school history teacher, Mary holds a Bachelor of Arts degree in history and American literature from Miami University in Oxford, Ohio. She lives outside of Chicago with her husband and two children, where she enjoys photography, gardening, and caring for animals at a local shelter.

Our talk took place in 2016.

Q. The first lines of your novel *Don't You Cry* are, "In hindsight, I should have known right away that something wasn't quite right. The jarring noise in the middle of the night, the open window, the empty bed." Tell us your thoughts about the opening lines of a thriller.

A. The opening lines need to grab and suck the reader in. I want to lay the groundwork of a problem at the beginning of the book. We know right away that something is wrong, that a sinister event happened or will soon occur. The protagonist, Quinn, has discovered something and, hopefully, that will grab the reader. The reader wants to know "What's this jarring noise and why is the bed empty?" I think those first lines propel the reader into the story.

Q. Your novels are all written in the first person, present tense. What makes you prefer this style?

A. I love getting into my characters' heads; I want to be "at one" with them. I feel a character is presented more effectively when I'm inside his or her head, when I feel those things intrinsically, rather than as an outsider. I feel the first-person perspective does it best.

To me the present tense creates a sense of urgency. Whatever is happening is going on *now*, not in the past. The narrative is propelled forward rapidly.

Q. Your protagonists often make crucial mistakes. Don't most readers love flawed and very fallible characters?

A. Yes, we all do. They're real. We *all* make mistakes. We can relate to that, and though a reader may wonder why Quinn is making such obvious errors in judgment, it's clear she's very human, and more like we are, not just a character in a novel.

Q. Both *The Good Girl* and *Don't You Cry* have dual narratives. What makes this form so effective?

A. I love writing a novel from two or more perspectives because I can tell two stories and then at some point, merge them. At times one character will see a situation one way, while the other narrator portrays it differently. It keeps readers on their toes. They wonder whom they can trust. Is there an unreliable narrator mixed in?

With *The Good Girl*, I told the story from three perspectives. If I'd told the story from only one point of view, it would have been a very different one. And much of the plot and certain relationships between characters would have been excluded from the novel. The same thing is true with *Don't You Cry*. I don't think I'd have been able to tell the same story with only one narrator.

Also, the *mystery* element of the novel is enhanced by there being two stories because the reader may wonder, "When are these two stories going to come together?" That's one of the unanswered questions in the book.

Q. Which of the characters in your novels thus far has been the most compelling to write, and why?

A. Willow in *Pretty Baby* was the character who got the most under my skin. When the novel begins, she's living on the streets of Chicago, caring for a baby though Willow herself is only a teenage girl. The novel goes back in time to explore how Willow came to be homeless, and her story is one I'm not able to easily forget.

Q. What draws you to writing suspense novels?

A. I didn't start out writing suspense. Before this I wrote quite a bit of women's fiction, though nothing was published. I felt something was missing in my writing—I'd create characters, but wasn't grabbed by the story line.

When I started writing *The Good Girl*, I was captivated as an author by having a mystery to solve. I found I loved putting together intricate puzzle pieces and figuring out how they would come together. It was also a challenge to think of ways to surprise the reader.

Once I'd written *The Good Girl*, I knew the suspense element was what had been missing from my previous writing. Now I can't see myself writing anything other than suspense.

Q. Is there anything about your writing process that might surprise our readers?

A. I don't write my novels linearly. Because there are multiple narratives in each of my novels, I pick one character's narrative to write at a time and then go back and do another. This gives me the opportunity to fully flesh out one character at a time and to create a voice that is unique to that person without hearing an array of voices in my head at a given time.

Q. What's the best thing about the writing life?

A. I love creating. It's a job, but it rarely feels like one to me. I generally write early in the morning before the rest of the house is awake. Before going to bed each night, I feel a sense of excitement that in eight hours, I get to wake up and rejoin my characters. It's great to forge these people on the page, to give them personalities. It's a thrill to craft these characters and make them do and say what I want in the story.

Q. Has success affected or changed your life?

A. In truth, I don't think it has other than the fact that writing is now at the forefront of my life. It's second only to my family, whereas it used to be a hobby, something I rarely had the time to focus on. But beyond that, I'm pleased to say my life has remained relatively unchanged.

Q. **If you weren't a writer, what would you be doing?**

A. I was a high school history teacher before my daughter was born. If I wasn't writing, now that my kids are a little bit older, I'd go back to teaching. I also volunteer at an animal shelter. My bucket list includes owning my own animal shelter.

Q. **If you could meet *one* fictional character in real life, who would it be and why?**

A. Lieutenant Frederic Henry from Hemingway's *A Farewell to Arms*. I read this for the first time in a college course and fell pretty hard for Henry. It's the type of novel—a war novel, masculine in nature—that I was certain I wouldn't like very much, and in truth had some difficulties getting into it, but I was soon swept off my feet by the romance between Frederic and Catherine. Just beautiful, with an ending that broke my heart.

Q. **If you could reread any two books as though you were reading them for the first time, which ones would they be? And why?**

A. Maggie O'Farrell's *The Hand That First Held Mine* for the moment when two divergent story lines came perfectly together in a way I hadn't anticipated, and S. J. Watson's *Before I Go to Sleep* because, for me, it's the crème de la crème of psychological suspense. I spent the entire novel marveling at Watson's gift, and would love the chance to relive the experience of reading it without knowing how the novel ends.

Congratulations on writing *Don't You Cry*, a suspense-packed follow-up to *The Good Girl*, with both novels plumbing each protagonist's psychology and each ending with mind-boggling twists.

ANDREW GROSS
A BRIEF MOMENT IN TIME

Andrew Gross is the bestselling author of several thrillers, five of which were written with James Patterson. His novels have been translated into more than twenty-five languages. His thrillers *No Way Back*, *15 Seconds*, *Eyes Wide Open*, and *Everything to Lose*, and others are deeply imagined thrillers taking the reader on pulse-pounding chases through current events and deadly circumstances.

Our talks took place in 2014, 2016, and 2017.

Q. **Your novel *Everything to Lose* begins with the line "Every life is the story of a single mistake, and then what happens after." Tell us why you began the novel this way.**

A. I think this is a compelling theme, not only for mystery and thriller writers, but about life in general. When you look at your own life, you can see how much was actually quite random and could never have been predicted. Many things happen in our lives—good and bad—arising from events that were completely beyond our control.

It's a way of looking at life: there can be moments in time upon which life hinges. For many people, unforeseen—and sometimes drastic—consequences spring from a single, life-altering bad decision. And that's what happens in *Everything to Lose*. At the beginning of the story, the protagonist makes a mistake leading to a series of unforeseen events.

Q. **And that certainly can be the nidus for a thriller.**

A. That's exactly what we thriller writers do. If you look at all my thrillers, a character makes a mistake—one that may occur in a moment in time—which leads to a series of drastic consequences. That mistake resonates profoundly and things fly wildly out of control. Even though most of these are forgivable moments in life, they unleash a torrent of consequences.

Q. **You once told me about a personal incident that led to an idea for a thriller. It involved a single moment in time. Will you tell us about that?**

A. Sure. I was in another city and driving a rented car. I rolled through a stop sign and was pulled over by a cop. Before I knew it, I was handcuffed and sitting in the back of his patrol car. It was a scary situation. It dawned on me that a scenario based on a police stop of an innocent person could be a starting point for a thriller plot. That led to my writing *15 Seconds*, in which Henry Steadman never knows what's about to happen when he's stopped by a police officer for a minor traffic violation, pulled from his vehicle, handcuffed, and told he's under arrest.

Q. **Tell us a bit about the role of conflict in your novels.**

A. I think every good novel involves conflict—both internal and external—involving other characters. The plot developments follow from that point. That's the essence of thrillers and, really, of all storytelling. Without human conflict, there's very little story to tell.

Q. **You once mentioned the term *MacGuffin* when describing how to construct a thriller. Talk about *MacGuffins* and how you use them.**

A. Yes, I dedicated the novel to Michael Palmer, a great friend and fine human being. His concept of creating a thriller was to create a story whose essentials could be told in a thirty-second summary. Some people call it an *elevator speech*. You know, if you're in an elevator, going to the twentieth floor, and you're asked to summarize your novel in the time it takes to get there, then you have that thirty-second summation.

I believe the term *MacGuffin* was popularized by Alfred Hitchcock. It's difficult to define accurately, but a *MacGuffin* is really the lynchpin of a plot—whether it's for a novel or a movie. It's the driving force that provides a story's momentum. Probably every thriller novel has a *MacGuffin*—something driving the plot and giving it a narrative arc.

Of course, a novel is an organic thing. It grows and morphs as it's being written. It expands and can take different directions. Hopefully, the final product provides a much richer experience for the reader than could a thirty-second summary, or a *MacGuffin*. After all, there's character and description and the flow of prose. So a novel is far more than simply a plotline, but a compelling *MacGuffin* can help fashion a thrilling story.

Q. **You publish a new novel about once a year. Is there external pressure to publish, or does it come from within?**

A. There's definitely external pressure—the primary one being to have a check in my bank account. [Laughter.] And there's internal pressure as well. After all, this is what I do. I want to keep doing it and doing it well. I think most writers feel an internal pressure to create, to tell stories, and in so doing, create order out of chaos.

Q. **Do you search actively for ideas for your thrillers?**

A. Yes. I'm constantly on the lookout for new hooks and plot sequences. I think many, if not most, writers do it. But an idea must be compelling to me and must be something with substance. After all, I have to live with a novel for a full year— being interviewed, making appearances—and if it doesn't excite me or stoke my imagination, I can't feel good about it.

Q. **Some writers won't read another author while writing a novel. They fear they may be influenced. Do you read other thriller writers when writing one of your novels?**

A. I've never subscribed to the line of thinking that somehow my own style or voice will be polluted by reading someone else's work. If you know your own voice, you won't fall prey to that sort of thing. In fact, I feel quite the opposite about it. I can actually read someone else's work and find inspiration in what I'm reading. Reading another writer can improve my own work. It may even solve a problem I'm having with a plotline or a character. It may even enhance my style. But truthfully, after a full day of writing, I'm quite tired, and I find it easier to watch TV or some sports than to sit down and read a novel.

Q. **Your most recent novel, *The One Man*, is riveting World War II historical fiction. As an internationally known author of "suburban" thrillers, what made you undertake this radical departure into writing a historical thriller?**

A. I wanted to write stories with bigger bones. Publishing, and to some degree your own readers, typecast you into a familiar role. While I was comfortable writing stories in which you can look at a character and hold up a lens and see yourself, I felt constrained by that genre of suburban thrillers. I felt it was holding me back as a writer, and I wanted to write books more in line with what I would like to read. I wanted to expand my horizons.

Q. ***The One Man* is richly evocative with descriptions of military intelligence, Auschwitz, and many other World War II details. It reminds me of some of Leon Uris's books. Tell us a bit about your research for this novel.**

A. When you're writing suburban fiction, you can always wing it. In that kind of storytelling, very few elements of reality are sacrosanct. When writing about the Holocaust, you can't just make stuff up. For me, as a Jew writing about the Holocaust, it's sacred territory—in a way, it's ground zero for me. I felt an obligation to represent things not only accurately, but compellingly. I've visited several concentration camps.

Over the years, I've read the litany of Holocaust books, including *Night* by Elie Wiesel, *Sophie's Choice*, and many others. I had to immerse myself in many different aspects of those events: from the American attitude toward Jews during World War II, Franklin Roosevelt's thinking, and to atomic physics, which is an important component of the book.

But it was my goal to write a story about heroism, not about atrocity—so, while I wanted the landscape of the death camps to be real for the reader, I wanted to write about one man in an extraordinary situation who stood up and demonstrated heroism. I didn't just want to add my name to the canon of Holocaust literature describing atrocity or the will to survive. But the setting was important to portray accurately.

Q. **I know *The One Man* has some very personal meanings for you. Will you tell us about that?**

A. My father-in-law, who recently died at ninety-six, came to this country six months before Poland was invaded during World War II. He never knew what happened to his entire family. He was the only one in the family to survive the war. Because of that, he carried a mantle of guilt and loss that no one really could understand. He would never talk about any of that and never wanted to go back to Warsaw because it conjured up such sad memories for him.

I very much wanted to understand what was behind this burden of guilt and shame that followed him here and remained with him for his entire life. He was never happy and never free of his memories. His survivor's guilt intrigued me. In composing this book, I wanted to write a story that was almost the story he would have told if he could have opened up enough to tell it.

He joined the US Army and was put into the OSS. He never talked about what he did there, either. While the rest of the novel is fiction, it's really my putting into his mouth what I think he might have said had he ever talked about these things.

Q. **Do you feel you've taken a personal career risk in writing this historical thriller as opposed to continuing with suburban thrillers?**

A. Absolutely. The risk began when I ended one contract with my previous publisher and began trying to sell the outline of *The One Man*. Various publishers wanted to take me on provided I continued to write conventional thrillers. They wanted more of the same from me. Others didn't want to take the risk of finding out whether or not I had the chops to write a historical novel. And, of course, there was the chance some of my readers wouldn't follow me. But really, people always crave a great story.

So I'm exploring new territory with this novel and hoping I can establish myself in this genre. The business of writing commercial fiction involves a great deal of risk.

Q. **This brings me to my next question. As a successful author of thrillers, what thoughts do you have about writers being relegated to certain genres?**

A. Publishing is a tough industry. From a business perspective, everyone talks about *branding* an author. It's hard to sell books and especially more difficult if you're trying to convey a new image or present a different brand, especially if you've been typecast or branded in a familiar way for a period of time. Name recognition and salability are really the defining parameters in the industry, and most authors find themselves locked into a specific genre.

The bottom line is this: I have to write what's in my heart. When you do that, the best stories emerge. I'll make this analogy: when I go to funerals, people eulogizing the deceased are often filled with an innate eloquence coming from the heart. Even those who aren't storytellers can convey compellingly things about the dead person because their words are truly heartfelt. That's a worthwhile thought to keep in mind when it comes to writing: write what's in your heart.

Q. Looking back at your career, have your writing process and style changed?

A. My process hasn't changed. I learned a great deal from working with James Patterson. I outline my stories and keep the chapters relatively short. My work regimen is still the same.

My style has evolved. In the beginning, I started out writing sixty percent for pacing and forty percent for character; I now spend more time on developing characters and settings than formerly. I want to deal with larger themes, and that requires a different style and more richness in my prose.

Q. Do you have any mixed feelings about the writing life?

A. On the positive side, I feel blessed to be able to do this. I'm so lucky I don't have to be on a train going into Manhattan for a day's work. I still manage to get paid for what I do during the course of a year. So, the flexibility of the writing life has changed me. It's made me a much easier person to be around.

Negatively, it can be a frustrating life. The business is often irksome because it's very difficult to market one's self these days. On any given week, the bestseller list resembles the same one from ten years ago.

Unless you enjoy that fully branded status, it's challenging to market yourself successfully in today's publishing world.

Q. **If you could reread any one novel as though you're reading it for the first time, which one would it be?**

A. I recently reread *All the King's Men* by Robert Penn Warren. I've picked that one because it might be the most beautifully written book ever written by an American. We're all taught it's a book about a Huey Long figure, Willie Stark, and it's a political novel. But my take on it is now through completely different eyes. To me it's the Telemachus myth about a son's search for his own father. And that made this book incredibly beautiful for me.

Congratulations on having the guts to change the direction of your writing career and for penning *The One Man*. It's a historical novel David Morrell called, "suspenseful, taut, terrific" and about which Steve Berry said, "The characters are intriguing, richly drawn, and wrestle with the unforgivable triangle of evil, guilt, and the choices they must make."

J. A. JANCE
LIVING THE DREAM

J. A. Jance was born in South Dakota, raised in Arizona, and graduated from the University of Arizona. Before becoming an author, she also worked as a school librarian on a Native American reservation, was a teacher, and sold insurance.

Her first book, *Until Proven Guilty*, was published in 1985. In the succeeding thirty years, she's written sixty-eight novels and novellas, including the popular J. P. Beaumont mysteries, the Joanna Brady mysteries, the Walker Family novels, and the Ali Reynolds novels.

In her latest novel, *Dance of the Bones*, protagonists from two different series intersect: J. P. Beaumont and Brandon Walker.

Our talk took place in 2015.

Q. **What made you use the initials *J. A.* instead of your full name?**

A. When I started out, my publisher felt it would be best to use my initials rather than Judith Ann. They felt revealing my gender would be a liability for a book about a male detective.

Q. **In *Dance of the Bones*, you cross-pollinate two characters from different series. Why did you do it?**

A. The reason is to bring readers of one series to the other and vice versa.

I encountered a problem I hadn't anticipated while I was writing the book: *J. P. Beaumont would not share.* He kept walking in and taking over the book. The only way to remedy that was to take part of his story out and put it in a novella called *Stand Down.* Since Beaumont was being so pushy, I had to include him in *Dance of the Bones.*

Q. **So, your characters are really alive for you?**

A. Yes, they are. I'd be writing a Brandon Walker part and Beau would come in and take over the scene. I had to get him under control before I could finish writing this book. [Laughter.]

Q. **You live in Seattle, Washington, and Tucson, Arizona. At least two of your series occur in these areas. Will you talk about settings for your novels?**

A. If I wanted to invent a universe, I'd be Frank Herbert writing *Dune.* But I'm too lazy to invent a universe, so I set my books in familiar places. When my characters are traveling a highway, when they're facing a summer monsoon, or anything else, I have those familiar settings in my mind, which allows me to focus on what the characters are doing or thinking.

Q. **Do you have a specific method by which you construct a mystery?**

A. I don't prepare an outline. I was forced to outline things in my sixth-grade geography class. I hated it then, and nothing that's happened to me over the decades has changed my mind about outlining.

Q. **So you construct the story as you go along?**

A. It didn't happen much in *Dance of the Bones*, but I wrote *Hour of the Hunter* in a nonlinear way. In some of my books, the action only goes forward. It's unidirectional. In the Brandon Walker books, the timelines are elastic, like rubber bands. You're in one chapter in a certain place, and in the next chapter, you're somewhere else and with someone different. And they move back and forth in time.

Writing that way, I discovered at a certain part of the story, the action would stop and I'd walk away and begin writing about another character. Ultimately, it all meshes at some point. It's not a matter of figuring out the end in advance. I just can't write that way. For me, writing those rubber-band timeline books is like going on vacation. I enjoy doing it so much.

Q. **You're very prolific, having written sixty books. Do you ever encounter writer's block?**

A. Yes. It's hell. Once, I was writing a book based on an encounter with a real killer. I didn't want to use him in the book, so my publisher said, "Just rewrite it." I needed a different character to be the bad guy. That caused writer's block so severe, it lasted a year. I ended up reading my alumni magazine from the University of Arizona, in which it described the creative writing program. I had once before tried enrolling in the program and was told by the professor, "Girls become teachers and nurses; boys become writers." He wouldn't let me into his class. Now, at that time, I had *eight* Beaumont books published as original paperbacks. I had thought I might become a writer-in-residence at the University of Arizona. I was told, and this is a direct quote, "We don't do anything with genre fiction. We only do *literary* fiction."

Well, reading that alumni magazine was something of a miracle. I was healed of writer's block on the spot. I used that professor as a model for the crazed killer in *Hour of the Hunter.* [Laughter.]

Another time when I had writer's block, I was watching the news and the station had just fired a popular newscaster because the thirty-five-year-old male news director thought she was over the hill at age fifty-three. Within minutes, I was writing about Ali Reynolds being thrown off her news anchor desk.

The thing is, it's a bad idea to make mystery writers angry at you.

Q. I understand your ambition to become a writer was frustrated both in college and by your first husband. Will you talk about that?

A. In 1964 at the University of Arizona, I wasn't allowed in the creative writing program because, as the professor told me, I was a *girl.* My first husband, who *was* allowed in the creative writing program, told me in 1968 that there was only going to be one writer in our family, and *he* was it.

As a consequence, in my first hardback, *Hour of the Hunter,* it's only the smallest of coincidences that the woman who's the main character always wanted to be a writer and her husband is dead at the beginning of the book. It's a similar coincidence that the crazed killer in that book turns out to be a former professor of creative writing from the University of Arizona.

Q. **The first book you wrote, a slightly fictionalized version of a series of murders that happened in Tucson in 1970, was never published. Can you tell us why?**

A. Because I was never allowed in the creative writing program, no one told me that there were some things I should leave out of the book. When I put everything in, it was fourteen hundred pages long, more than three times too long for an ordinary mystery. That's why the first book was never published—it was too long.

Q. **You once said one of the wonderful things about being a writer is that "even the bad stuff is usable" and gave some examples from your own life in relation to your books. Will you describe them to our readers?**

A. When it came to being a husband, my first husband didn't amount to much. But as the partner of a mystery writer— namely, me—the man was a gold mine. It's no accident that J. P. Beaumont originally had a problem with booze. My first husband died of chronic alcoholism at age forty-two, a year and a half after I divorced him. That was "bad stuff" in my life, but I turned it into something in my books that's reso- nated with my readers for more than thirty years.

Q. **I understand when you go to bookstore signings, you ask the stores to donate a percentage of their profits to causes. Which causes are important to you?**

A. I don't do that very much anymore since bookstores have become causes in and of themselves. In the thirty years during which I've been writing, the bookstore world has changed completely. It isn't fair to ask them to donate at this time. In the past, I've asked them to donate to the American Association of University Women, the YWCA, and a women's service organization awarding scholarships to young women.

I try to do events for organizations that help young women get a foothold. You and I wouldn't be talking today if I hadn't received a scholarship as a high school senior to attend college. In September, when I go to Bisbee, Arizona, my hometown, I'll be doing a benefit for the Bisbee High School Alumni Scholarship Fund.

Q.   **If you weren't a writer, what would you be doing?**

A.   I would probably be selling life insurance. It was a job with a flexible schedule and allowed me to raise my kids. I was able to care for my children without the benefit of child support from their father. Selling life insurance was never my dream job, but it paid the bills. I dreamed of being a writer from second grade on.

Q.   **So you're someone whose dream has come true.**

A.   I often close my presentations with Janis Ian's song, "At Seventeen."

I was six feet tall in the seventh grade and wore thick glasses. Junior high and high school were hell for me. So the line of her song that really resonated with me was: *When dreams were all they gave for free / to ugly duckling girls like me.* And yes, I *have* made my dreams come true.

Q.   **You're hosting a dinner party and can invite any five people, living or dead, from any walk of life. Who would they be?**

A.   I would want to invite Agatha Christie; Daphne du Maurier; Zane Grey, who, though he was a Western writer, was a dentist and a naturalist; Winston Churchill; and Dwight D. Eisenhower. It's an eclectic group of people who would have a great deal to talk about.

Congratulations on living your dream and on writing so many successful series.

STUART WOODS
FOUR BOOKS A YEAR

Stuart Woods's website notes he was born in Georgia, attended the local public schools, and graduated from the University of Georgia with a BA in sociology. He doesn't remember why.

After college he spent a year in Atlanta and two months in basic training for what he calls "the draft dodger program" of the Air National Guard. Then, in the autumn of 1960, he moved to New York in search of a writing job. The magazines and newspapers weren't hiring, so he got a job in a training program at an advertising agency, earning seventy dollars a week. "It is a measure of my value to the company," he says, "that my secretary was earning eighty dollars a week."

At the end of the sixties, he moved to London, where for three years he worked in various advertising agencies. In early 1973, he decided that the time had come for him to write the novel he had been thinking about since the age of ten. He moved to Ireland and supported himself by working two days a week for a Dublin ad agency while he worked on the novel. Then, about a hundred pages into the book, he discovered sailing, and "everything went to hell. All I did was sail."

The next few years were spent in Georgia, writing two nonfiction books: *Blue Water, Green Skipper*, an account of his Irish experience and a transatlantic race, and *A Romantic's Guide to the Country Inns of Britain and Ireland*, a travel book, done on a whim. He also did more sailing.

In the meantime, the British publisher of *Blue Water, Green Skipper* sold the American rights to W. W. Norton, a New York publishing house, which also contracted to publish his next novel, on the basis of two hundred pages and an outline, for an advance of $7,500. "I was out of excuses to not finish it, and I had taken their money, so I finally had to get to work." He finished the book and it was published in March 1981, eight years after he had begun it. The novel was called *Chiefs*.

The book enjoyed large sales in paperback and was made into a six-hour CBS TV drama starring Charlton Heston and a cast that included Danny Glover, Billy Dee Williams, and John Goodman.

Chiefs established Stuart Woods as a novelist. The book won the Edgar from the Mystery Writers of America. He has also been awarded France's Grand Prix de Littérature Policière for *Imperfect Strangers*. He is a prolific author, having written more than sixty novels, fifty of which have been *New York Times* bestsellers.

Our talk took place in 2015.

Q. **You've written four novels this year. How do you remain so prolific?**

A. I suppose my writing life has evolved into a system that works for me. I write in an improvisational way. I begin with a scene. The next day I reread it and make small corrections. That catapults me into the next chapter, and I keep writing a chapter a day until I'm done. When I get about fifty chapters into the story, I start looking for a way to get out of the corner I've painted myself into. So far, I've always found a way out.

Q. **So you don't outline the plot?**

A. I gave up outlining a long time ago. It seems to me that going by the seat of my pants is a more interesting way to write a novel. If I can't figure out what's happening, then I don't think the reader can, and that's very important to me. There's that old adage, "No surprise for the writer, no surprise for the reader."

Q. **What are the sources for your ideas?**

A. I don't really know. It can involve almost anything. It can be a story in a newspaper. I'm using drones in my next book because drones have been in the news lately. I've never had any trouble coming up with ideas. I can go online or use any thoughts or fantasies for ideas. All of them combine in my imagination and are rich sources for me. The world is filled with ideas. They grow like weeds, and it's just a matter of doing some weeding.

Q. **Did you once say in an interview, "I have a fevered imagination and a rich fantasy life, which helps with the sex scenes"?**

A. That's absolutely true. And it's on my website.

Q. **You have homes in New York City, Florida, and Maine, pilot and own a Cessna Citation M2, and are an avid sailor. How do you find time to write?**

A. Well, if you're working only an hour a day, it's not that tough. We spent a month in Paris last year, and I managed to write twenty-five chapters there. Wherever I go, I take the laptop and I do some work. A day's work for me is from eleven in the morning until twelve noon. I keep a fairly rigid writing schedule. Someone once said, "You should think like an artist and work like a farmer." With my schedule, it takes me about two months to write a novel. If you add it up, I'm working about eight months a year.

Q. **How much of Stone Barrington's life mirrors the life of Stuart Woods?**

A. Well, there are a few similarities. We once shared a tailor. [Laughter.] I think Stone and I share fantasies more than anything else. His life is quite different from mine, except in small ways. Flying airplanes is the biggest similarity between Stone and me.

Q. **He's quite a ladies' man.**

A. It would be pretty dull if he weren't. [Laughter.] I was a confirmed bachelor for a fairly long time. I didn't get married until I was forty-seven. I think I was still too young for it at the time. [More laughter.]

Q. **You've penned so many novels. What about writing has surprised you?**

A. I was surprised that things actually turned out the way I'd planned them. The biggest surprise for me has been my success. Everybody has dreams, and I managed to make most of mine come true.

My first novel wasn't published until I was forty-three. By then my contemporaries had well-established careers. I was a straggler. On the other hand, I was having an awfully good time before I stopped straggling and before I got married. I lived in various places and did things I could never have done if I had been married.

Q. **And you've incorporated those things into your novel writing?**

A. Yes. A lot of them have found their way into my novels. I also wrote a memoir, *Blue Water, Green Skipper*, about my sailing adventures. I began writing it while I was living in Ireland and finished it when I got back to the United States. That was before I began writing novels.

Q. **What do you love about writing?**

A. I love the freedom. I like not having a boss. I like being able to pick up and travel somewhere if that's what I want to do. Or even move somewhere if I want to. I don't have to worry about finding a job. My work is portable. It moves as easily as I do.

Q. **Do you watch much television?**

A. I do. My wife and I watch television on a fairly regular basis. We really love the Roosevelt series. I saw the first two seasons of *Breaking Bad* and it wore me out. One of these days, I'll catch up. We're big fans of the series *Ray Donovan*. I think Jon Voight is tremendous. Mickey Donovan is probably the best character he's ever played. And we finally caught up on *House of Cards*.

Q. **Is another Stone Barrington novel coming from Stuart Woods?**

A. Yes. Part of my deal with the publisher is that all my novels will be Stone Barrington books. However, I've tricked them by bringing my characters from the Holly Barker series into Stone's novels. My wife and I are spending a month each year in different countries. This year we'll be in Rome, and Stone will be going with us. I'm just going to keep writing as long as I can think and move my fingers and hope people will keep reading what I write.

Q. **If you could have dinner with any five people, living or dead, who would they be?**

A. For a start, I would have Mark Twain. I wouldn't have to do much talking if he were my guest. Jack Kennedy would be very interesting. It would be great to talk with Clark Gable and David Niven, too. He was a wonderful raconteur. Eleanor Roosevelt would be at the table. Of course, I wouldn't be doing much talking; I'd be listening and learning. Afterward, I'd probably write about them.

Congratulations on having written so many successful books. You're certainly one of the most prolific authors on the planet.

HEATHER GRAHAM
THE SLUSH PILE BAND; 150 BOOKS AND COUNTING

Heather Graham is an internationally renowned author of more than 150 novels and novellas published in twenty-five languages. She has been honored with nearly every award available to contemporary writers. She's had more than seventy-five million books in print.

In 1982, she sold her first novel, *When Next We Love*. She's a winner of the Romance Writers of America's Lifetime Achievement Award and the Thriller Writers Silver Bullet. She is an active member of International Thriller Writers and Mystery Writers of America. Heather is known as an author who writes in different genres, including thrillers, romance, romantic suspense, Gothic, historical thrillers, and paranormal suspense.

Our conversations took place in 2017.

Q. **How did you arrive at a conceptualization of your paranormal series involving the Krewe of Hunters?**

A. I conceptualized this group of paranormal investigators as being people with the ability to communicate on some level with the dead. The man leading the group is Jackson Crow, who was introduced in the first book of the series, *Phantom Evil.*

Jackson is an extremely brilliant, very wealthy man who lost his son and who realized that, although his child was dead, a line of communication remained open to him.

He went to the FBI and convinced them to start this special unit, dubbed the Krewe of Hunters, and Crow was made its field director.

Q. **Many of your books, whether paranormal suspense or thrillers, connect the past and present. Is the past ever truly dead?**

A. I like to hope not. [Laughter.] We Americans have a terrible tendency to tear down history instead of acknowledging the bad things that happened in our country. We need to remember everything that has happened—the good and the bad—and not repeat our misdeeds.

I think the past is never really dead. As William Faulkner said, "The past is never dead. It's not even past." The past becomes part of us and influences us—individually and collectively—in more ways than we can ever realize.

Q. **You've written more than 150 novels and novellas as Heather Graham, as Heather Graham Pozzessere, and as Shannon Drake. Why use different names?**

A. I used different names because I was writing in different genres—for instance, I wrote contemporary thrillers for one publisher and historical thrillers for another. Writing them all under the same name could be a problem because I didn't want someone buying a historical thriller who really wanted to read a contemporary thriller, or a horror or a paranormal novel. Using a pseudonym was a wise thing to do so readers preferring one genre over another wouldn't be disappointed after buying the wrong genre of book.

Q. **How did the pseudonym *Shannon Drake* come about?**

A. The name *Shannon Drake* came about because I was on the phone with the publisher who told me they wanted to publish one of my books under a pseudonym. I asked how long I had to think about conjuring one up and she said, "You have sixty seconds." At that point, two of my sons, Shane and Derrick, walked into the room, so I came up with the name *Shannon Drake*.

Q. **Tell us about your journey to become a published author.**

A. I went to the University of South Florida and majored in theater. I then spent several years performing in dinner theater. I sang backup for the Rhodes Brothers, who made recordings at that time. I also performed in theater venues, bartended, and worked as a waitress.

    None of it paid very well. Auditions and dinner theater involved hours and hours away from home, and I wasn't earning enough money to make up for the time I was missing out with my children. That was when I began staying home and writing.

    After we had our third child, Derrick, it was getting to be overwhelming. My husband said, "You always wanted to write a book . . ." He came home with a typewriter that was missing an *e*. Every night I filled in the *e*'s on whatever I'd written. I bought a copy of *Writer's Digest* and another of *Writer's Market*, to which I still subscribe, and started sending things off to publishers because I didn't know anyone in the field.

I had a couple of stories published with horror magazines and eventually sold the first book to Dell.

I then realized my strength was writing novels with murder, mystery, and mayhem. I learned if I was going to survive as a writer, I had to produce a lot of books. I learned to simply sit down and write. And write some more. The notion of having a deadline keeps the fires burning for me. I must say that now I can't imagine *not* writing. It's what I absolutely adore doing. If I won the lottery, would I stop writing? No.

Q. **Were there early influences in your life that sparked your interest in writing?**

A. My father and mother came from Scotland and Ireland respectively. They left very tough circumstances and arrived in the United States. My parents were avid readers; they read everything. My mother loved Gothic novels and mysteries of all kinds; my father loved reading anything that had to do with water and the navy. They were both huge fans of Edgar Allan Poe.

As a child, I was a voracious reader. I don't ever remember not having a book in my hands. When I began writing, the industry notion of a writer sticking strictly to one genre surprised me. That concept has changed over time, and now many popular books straddle various genres.

Q. **You're immensely prolific and write in many genres. Do you have to switch your frame of mind to write a suspense novel after a Gothic tale, a paranormal, or a vampire story?**

A. I really don't switch gears to enter into a different genre. It's just a matter of thinking about whatever it is I'm writing. For me it's similar to this: if I'm reading a Jack Reacher novel, I expect a lot of excitement and action; if I pick up a Lisa

Scottoline book, I expect a courtroom drama. A Harlan Coben novel will very likely be domestic or suburban noir.

I have no trouble going from one genre to the other. I find myself simply thinking in whatever direction I'm writing. Maybe it's the way I grew up—reading everything—and now I just enjoy writing everything. I love reading everything, too. If I have nothing to read, I'll read the cereal box.

Q. You've been a performer and a writer. How has each of these been gratifying?

A. I'm the luckiest person in the world to be able to do something I love so much for a living. In itself, that's been gratifying. People have been wonderful to me. I've been on a USO tour with other writers and have gotten to experience so many things that have been a pleasure to do. As for the performance part of my career, we still have a little dinner theater skit every year at the *Romantic Times* convention, and I'm still a member of the Slush Pile Band. [Laughter.] We chose the name *Slush Pile* because we were all writers who were lucky enough to get pulled out of that place.

Q. With more than 150 books out there, procrastination must be a foreign concept for you.

A. It is, because writing is how I make my living. It's what I do. I'm always busy, even though the kids are older—I now have grandchildren—and I belong to all these different writing groups: horror writers, mystery writers, thriller writers, and romance writers' groups. So, I just keep going.

Q. What's a typical writing day like for you?

A. I don't think I have a typical day, and never did. I had five children in the house, and I learned to write anywhere at any time—in a car, on a train, anywhere. I grew accustomed to a lot of commotion around me, so I can work anywhere.

Q. **If you could host a dinner with any five people, real or fictional, living or dead, from any walk of life, who would they be?**

A. I only get five? [Laughter.] Historically, I would love to have Abraham Lincoln and Jefferson Davis over for dinner. Can you imagine their conversation? I would love to invite Edgar Allan Poe, who's my ghost in the third book of the Krewe of Hunters. I'd invite Charles Dickens because *A Tale of Two Cities* is one of my favorite books. I'd also love to have Michael Shaara, who wrote *The Killer Angels*, which is more about the relationships between people than about the Civil War. If I could have one more person, it would be Vincent Price. I *love* him.

Congratulations on such a multifaceted career and on writing chart-topping and heart-stopping books spanning so many genres.

DANIEL SILVA
AN ASSASSIN'S ART

Daniel Silva is the international award-winning author of the Gabriel Allon series of spy thrillers, which have topped the *New York Times* bestseller list many times. He burst onto the literary scene with his debut novel, *The Unlikely Spy*, which made the *New York Times* bestseller list. He soon began writing books about Gabriel Allon, an Israeli art restorer, assassin, and spy. These novels have been translated into twenty-five languages sold in more than thirty countries. Before becoming a novelist, Daniel was the chief Middle East correspondent for UPI in Egypt and the executive producer of CNN's *Crossfire*.

We talked in 2016 and 2017.

Q. **In your novel *The Black Widow*, you wrote about the Paris bombing by ISIS *before* that horrific attack occurred. How did it feel to see your own plot element play out in real life?**

A. It felt so terrible that I seriously considered setting the book aside and writing something else. In the end, I chose to pretend the Paris attack in November had not happened in the very same universe where my characters live and work. The similarities between the attack—the use of bombs and guns, the links to Molenbeek in Brussels—were all written before the actual Paris attack.

I think people like me, who've been writing about jihadism in Europe and have been watching and listening carefully to ISIS, were not at all surprised by what happened in Paris. We all knew because of the number of foreign fighters who have gone to Syria and who then return to Europe with their European passports, which allow them freedom of movement within the EU, that Europe is low-hanging fruit for ISIS.

Q. **And then again something similar occurred with your latest book, *House of Spies*, relating to the London attacks on Westminster Bridge, the Houses of Parliament, and the suicide bombing at the Manchester Arena. Is this a matter of prescience, or do you have intelligence contacts? Or both?**

A. It's a little of both. Anyone who seriously follows these issues knew ISIS was desperate to attack the United Kingdom. ISIS painted a bull's-eye on the UK. There were twelve or thirteen plots British intelligence and security services thwarted and disrupted, but it was only a matter of time before one slipped through the cracks. The director general of MI5 told the British people point-blank there would be attacks in Britain. That's why I chose to use Britain as a jumping-off point for the story of *House of Spies*. While I was deeply saddened to see certain aspects of my book actually happen, I was not at all surprised.

Q. **How did you learn so much about intelligence and spy craft as exemplified in your novels?**

A. I have read every single major work on the history and practice of intelligence. Then, quite frankly, some of my best friends are spies and I spend a lot of time around them. I don't go to an Israeli who's a former spy or intelligence officer and ask, "How do you do that?" I can make that stuff up. But I do like to capture their view of the world, their characters, and their sense of humor.

Q. **Everyone who reads international thrillers and spy novels knows about Gabriel Allon. Is it true you never intended him to be a character in an ongoing series?**

A. It's true. When I wrote about Gabriel in the first book, he was going to appear only in that novel and then, quite literally, sail off into the sunset. My publisher at the time, Putnam, wanted another book on Gabriel. My editor was the great Phyllis Graham, and I explained to Phyllis all the reasons why an Israeli continuing character was *not* going to work. [Laughter.] I felt there was too much anti-Israeli sentiment and, frankly, too much anti-Semitism in the world for Gabriel Allon to work in a mass-market way. No one has been more surprised than I to see an Israeli character appear at the top of the *New York Times* bestseller list on a regular basis.

Q. **What happened after book two?**

A. Well, then came book three. [Laughter.] My third book in the Allon series is called *The Confessor*, and I originally conceived that book as a non–Gabriel Allon novel. After the success of that book, I had the sense I had a series going.

Q. What do you think makes Gabriel Allon such an enduring and popular character?

A. I really think it's the fact there are two distinct sides to his character. He's a man of violence, a soldier and assassin, but he's also an art restorer. His duality allows me to construct my stories in a way that makes them appeal to someone who might not necessarily read spy fiction. I know for a fact that many of my readers really don't read much in the genre besides the Gabriel Allon books. I think that's a testament to the character. He makes the books appealing to a broader range of people.

I also think the abundant controversy about Israel and the Middle East gives him a certain heft and significance. It gives him some personal heat because the subject matter is both real and critical. Many historical tides move the character of Gabriel.

Q. Is there some significance to your having decided to make Gabriel Allon, a spy-assassin, into an art restorer?

A. When I created Gabriel, I wanted him to have a distinct and prominent "other side" to his character. He had been a gifted painter until he lost his will to create art because of his work as an assassin for Israeli intelligence.

Art restoration not only provides the perfect cover for him, but allows him to stay connected to art, which is his passion.

He's a complex man, and it's important to me that the reader see him in all his dimensions.

At the time I was creating Gabriel, I happened to be having dinner with one of the world's foremost art restorers. He helped me turn this Israeli assassin into a restorer of Italian masterpieces.

Q. Let's talk about your writing process. You publish a new book during the second week of each July. Is there any significance to that date?

A. If you look at the publishing calendar, many authors publish books around the same date each year, whether it's John Sandford, Lee Child, Michael Connelly, or myself. We all have our "slots." Mine became the second Tuesday of July. I've had at least ten books published on that day: it helps the industry with such things as production schedules and ordering, and hopefully, I've got readers who know to look for my next book at that time.

Q. How long does it take you to write a novel?

A. Roughly, from Labor Day until April Fool's Day. I finish my draft by about March 1, and spend the next month rewriting and editing.

Q. Do you have first readers for your novels?

A. I rely on two people only: my wife and Louis Toscano, my editor. Louis has been editing my manuscripts and making them better since I was a twenty-four-year-old kid.

Q. I've heard you write in longhand on a legal pad. Is that true?

A. Yes, that's true.

Q. Why not use a computer for that first draft?

A. I do use a computer for parts of that first draft, but I sit comfortably and quietly while I write in longhand. I think better by writing in longhand. I love the quiet atmosphere of it. I prefer not staring at a computer screen all day. For me, the pace of putting words on paper with the human hand lets me form my sentences as I go. I end up with a skyscraper-tall pile of legal pads by the end of a book.

I'll tell you something: you could go through those papers and pull out large sections of the novel written in one take from beginning to end. For me, writing in longhand produces a far more polished first draft than I could ever produce by typing on a keyboard. I think it has to do with the slower pace of physically executing words and sentences. Thoughts go from my brain to my fingers and onto the paper via my pen.

Q. **All your novels have plot twists and explosive turns. Do you usually preplan them, or do they arise as you write?**

A. For the most part they arise as I write.

I don't outline at all. My first draft is my outline. [Laughter.] I tried outlining once and felt it was a complete waste of time. Basically, I have a sense of the story and some touchstones and landing pads before I start, but I begin writing with very little plotted out.

Q. **Tell us about the deal with MGM Television to turn Gabriel Allon's adventures into a series. And why TV instead of a feature film?**

A. It's the deal I've been waiting for. We're moving forward at full speed.

I had to make a basic choice: film versus television. That decision became easy when I considered having the prospect of twelve hours of a television series devoted to Gabriel Allon versus two hours of film.

There's a vast amount of material to capture and explore, and I'm fascinated by the prospect of seeing some of the older material updated.

Television has become quite innovative, and I think it was the way to go.

Q. **You once said you wanted Gabriel to live solely on the page. What changed your mind?**

A. For many years I was convinced Gabriel should live only on the page. But after *The Black Widow* was published, I was inundated with so many offers, I was finally able to feel pretty confident that the offer I would ultimately select would get the complex character of Gabriel and the tone for the series done correctly.

Q. **Do you see Gabriel Allon continuing for many more books?**

A. That's a difficult question to answer. Let's just say that I'm working on another Gabriel Allon novel right now. [Laughter.]

Q. **What's the most important lesson you've learned about writing?**

A. I always thought the dumbest piece of advice I ever heard was "Write what you know."

I disagree. Write what you're *passionate* about. Write what you're interested in writing. Choose your material and then bury your face in it. I learned not to worry before starting a project. I've never quite understood the fear some writers have about beginning a novel. I never fear beginning something; I know I can always fix the book.

The other very important lesson I learned is to try to enjoy the writing of that *first* novel, because once you're a published author, it's never quite the same again. It's important to make sure you're doing something that's a lot of fun to do.

Q. **You're hosting a dinner party and can invite any five people, living or dead, real or fictional, from any walk of life. Who would they be?**

A. Churchill would be there. I'd invite George Orwell, who might be coughing and wheezing and not feeling well, but

I'd love to talk to him. It would be fun to have FDR along with Churchill—to have the two leaders who saved the world sitting at the same table. How about inviting the acerbic Graham Greene? And then I'd love to have Hemingway join us. Can you imagine the amount of drinking going on with Churchill and Hemingway there? [Laughter.] I'd watch the whole evening explode.

Congratulations on having penned twenty bestselling novels, seventeen of which are about an iconic protagonist who will soon be depicted in what's certain to be a blockbuster television series.

LAURA LIPPMAN
A WRITER'S DESTINY—THE BREAKTHROUGH

Laura Lippman was a reporter for twenty years, including twelve years at the *Baltimore Sun*. She began writing fiction while working full-time as a reporter and published seven books about "accidental PI" Tess Monaghan before leaving journalism in 2001.

Her bestselling works have been awarded the Edgar, Anthony, Agatha, Shamus, Nero, Gumshoe, and Barry Awards. Her books have been translated into more than twenty languages.

She also has been nominated for other prizes in the crime fiction field, including the Hammett Prize and the Macavity Award.

Our conversations took place in 2016 and 2017.

Q.   **Many of your novels could be considered family sagas just as much as crime thrillers or mysteries. I'm thinking of *Wilde Lake* and your latest, *Sunburn*. Will you talk about that?**

A.   I define crime novels very broadly. To me, a crime novel is one in which a crime propels the story. There would be no story if not for a crime.

But sometimes these genre definitions can trip us up because there can be much more to a novel than the crime.

Many of my novels are about a crime, but they're about family and reconciling how we view the past with our present sensibilities. In the present, we often feel superior, as though we've figured everything out in the ten or twenty years that have elapsed since something occurred. We tend to forget that if we go into the future and look back at our past—which is our present right now—people might consider us as having been backward or wanting. That should make us a little more forgiving of the mistakes made by our ancestors.

Q.   **From reading your novels, I get the sense that you consider many of our early memories unreliable, that we create our own versions of the truth. Will you talk about that?**

A.   Everyone has had the experience of looking back at something from the past and suddenly realizing what *really* happened. We end up saying, "This is what truly happened. This is the perspective I didn't have as a child."

Memory *isn't* reliable. Telling a story over and over again doesn't make it any more factual. There's evidence in the study of the human brain that every time you tell a story, you introduce errors into that story. It's like lifting a very old piece of lace from a box where it's been kept. Every time you pick it up, you risk damaging or changing it.

But memory is often the only thing we have. After all,

other than factually verifiable incidents, what can we really "know" about past events? If we limit ourselves to primary documents, videos, and photographic evidence, we won't know very much. In journalism and other forms of communication, we have to rely on people's memories, which are almost universally imperfect.

Q. **Your latest novel has a very different kind of woman protagonist than we've been seeing in recent fiction. Will you talk about that?**

A. We've been going through a phase in crime fiction with unreliable female characters in books like *The Girl on the Train*, *Gone Girl*, and others. Instead, I wanted to write about a very *reliable* female character. In *Sunburn*, Polly, my protagonist, is extremely direct, generally doesn't lie, and very early in the novel thinks: "Pay attention. I just told you who I am, and you didn't notice." She tells her lover, Adam, a good deal about herself, but he doesn't pay attention. That was my premise: a novel based on a woman abandoning her child, a dark theme that's had many iterations in literature. But above all, Polly is a very reliable protagonist. It's simply that other people don't realize that about her.

Q. **Your latest book, *Sunburn*, is truly a noir novel and a bit of a departure for you. Isn't it?**

A. Yes, it is. I never tried to write noir. I didn't think I could do it. I thought my own innate view of human nature is what I'd call ruefully optimistic. I'd sort of put writing noir away in a box, knowing it's what I like to read and realizing it's a genre that's produced some of my favorite films, but felt it wasn't *me*. But then I decided to write something really mean and nasty. When the idea came to me, it was really different.

I'm always trying to do something challenging from book to book. Within the Tess Monaghan series, I tried never to write the same book twice. In the stand-alones I've tried to make each one quite unique.

Q. **Will you talk about the different expectations people have about men and women concerning child-rearing in real life and as depicted in novels?**

A. We expect nurturing to come naturally to women. We expect they'll have a single-minded maternal devotion to a child. If a woman feels somewhat bored raising a child or misses the life she had before the child was born, it's considered somewhat shocking. Women are supposed to embrace motherhood and everything about it. They're never expected to abandon a child. A woman walking away marks her as someone who is flawed and different. I disagree with those assessments.

In *Sunburn*, I depict a woman who sees her marriage ending and is confident her husband will walk out on her and her child. She'll have to fight for him to send a support check each month, and with few skills, she'll be ill-equipped to enter the job market. But she has a long-term plan. She tells herself, "I'll get the jump on him. I'll seize control of the situation."

It seems to me that men and women see things very differently. Early in my relationship with my husband, David, I noticed that he really lived in the moment, as do many men. On the other hand, I carry the family calendar around in my head all the time. I once drew a cartoon of David and me: The drawing of him showed a huge round head with the word *now* in the middle. The one of me had a rectangular *calendar* for a head. I think that's typical of things between men and woman.

Q. **Many of your novels feature women haunted by and barely surviving their pasts. Will you talk about that?**

A. I think we're all haunted by our pasts. Our culture has an extremely dissonant relationship with the concept of redemption and forgiveness. We talk a good game about it, but the culture doesn't really work that way. Our prisons are filled with people who barely had a *first* chance. I know we'd like to think we all believe in redemption, but to my mind, redemption and forgiveness are often withheld from many people. It's a carrot dangling on a stick, and it's out of reach for many people. But yes, many of my characters—men and women—are haunted by their pasts.

Q. **Is there one book you wrote that was the breakthrough novel for you?**

A. Yes, my big breakthrough novel came in March of 2007. *What the Dead Know* was my twelfth novel. Conventional wisdom says you get maybe three or four chances to break through. After that you're done. You'll be stuck in the midlist forever. I was lucky. I received amazing support from William Morrow, my publisher, and that twelfth book was a *New York Times* bestseller. No one really knows what shapes a writer's destiny.

Q. **Your essay in *Bad Girls* detailed employer abuse you suffered working at a newspaper. Will you talk about that and discuss how it may have affected your views and writing?**

A. I worked in the newspaper industry for twenty years. I eventually made it to the *Baltimore Sun*, where my father was still working at the time. Eleven of my twelve years were very good. The last one was miserable. The managing editor didn't like me very much and didn't appreciate that I was also writing my novels outside my job at the paper. He felt he wasn't getting 100 percent of my time, even though I was working forty hours a week and was giving them the full benefit of those forty hours. I received what I would call a psychological demotion: I was sent from the feature staff to the suburban offices—a department where young people were on their way up the ladder and middle-aged people were on their way out.

I had to make a little noise because the paper tried to violate my rights time and again. The union backed me up and I left the paper with a confidential settlement. The timing was lucky because I also got a contract that allowed me to become a full-time novelist.

Q. **Did that experience work its way into any of your novels?**

A. The emotions of what happened surely worked their way into my novels. The feelings were primarily those of anger and impotence. At the time I felt rage. As I detailed in the essay in *Bad Girls*, one day at work I ground my teeth to the point I spit out my back molars. I recall spitting them into my hand and showing them to my supervisor, who was appalled.

Yes, these feelings seeped into my novels, especially situations in which a female character has very little control and has to be nice to despicable people.

Q. **Will you complete this sentence: Writing novels has taught me____?**

A. Writing novels has taught me that sometimes dreams do come true.

Q. **I take it you always wanted to be a writer.**

A. Ever since I was five or six years old.

Q. As a highly successful novelist, what's the most important lesson you've learned about writing?

A. To do it. [Laughter.] To get up and write, and to do it regularly. I think people make a mistake in talking about developing discipline. Discipline is a scary word. It doesn't sound like fun, and it's difficult to maintain. It's the conscious act of overcoming one's own will—like following a diet or exercise program—which almost always fails.

What really works for people isn't discipline, but habit. It's crucial to develop the *habit* of writing. It's best to start small. My big mistake when I started was trying to write all weekend. It was impossible—it was exhausting and there were other things I needed or wanted to do.

Instead, setting a goal of writing for thirty minutes a day, four times a week, is more realistic. My writing goal to this day is to write a thousand words a day. If I do that five days a week, in twenty weeks I'll have a novel. That's the important lesson I've learned—to build writing into becoming a habit.

Q. What do you love most about the writing life?

A. I love working for myself. I have a great editor whom I love, but I really work for myself. I set my own hours, have my own goals, I come up with my own ideas, and I'm treated as a full partner in the enterprise. It's very different from the newspaper work I once did. I love the independence of being a writer.

Q. You're hosting a dinner party and can invite any five people from any walk of life, living or dead, fictional or real. Who would they be?

A. I'd definitely invite Stephen Sondheim. I'd love to have Ferran Adrià, the chef from elBulli; he is one of the seminal figures in the world of cooking. My husband would be there because I love him, and he's great company. I would also invite a friend who's the most provocative, no-holds-barred person I know, Rebecca Chance, and I'd love to invite Michelle Obama to the dinner.

I wouldn't invite any dead people because I'd have to spend so much time bringing them up to speed on stuff. Imagine saying to Shakespeare, "The other day, I googled someone . . ." and he would look at me like I'm insane. [Laughter.]

It's been a pleasure talking about a writer's destiny, your breakthrough novel, and so many other things, and thanks for sharing some personal anecdotes.

FOUR AUTHORS TRULY WORTH DISCOVERING

The authors noted below are enormously gifted writers who do not yet have the worldwide following of those included in this volume. I've interviewed them all and have read many of their novels.

They are creative wordsmiths whose works I've enjoyed immensely, and I invite you to discover them. You won't regret immersing yourself in their intriguing and entertaining books.

They are listed in alphabetical order along with brief excerpts from each of their interviews.

STEVE HAMILTON

Steve Hamilton has either won or been nominated for virtually every major crime fiction award, including the Edgar, Dagger, Shamus, Anthony, Barry, and Gumshoe, among others. His Alex McKnight series involves ten bestselling and highly acclaimed books. His stand-alones include *Night Work* and *The Lock Artist*, which won the Edgar and Barry Awards for best novel of 2011. *The Second Life of Nick Mason* was Steve's first entry in a new series. The novel is in development by Lionsgate to be released as a major motion picture.

Steve is one of the most talented authors writing contemporary suspense/thriller novels. He paints vivid portraits of people in situations from which it seems impossible to extricate themselves.

Q. **Nick Mason is a very different character from Alex McKnight, your first series protagonist. Talk to us about character development in your novels.**

A. He's different from Alex McKnight, yet they actually have things in common. They're both very loyal people and are dedicated to what they do. Mason was very careful about what he did as a criminal and does his best to live by a certain code, as does Alex McKnight. I think they're sort of mirror images of each other.

If you recall the diner scene in the movie *Heat*, Robert Di Niro and Al Pacino sit across the table from each other and realize they've got a lot more in common than they thought.

When I create any character, I'm looking for a fully realized person in every way. Even if I'm writing a villain like Darius Cole, I try to construct understandable reasons for what he does.

People are multifaceted and there are often complicated reasons behind their actions, and I do my best to portray that in my novels.

JON LAND

Jon Land is the prolific author of more than thirty novels, many of them *USA Today* bestselling books. As his senior honors thesis before graduating from Brown University, Jon wrote a thriller novel. He is well-known for his Blaine McCracken series, among others, as well as more than nine stand-alone novels.

His latest series features fifth-generation Texas Ranger Caitlin Strong. Her courage and tenacity often land her, along with her paramour, Cort Wesley Masters, on perilous terrain.

In my view, Jon's books have some of the best action scenes ever written. They are quintessential thrillers combining current technology with the charm and romanticism of earlier times.

Q. **I've read many of your novels, and they've all tied the protagonist's present investigation to events that occurred many years earlier. Tell us about these connections of past and present.**

A. I've always believed what William Faulkner said, "The past is never dead. It's not even past." In this future-obsessed culture, we forget how vital the past is. In the Caitlin Strong series, I use the past to highlight the tradition of the Texas Rangers in Caitlin's family. We see how crimes were solved in 1883, in the 1930s, and in the present. It shows that no matter how things may change, they really stay the same. If it were possible for Caitlin, her father, and her grandfather to team up today with Judge Roy Bean, you would probably have the same result.

These historical subplots also allow me to pick wonderful snippets from history and present them in a way that integrates past and present. In *Strong Darkness*, I touch on the railroad tradition of the Old West and Texas. The railroads were crucial in American history because people became mobile, which ended the era of the Wild West and lone gunfighters. Gunmen became Pinkerton men or contract killers.

I love relying on history as part of telling a story. History can fuel a plot that spills over into the present. It makes the past completely relevant.

MARCUS SAKEY

Marcus Sakey has written thrillers that have been nominated for multiple awards, including an Edgar Award nomination for *Brilliance*, the first book in the outstandingly creative Brilliance Trilogy. The two others in the trilogy are *A Better World* and *Written in Fire*. His novel *Good People* was made into a movie starring James Franco and Kate Hudson. *Brilliance* is now in development with Legendary Pictures.

After graduating from college, Marcus worked in advertising and marketing. His debut thriller, *The Blade Itself*, was published to wide critical acclaim, allowing him to work full-time as a writer. His stand-alone novels are beautifully written suspense thrillers.

In my view, Marcus Sakey writes intense stories that are brilliantly conceived and are among the richest and most deeply imagined on the literary scene today.

Q. **The entire Brilliance Trilogy is an amazing mixture of futurism, genetics, finance, the military, politics, psychology, and technology. Tell us a little about the research you did for these books.**

A. The notion of the *brilliants* themselves came from my wife, who has a master's degree in child development. She was fascinated by autism, and that triggered in me the question, "What if the one in one hundred people who have autism had something that had no negative social consequences?" As a writer, I took it a step further: "What if they had gifts taking them closer to savant-like?"

The research started there, but I quickly realized the important element is the *story* I'm creating and the actions of the people in that story. Research can be a rabbit hole. I made myself a promise: I would look up whatever I needed to get things right rather than do a mountain of research and have the story derive from that.

SIMON TOYNE

Simon Toyne was a highly successful writer, director, and producer in British television. He worked on many award-winning shows. Now he is a full-time novelist, whose first book, *Sanctus*, became part of an internationally bestselling trilogy known as the Sanctus Trilogy.

Simon Toyne is an uncommonly brilliant man whose novels are not only thrillers, but explore political, philosophical, and religious issues, along with the meaning of identity.

Simon's novels are beautifully written, multitiered thrillers transcending time, place, and person. His second series features a mesmerizing character, Solomon Creed.

Q. **There's something mystical and mythological in your books. I'm reminded of the *Myth of the Birth of the Hero* by Otto Rank. Will you talk about the "myth" of Solomon Creed?**

A. Even though the Solomon Creed books are modern thrillers, they have historic backstories, whether it's *The Searcher* or *The Boy Who Saw*. And though the books are thrillers, Solomon isn't a stereotypical action hero. He's somewhat ethereal. Typical action heroes have solid pasts—they're ex-cops or ex-military who use their skill sets to solve crimes. With Solomon, the biggest mystery is himself. He lacks that centeredness. He has a mythological—nearly a supernatural—quality.

Yes, he bleeds and is mortal, but I wanted him to have a somewhat mythical dimension. And the novels raise the question—perhaps even the possibility—that he's been reincarnated. There's a tension and a question about the reality of Solomon, and he keeps cropping up in these historical contexts. I like playing with that possibility. As a reader, I enjoy a character who assumes a quality of being slightly larger than life, someone who's slightly *other*, or heroic. In fact, this Solomon Creed series is effectively an odyssey of self-discovery.

ACKNOWLEDGMENTS

I owe an enormous debt of gratitude to Shane Salerno, a great agent and a man of his word.

The Storytellers is of course, a collaborative work. I wish to thank each of the authors I had the pleasure of interviewing. They are creative and generous people, having given me so much of their time and talent. Many hours were spent with them, either at conferences, dinners, lunches, on the telephone, or communicating by email. They provided candid thoughts, insights, and observations about their writing, their inspirations, and above all, about themselves and their lives.

Many thanks to Sharon Goldinger who taught me plenty about the book business.

Thank you Penina Lopez.

And to Randall Enos, an incredibly talented graphic artist.

My wife, Linda, as always, is my greatest collaborator and source of strength.

ABOUT THE EDITOR

Mark Rubinstein graduated from NYU with a degree in business administration. After college, he served in the US Army as a field medic at Fort Bragg, North Carolina, tending to paratroopers of the 82nd Airborne Division. That experience impacted him profoundly. After discharge from the army, he returned to college, studied the premedical sciences, and gained admission to medical school. He became a physician and then a psychiatrist.

He worked as an attending psychiatrist at Kings County Hospital, both on the wards and in the psychiatric emergency room. Maintaining private practices in New York City and Connecticut, he became involved in forensic psychiatry and testified as an expert witness at many hearings, inquests, arbitrations, and jury trials.

As an attending psychiatrist at New York–Presbyterian Hospital and the Payne Whitney Clinic, and a clinical assistant professor of psychiatry at Cornell University Medical School, he taught psychologists, psychiatric interns, residents, psychiatric nurses, and social workers while practicing psychiatry.

Before turning to fiction, he coauthored five nonfiction books in the medical-self-help genre. He is a contributor to the Huffington Post and has contributed to *Psychology Today*. His novels and novellas have either won or been finalists for multiple awards, including the Foreword Indies Book of the Year Award, the Benjamin Franklin Gold Award for Popular Fiction, and the IPPY Award for Suspense and Thriller Fiction.

You can contact him here:

Website: http://markrubinstein-author.com
Twitter: @mrubinsteinCT
Email: author.mark.rubinstein@gmail.com